CARIBBEAN WOMEN WRITERS

Caribbean Women Writers

Fiction in English

Edited by

Mary Condé

and

Thorunn Lonsdale

St. Martin's Press
New York

CARIBBEAN WOMEN WRITERS

St. Martin's Press, Scholarly and Reference Division,
175 Fifth Avenue, New York, N.Y. 10010

First published in the United States of America in 1999

This book is printed on paper suitable for recycling and
made from fully managed and sustained forest sources.

Printed in Great Britain

ISBN 0–312–21861–3 clothbound
ISBN 0–312–21863–X paperback

Library of Congress Cataloging-in-Publication Data
Caribbean women writers: fiction in English / edited by Mary Condé
and Thorunn Lonsdale.
p. cm.
Includes bibliographical references (p.   ) and index.
ISBN 0–312–21861–3 (cloth). — ISBN 0–312–21863–X (pbk.)
1. Caribbean fiction (English)—Women authors—History and
criticism. 2. West Indian fiction (English)—Women authors—History
and criticism. 3. Women and literature—Caribbean Area—History.
4. Women and literature—West Indies—History. 5. Women—Caribbean
Area—Intellectual life. 6. Women—West Indies—Intellectual life.
7. Caribbean Area—In literature. 8. West Indies—In literature.
9. Women in literature. I. Condé, Mary, 1943– . II. Lonsdale,
Thorunn, 1958– .
PR9205.4.C37   1999
813.009'9287'09729—dc21   98–28418
                                                            CIP

For Jasmine and for Arthur

Contents

Acknowledgements

Our thanks go to Queen Mary and Westfield College, University of London, and to the Central Research Fund, University of London, for providing funding for conferences in the Caribbean and for library visits to the United States, to the Reverend Jesús Riveroll, SJ, for his invaluable sociological and historical advice, to Joan Anim-Addo for her pioneering work in Caribbean studies, to Jeanne Devoize for her conference on the Caribbean short story at the University of Angers, and to Adisa Banjanović and Guy Rawlings for their indispensable practical help.

Notes on the Contributors

Laura Niesen de Abruna teaches at Ithaca College.

Merle Collins is a writer, now at the University of Maryland.

Mary Condé teaches at Queen Mary and Westfield College, University of London.

Alison Donnell teaches at Nottingham Trent University.

Vernella Fuller is a writer, living in Britain.

Beryl Gilroy is a writer, living in Britain.

Thorunn Lonsdale is a director of the Yamani Cultural and Charitable Foundation and a PhD candidate at Queen Mary and Westfield College, University of London.

Heidi Slettedahl Macpherson teaches at the University of Central Lancashire.

Denise deCaires Narain teaches at the University of Sussex.

Adele S. Newson teaches at Florida International University.

Velma Pollard is a writer, living in Jamaica.

Charlotte Sturgess teaches at the University of Tours.

Sarah Lawson Welsh teaches at the University College of Ripon and York.

Introduction

Mary Condé

To speak of Caribbean women's fiction in English is already to have imposed four separate classifications. What further classifications might be used? The area from which writers come, the area in which they now live, the settings which they use, their ethnic descent; the generation to which they belong, or their political agenda? A grouping under 'Guyana', for example, would include Beryl Gilroy, who left 'British Guiana' for Britain over 40 years ago; Grace Nichols of the next generation; Meiling Jin, who is of Chinese descent; Narmala Shewcharan, who is of Indian descent; Pauline Melville, who is of Afro-Guyanese and English descent; Joan Cambridge, who has set her novel *Clarise Cumberbatch Want to Go Home*[1] in New York City; and Norma DeHaarte, who lives in Canada. The group 'Trinidad' would include the African American writer Rosa Guy, and works as different as Valerie Belgrave's utopian historical romance *Ti Marie,*[2] and the experimental and socially conscious writings of the Canadians Claire Harris and Dionne Brand. Brand's preferred identification of herself as 'black Canadian', incidentally, eliminates the classification 'Caribbean' altogether.

Even within the English-speaking Caribbean, people from different areas are intensely, and proudly, conscious of their difference from each other. The Prime Minister of Barbados, Errol Barrow, remarked long ago of the ill-fated West Indies Federation that 'We live together very well, but we don't like to live together together'.[3] Audre Lorde opens her 'biomythography' *Zami: A New Spelling of My Name* with a statement of difference: 'Grenadians and Barbadians walk like African peoples. Trinidadians do not.'[4] Lorde herself is a 'different' kind of Caribbean, because, like Paule Marshall, she was born of Caribbean parents in New York City. Carriacou, her mother's birthplace, writes Lorde, did not appear

> on any map that I could find, and so when I hunted for the magic place during geography lessons or in free library time, I never found it, and came to believe my mother's geography was a fantasy. . . .[5]

1

Paule Marshall uses Carriacou as a real island in her novel *Praisesong for the Widow*,[6] but also as a 'magic place' where her heroine Avey is spiritually regenerated. Although Barbados, her parents' real island, constantly informs the action of most of her fiction, for her latest novel *Daughters*[7] she has invented the imaginary, composite Caribbean island of 'Triunion'. Similarly, Brenda Flanagan from Trinidad has invented 'Santabella' for her novel *You Alone Are Dancing*,[8] Merle Collins from Grenada has invented 'Paz' for her novel *The Colour of Forgetting*,[9] and Beryl Gilroy uses an island, referred to simply as 'the island', for her novel *Boy-Sandwich*,[10] which corresponds to no exact geographical reality. Jean Rhys in her novel *Voyage in the Dark*[11] left her island of Dominica unnamed. Elaine Potter Richardson, from Antigua, explained her decision to change her name to Jamaica Kincaid as 'a kind of invention', saying of the Caribbean, '"Jamaica" was symbolic of that place. I didn't come from Jamaica'.[12]

Nostalgia is a powerful element in much Caribbean women's fiction, and usually regarded as a dangerous element within it. This may be partly the consequence of what Marlene Nourbese Philip, a writer from Tobago now living in Canada, has pointed out, that

> growing up in the Caribbean, you grow up knowing that you're going to leave home. For one thing, the societies are too small to absorb all their trained people, so you have to leave.[13]

As Carole Boyce Davies has remarked of Caribbean women's writing in the United States, 'Migration creates the desire for home, which in turn produces the rewriting of home.'[14] *Home* is signalled as the important concept in the titles of many works of fiction by Caribbean women: for example, Erna Brodber's *Jane and Louisa Will Soon Come Home*,[15] Joan Cambridge's *Clarise Cumberbatch Want to Go Home*, Velma Pollard's *Homestretch*,[16] Vernella Fuller's *Going Back Home*,[17] June Henfrey's *Coming Home*.[18] Yet in all these works, *home* is elusive, and treated in varying ways as a 'magic place'.

Father Pedro Alonso O'Crovley wrote in 1774 that 'The conquest of the Indies filled all the vague diffusion of the imaginary spaces of man'.[19] These imaginary spaces have been constantly under reconstruction. As Dionne Brand has said of her birthplace, Trinidad, and Toronto, where she now resides, 'I live somewhere between these two places – and it's a place too – a new place we're making – a place a lot of people live in.'[20] Moving from the Caribbean has not only created a collective Caribbean identity, as it did for many immigrants to Britain, and weakened the sense of Caribbean identity, as it has for many black people now living in Canada and the US, who have ranged themselves along colour lines, but it has created a 'new place' in literature.

The use of the colloquial voice and of local idiom is now commonplace in Caribbean women's fiction, as titles like *Abeng*[21] (Michelle Cliff), *Myal*[22] (Erna Brodber), *Baby Mother and the King of Swords*[23] (Lorna Goodison), and *Me Dying Trial*[24] (Patricia Powell) indicate. What is less commonplace, with a few notable exceptions such as Michelle Cliff's *Free Enterprise*[25] and Beryl Gilroy's *Stedman and Joanna*[26] and *Inkle and Yarico*,[27] is a direct confrontation with the story of Caribbean slavery, which Orlando Patterson has described as 'unique in World history'[28] and the sociologist Paul Gilroy has called 'capitalism with its clothes off'.[29] The continuing consequences of slavery are explored throughout the fiction, but slavery itself is not addressed as it has been in such celebrated novels by African American women writers such as Margaret Walker's *Jubilee*,[30] Gayl Jones' *Corregidora*,[31] Sherley Anne Williams' *Dessa Rose*[32] or Toni Morrison's *Beloved*.[33]

Beryl Gilroy in 'Reflections', the autobiographical piece she has contributed to this volume, does not speak of her historical works, but reminisces about her Guyanese childhood, and, appropriately for a distinguished educator, traces the early influences which formed her, and which she used, in turn, to form others.

The Jamaican writer Velma Pollard names as 'The most important reason I write' the desire to preserve and record the past, and identifies 'Gran' as being her favourite piece of short prose, partly because she believes it to be the most autobiographical of her writings. The figure of the grandmother as an obvious emblem of the continuing influence of the past is pervasive in Caribbean women's fiction, often, like Velma Pollard's 'Gran' who is a master baker, recollected in terms of a practical skill: Ma Chess in Jamaica Kincaid's *Annie John*[34] is a healer, Granny Ruby in Joan Riley's *Romance*[35] does exquisite crochet work, Ma Tan in Jean Buffong's *Under the Silk Cotton Tree*[36] makes delicious coconut cakes and fudge. They can also, like Paule Marshall's Da-duh,[37] Beryl Gilroy's Gran in *Boy-Sandwich*, Erna Brodber's Granny Tucker,[38] Lorna Goodison's Miss Cordy[39] or Olive Senior's Ma Bell[40] be snobbish, rigid, or cruel, but they are almost invariably directly connected

with the history of their countries, whether through an association with its political independence, like Sarah in Jan Shinebourne's
Timepiece,[41] Granny Ivy in Zee Edgell's *Beka Lamb*[42] or the grandmother in Dionne Brand's short story 'Photograph',[43] or an association with its rural beauty, like Ma in Merle Hodge's *Crick Crack,
Monkey*[44] or the grandmother in Marlene Nourbese Philip's *Harriet's
Daughter*.[45] Merle Collins' 'Gran' has literally helped to make her
island, Grenada: as her daughter says at Gran's last illness,

> 'She don't have nothing to show for it, but this country is hers
> for sure! If is not hers is nobody own! She body *must* be hurt-
> ing her, yes, because all she strength in the cracks in the road
> in this country.'[46]

In Merle Collins' autobiographical piece, 'Writing Fiction, Writing Reality', she tells of her own observations of the 'making' of
Grenada in its recent history, and of her gradual development as
a writer. The Jamaican writer Vernella Fuller in her piece 'The
Development of My Art as a Fiction Writer', comments on all
three of her novels, and her growing confidence in herself as
the manager of her own work.

Vernella Fuller writes novels of social realism, and there is a
strong tradition of this in Caribbean women's fiction, *Every Light
in the House Burnin'*[47] and *Never Far From Nowhere*[48] by the London-
born Andrea Levy being typical recent examples. Erna Brodber,
despite being a professional sociologist of the Caribbean, is not
in this tradition, and, while Vernella Fuller reveals that she has
worried that her first novel was 'too simplistic and accessible',
Denise deCaires Narain in her article 'The Body of the Woman
in the Body of the Text: the Novels of Erna Brodber' comments
on the notorious difficulty of Brodber's fiction, and suggests some
appropriate critical responses.

A variety of theoretical and critical responses are represented
by chapters in this volume, appropriately for such a diverse
collection of texts. Thorunn Lonsdale in 'Literary Allusion in the
Fiction of Jean Rhys' discusses the significance of Jean Rhys's
literary borrowings and lendings. Heidi Slettedahl Macpherson
in 'Perceptions of Place: Geopolitical and Cultural Positioning in
Paule Marshall's Novels' gives a comprehensive account of location in Paule Marshall's work, and Alison Donnell in 'The Short
Fiction of Olive Senior', Laura Niesen de Abruna in 'Jamaica

Kincaid's Writing and the Maternal-Colonial Matrix' and Adele S. Newson in 'The Fiction of Zee Edgell' all combine political and literary readings of their material, setting their authors in the context of a complex colonial heritage.

In 'Dionne Brand: Writing the Margins' Charlotte Sturgess considers Dionne Brand's very particular status as 'a Trinidadian Canadian black lesbian feminist' through a theoretically informed analysis of stories from *Sans Souci*, and Sarah Lawson Welsh in 'Pauline Melville's Shape-Shifting Fictions' offers a similarly detailed reading of Melville's collection *Shape-shifter*. In Dionne Brand's recent novel *In Another Place, Not Here* one of the protagonists, Verlia, is shocked by her encounter with pure hatred at a Klan demonstration in Toronto, where she sees a woman who has had KKK engraved on her breast.[49] In Pauline Melville's *The Ventriloquist's Tale* one of the characters muses on the possibilities of turning the whole of Guyana into a theme park for tourists:

> People could act being slaves. Ships full of indentured labourers would arrive in the docks. Visitors would stare at Amerindian villages where the villagers would be obliged to return to traditional dress and costumes. Hollywood films could be made and package dramas created for the American and European education industries.[50]

Each of these passages encapsulates, in its different way, a warning to the reader to take Caribbean women's fiction seriously, as all our contributors have done, and to regard it neither as intrinsically celebratory nor as a museum-piece.

Notes

1. J. Cambridge, *Clarise Cumberbatch Want to Go Home* (London: Women's Press, 1987).
2. V. Belgrave, *Ti Marie* (London: Heinemann, 1988).
3. Quoted in D. Lowenthal, *West Indian Societies* (New York, London and Toronto: OUP, 1972) p. 9.
4. A. Lorde, *Zami: A New Spelling of My Name* (Trumansburg, NY: Crossing Press, 1982) p. 9.
5. Ibid., p. 14.
6. P. Marshall, *Praisesong for the Widow* (London: Virago, 1983).
7. P. Marshall, *Daughters* (London, Serpent's Tail, 1991).

8. B. Flanagan, *You Alone Are Dancing* (Leeds: Peepal Tree Press, 1990).
9. M. Collins, *The Colour of Forgetting* (London: Virago, 1995).
10. B. Gilroy, *Boy-Sandwich* (London: Heinemann, 1989).
11. J. Rhys, *Voyage in the Dark* (London: Constable, 1934).
12. S.R. Cudjoe, 'Jamaica Kincaid and the Modernist Project: An Interview' (1987) in S.R. Cudjoe (ed.), *Caribbean Women Writers: Essays from the first International Conference* (Wellesley, Mass.: Calaloux, 1990) p. 220.
13. M.N. Philip, 'Writing a Memory of Losing That Place', J. Williamson (ed.), *Sounding Differences* (Toronto: University of Toronto Press) p. 230.
14. C.B. Davies, *Black Women, Writing and Identity: Migrations of the Subject* (London and NY: Routledge, 1996) p. 113.
15. E. Brodber, *Jane and Louisa Will Soon Come Home* (London: New Beacon, 1980).
16. V. Pollard, *Homestretch* (London: Longman, 1994).
17. V. Fuller, *Going Back Home* (London: Women's Press, 1992).
18. J. Henfrey, *Coming Home: Stories* (Leeds: Peepal Tree Press, 1994).
19. Quoted in A. Pagden, *The Fall of Natural Man: The American Indian and the Origins of Comparative Ethnology* (Cambridge: Cambridge University Press, 1982) p. 10.
20. Speaking at the Voice Box, Royal Festival Hall, London, on 2 June 1992.
21. M. Cliff, *Abeng* (Trumansburg, NY: Crossing Press, 1984).
22. E. Brodber, *Myal* (London: New Beacon, 1988).
23. L. Goodison, *Baby Mother and the King of Swords* (London: Longman, 1990).
24. P. Powell, *Me Dying Trial* (London: Heinemann, 1994).
25. M. Cliff, *Free Enterprise* (London: Penguin, 1993).
26. B. Gilroy, *Stedman and Joanna – A Love in Bondage* (New York: Vantage Press, 1991).
27. B. Gilroy, *Inkle and Yarico* (Leeds, Peepal Tree Press, 1996).
28. O. Patterson, *The Sociology of Slavery: An Analysis of the Origins, Development and Structure of Negro Slave Society in Jamaica* (London: Macgibbon and Kee, 1967) p. 9.
29. P. Gilroy, *The Black Atlantic: Modernity and Double Consciousness* (London and New York, Vervo, 1993) p. 15.
30. M. Walker, *Jubilee* (New York: Houghton Mifflin, 1966).
31. G. Jones, *Corregidora* (New York: Random House, 1975).
32. S.A. Williams, *Dessa Rose* (London: Macmillan, 1986).
33. T. Morrison, *Beloved* (London, Chatto and Windus, 1987).
34. J. Kincaid, *Annie John* (London: Picador, 1983).
35. J. Riley, *Romance* (London: Women's Press, 1988).
36. J. Buffong, *Under the Silk Cotton Tree* (London: Women's Press, 1992).
37. P. Marshall, 'To Da-duh, In Memoriam', *Merle: a novella and other stories* (London: Virago, 1983).
38. E. Brodber, 'Voices', *Jane and Louisa Will Soon Come Home*.
39. L. Goodison, 'The Big Shot', *Baby Mother and the King of Swords*.

40. O. Senior, 'Country of the One Eye God', *Summer Lightning and other stories* (London: Heinemann, 1986).
41. J. Shinebourne, *Timepiece* (Leeds: Peepal Tree Press, 1986).
42. Z. Edgell, *Beka Lamb* (London: Heinemann, 1982).
43. D. Brand, 'Photograph' *Sans Souci* (New York: Firebrand, 1989).
44. M. Hodge, *Crick Crack, Monkey* (London: Heinemann, 1970) p. 14.
45. M.N. Philip, *Harriet's Daughter* (London: Heinemann, 1988) p. 9.
46. M. Collins, 'Gran', *Rain Darling* (London: Women's Press, 1990) p. 54.
47. A. Levy, *Every Light in the House Burnin'* (London: Headline Review, 1994).
48. A. Levy, *Never Far From Nowhere* (London: Headline Review, 1996).
49. D. Brand, *In Another Place, Not Here* (Toronto: Alfred A. Knopf Canada, 1996) p. 173.
50. P. Melville, *The Ventriloquist's Tale* (London: Bloomsbury, 1997) p. 324.

Part I
Literary Autobiography

1

Reflections

Beryl Gilroy

My grandparents said that on the ninth day after I was born, I was taken out of the bedroom to show my face to the sun and the neighbours. I blinked, I was told. It was a good omen.

My village gave me a religious, family, and place identity, and my personal identity was represented by my given names, which I didn't really like. I think my names were meant to mean particular qualities by those who named me. Names are given, and children when grown may or may not validate them, and are thus open to condemnation, over-correction and blame within the family. Of course there are exceptions to this view. I was named Beryl after some kind of precious stone, and Agatha after Agatha Christie, a thriller writer whom my aunt had been reading. My mother loved Bertha Clay. Mercifully I was spared Bertha.

Our priest, who thought it good that I had the name of a saint, gleefully told me, just before my confirmation, that Agatha was the patron saint of bell-founders, and with mouthwatering relish rehearsed her story. A woman of noble birth, she caught the eye of a rakish Roman named Quintian, who had been sent to her village of Catania, in Sicily. She refused his advances, but he could not resist her vivacious disposition and her beauty. He obtained a harlot to show her the ways of such women. Agatha resisted and she was denounced as a Christian and sentenced by Diocletian to have a double mastectomy. St Peter appeared to her, to comfort her, but she passed away. Her breasts, now looking like bells, were taken to Quintian on a dish. He asked, 'Where is the maiden?' He was so stricken with grief, he too was converted to Christianity and was subsequently beheaded. Thereafter Agatha became the patron saint of bell-founders and is symbolized by two bell-like breasts on a dish. The story increased my dislike of the name. Here I was, a little black girl, bound to the reign of Diocletian, an evil ruler of Rome.

My identity consisted of different strands, woven together by guidance and experience, and by the freedom to learn by trying out new ideas. I liked to learn, and even now get excited by research. I learned to be thrifty and careful of debt from my grandfather, and to be responsible, committed and self-sufficient from my grandmother. Because I could choose what I did with my time, I did not become regimented at an early age. I learned to be original and creative, something I once won a prize for at school. When quite young I came upon 'words' and spent a great deal of time localizing them. I also knew that some people would make much of my 'difference,' – but that the problem would be theirs.

Rising above all my identities was my colonial identity. It also meant more to others than it did to me. It consisted of façade and charade. From time to time officials from Georgetown would come to our village. Houseowners would be told to clear their parapets of castor oil plants, shame bush and other shrubs. After the people had completed the tasks, a car with some whites in it would rush at breakneck speed through our village. The officials had come! We had cleared the parapet, but they had not noticed the absence of shrubs and trees and they had not stopped, and we had not seen them. Later there would be talk. Our visitor had spent the day drinking gin with his confederates on the plantations.

No one ever said what 'colonial' truly meant. The shops were full of goods, we could buy books at 2s 6d (2/6) a time, and on our exercise books was the face of a serious-looking person which we could deface at will. Over us were people with a duality of expectations about us. We were expected to be ignorant or competent, lazy or energetic, dirty or clean, honest or dishonest, and always able to smile, dance and respect the whites we happened to meet.

I grew up with a belief in competence. It is the pivot of my identity, for wherever I work, whatever I do, it is in the name of my grandparents who raised me and the country in which I happened to have been born. My grandparents said 'Do it once. Do it well else you waste time.' I agree entirely.

I had enrolled at the University of London before I came to Britain six years after the second world war, Britain was in the grip of reconstruction and rationing had not yet ended. I was excited by the prospect of being lectured to by some of the stalwarts of the educational world. When I started teaching in October of 1953 I became conscious of my attributed (Negro at the time) colonial heritage. Since Mimesis had produced me, I was not quite the thing – 'a mere Jackdaw in borrowed feathers'.

I had read about the Jackdaw in my Royal Reader Book 2 which children in the 'second standard' read, and had the metaphor explained as 'A carrion crow in parrot's feathers'. I was brought up in a highly literate family and subsequently pushed into teaching by our priest, the Reverend Headman. It was his idea that our parish should produce its own teachers. I have always approved of myself through my individuality and was known as a creative teacher, even if questioning and rebellious. My grandparents always forbade me to see with other people's eyes, hear with their ears or think their thoughts. When as a six-year-old I was competing to reproduce 'The Fox and the Grapes', I wrote the story from the point of view of the grapes.

I communicate well with children, and was co-opted into helping on a supplementary food programme by UNICEF. It was while working with undernourished children that I became interested in nutrition and its relationship to under-achievement. We were expected to teach a national curriculum, and I carefully studied the children's responses to what we taught. Young children, I observed, learn by doing, getting involved with choice, selection, sequencing and retrieving from within themselves the persistence to begin and end a task. Many of the concepts taught through chalk and talk, slates, pencil and the chalk board were hardly understood by some children. They were bored, as I had been in my school-refusing years. As dictated by the teacher's book, we taught them about the seasons, about squirrels, stoats, the Manchester Ship Canal. Up to that time I had never read a novel set in British Guiana, although I did subsequently read Mittelholzer's *Corentyne Thunder*. It was as if black people (barring the clown, the caricature or the savage) did not exist in literature. All the black writers of my childhood were American; Lilian Smith, Booker T. Washington, Paul Laurence Dunbar are some I can remember.

Our village, like most British Guianese villages, was a little island surrounded by opinion, speculation, and something known to the villagers as 'dem seh you seh' (benign gossip). I began to contribute to a weekly educational column which teachers read, and new ideas infiltrated our schools. For me, coming to Britain extended my ideas about the purpose of school. Research showed that hungry children could hardly learn and many children after the second world war were hungry, malnourished, sleepy and tired.

Our curriculum was based on faculty theory. Every child had the faculty to learn, and every teacher the faculty to teach. This faculty was based on patience, a sense of vocation, skill, love of children, knowledge, commitment, continuing re-entry into the world of the child, and the ability to monitor ourselves as well as the children. I enjoyed learning about teaching in Britain, for I began to know myself better. I found out that I was the product of centuries of mimesis, appearing first as compulsion in the lives of my forebears when they were forced to surrender everything that was theirs and yield to cultural dominance and its consequences. I understood how. I learned to despise anything that was of Africa. I never once considered the fact that my primary label, my name, had nothing whatsoever to do with me and as a consequence I cooperated with my own colonization. What saved me were the gifts of oral history I received from my grandparents and their friends. Nevertheless, I wrote stories, poems, minibooks in longhand and bartered them to my cousins in return for various objects. These were fun, but at school the teachers were carping, pseudo-ladies, patterning themselves on the vicar's wife and other plantation 'ladies'. They failed hopelessly to improve me. My grandmother said no one could be twice brought up and she had brought me up already.

Teaching in British Guiana during the fifties allowed teachers to be innovative. Children were keen and when there weren't books in the schools, they could be bought in the shops. There was a culture of reading as the gateway to learning. Scholarship was valued. Throughout the society there was a vibrancy – a mix of cultures, that stood me in good stead when I came to Britain. It did not matter from which part of the world a student was sent to Britain, we had a lot in common. We had the same educational heritage, prose or poetry, tragedy or comedy. We had kissed Shakespeare, Byron, Charles Lamb and all the rest on their literary cheeks and whispered how much we loved them.

Quite early in the fifties Ted Brathwaite wrote *To Sir with Love*, *Paid Servant* and *Choice of Straws* and uncannily reproduced the language of the white working class. No, this wasn't Dickens or Mayhew on their walks abroad among the poor of London. It was a black man, discriminated against, emotionally abused, healing himself by virtue of his own integrity and by persistently playing 'I spy' with 'the Lord of the Flies'. Later came Sam Selvon with whom I shared a platform on his last visit to Britain. I joked that people our age were waiting in life's departure lounge and he replied wistfully, 'I am nearer the exit than you, Beryl.' How prophetic! He introduced the idioms and rhythm of West Indian English spawned by colonialism itself, to their creators. Unlike the French who liberally offered their language to their natives for ulterior purposes, the English withheld theirs for purposes of cultural dominance. In both cases, they sowed the wind and reaped the whirlwind. One has ended up with mutations of French and the other with the pidgin of colonialism.

I began to write children's books when my class, mainly Cypriots and refugee Jewish children, fell asleep under the yoke of a series of school texts called *Janet and John*. They were written by an Australian, I believe, mainly for middle-class children. The family lived in a bungalow: mother, father, Janet and John with their dog whose name has long since vanished from my mind. My class had names like Costas and Androulla, Andreas and Katina, Syd and Amos, Sharon, Leah, Thalia and Rachel. I felt a kinship with all the children, as I knew the pain of exclusion and discrimination. Because the Jews were the first to accept foreign students into their homes in the fifties, along with British radicals who had fought for freedom, I spoke up in defence of Jewish children. There were very few black children in London schools at that time. In my school with a roll of 300, there were four children of Jamaican parents. I got fed up with the patronizing and the unfairness. I resigned. Just thinking of the mental anguish of those children in what is now called post-traumatic shock, droning 'Look Janet . . . Look John. Look! Look!' and other crass utterances, I developed school phobia rather than be stressed to extinction. These were my best years. A cocoon time, when I enjoyed my family.

I returned after ten years of absence from full-time teaching and was for two years a part-time teacher. After a while, I accepted full-time work, and six months later was appointed head of a Camden school. It was during those ten years that I wrote *The Green and Gold Readers* for Guyanese schools (Longman), *Yellow Bird* and other books (Macmillan) and *Compass Books* (Cassell). I wrote novels as well, but they could not get past the readers who were opiniated West Indian males playing the Gender Game. Women were peripheral creatures.

My school contained children from 55 countries and no one set of texts would meet all their needs. During this time I met Leila Berg, a prolific writer of the period, and a champion of children's rights. I wrote *Ten Nippers* for the series and *Three Little Nippers*. The children loved Nippers. It was not unusual to hear children saying, 'My mum does that', or 'My dad is just like that'. Nippers healed children because they introduced philosophical discussion to children. It made them aware of the eco-system of class. Reading should be therapeutic to children. Nippers were limited to class – race and gender had not yet been invented in Britain. There weren't enough of us.

I returned to the West Indies in 1968 and visited a friend who ran a superior nursing home for the mothers of successful West Indian professionals in the USA. If there were men, I did not see any. I thought of myself in that situation and I told my friend I would run away. Thus *Frangipani House* took seed. When later, I was coping with similar problems in the care of my ageing mother, I reflected on her life and 'Mama King' was the result. (My mother could never leave her nearby grandchildren to visit us. She liked to be needed and 'they needed her', she said. But my favourite aunt did visit and my children loved her stories.)

Along with *Black Teacher* and *In Praise of Love and Children*, *Frangipani House*, judging from the letters I receive, is my most read book. I have written to students at length about it. Actually I try always to answer all the letters I receive. I would have liked to rewrite *Frangipani House* one more time before publication, but alas, I was unable to do so.

Works by Beryl Gilroy

Black Teacher (autobiography) (1976)
Frangipani House (1986)
Boy-Sandwich (1989)
Stedman and Joanna – A Love in Bondage (1991)
Sunlight on Sweet Water (autobiography) (1994)
Gather the Faces (1996)
In Praise of Love and Children (1996)
Inkle and Yarico (1996)

2

The Most Important Reason I Write

Velma Pollard

Perhaps the most important reason that I write is that I have a great desire to record aspects of life, events and experiences which I think are worth keeping. I grew up in rural Jamaica in the forties. In the fifties I went to school in the capital city, Kingston, but continued to spend all my holidays at home in the country. I write from a memory of those times and those places. It is very easy to lose a sense of the past and have each generation evolve a notion of what existed at a time before the present. I consider that a tragedy.

There is a great deal that no longer exists in Jamaica today that was important to life in Jamaica yesterday. In my fiction I make these things affect imaginary people. There is an interrelationship between history and literature which when exploited gives a clearer picture of any given time than either discipline would have been able to offer independently. A picture or a description of any phenomenon can tell only so much. The reactions of people in a story give life to the picture. When I am lucky my things get published and eventually people read them. I will illustrate the point I have been trying to make by commenting on 'Gran', a long short story from the collection *Considering Woman*, and on *Karl – a novella*.[1]

'Gran' is my favourite piece of short prose, partly, I believe, because it is closer to being autobiographical than anything else I have written. I decided to write about my grandmother because I loved her, but also because she represents one kind of Jamaican woman, the kind that is called the backbone of this country. I wanted people to know about this kind of woman.

My grandfather died when my mother (the first of seven

17

children) was nine years old. He left my grandmother the house she lived in, several acres of land planted with sugarcane and a mill-and-copper. On that she singlehandedly brought up seven children. She was both man and woman on that farm, working from sun-up to sun-down supervising the cutting of cane and the making of sugar (as a cottage industry), which is what the mill-and-copper was about. She was a baker too, baking from a cottage oven, to supply bread and cheap pastry to all the shops around. When I was a child people still made basic sugar (wet sugar) by grinding the cane in an ancient mill and boiling the liquid to sugar in a copper vat housed in a thatch-roofed hut.

History books will carry pictures of the mill house but I believe that the literary treatment of it within Gran's story brings a new and important dimension to its appreciation. One short example should suffice. At the end of the story the reader is left with a picture of the mill without the mill house, which is gone. The metal of the mill looks like a carving ' . . . something struck in bronze'. But the memory it evokes in the grandchild turned woman who visits the ancient homestead after many years is nostalgic and emotional:

> On the left, the metal trunk of the cane-mill, like a work of art from an early civilisation, sat silent with its wooden arms ill-fitting and unsuitable, far too long for such a stubby trunk, dangling in the dust of the very last season's dead and juiceless cane.

> If you were quiet, as I was. . . . The last of the birds would pick up the echo of the years and quickly yoke a cow or a horse to those long and useless wooden limbs; would show the bulging muscles of the smooth-skinned black strong man in his flour-bag vest feeding the cane between the black and heavy metal gums confident that barrel on barrel of yellow liquid frothing white would pour from the bamboo gutter set there to receive it. . . .

> Or you could look at the silent broken-down top of a forgotten thatched hut and see rockets of smoke shoot upward from a white-marl chimney while the smell of boiling sugar sweetened miles and miles of air.[2]

In today's local Jamaican parlance one could say 'Gran' is an excuse to 'big up' a strong black female symbol of Jamaican peasantocracy.[3]

She worked hard all week and spent almost the whole of Sunday in church. Her propensity for hard work, her kindness and her high principles all made her an outstanding woman.

The novella *Karl* looks at the product of an environment similar to Gran's and marks how Karl's psyche buckles under when confronted with the mores of the brown middle and upper classes.

I grew up in a situation where the written word was king and where education was king (or perhaps queen). Of course I know that many people feel that country people are ignorant and do not read. They would have been surprised to find Gibbon's *Decline and Fall of the Roman Empire* and Tennyson's complete works rubbing shoulders with *The Rosary* and *The Basket of Flowers* on the bookshelf in our living room (drawing room then). But those were my early companions. I say that to emphasize that stereotypes have exceptions, and that urban non-readers and rural readers are equally part of the Jamaican landscape.

Long after I had left my village I learnt of other dichotomies to do with money and skin colour and family history in a severely stratified society. One wonders why poor whites, poor blacks, and poor Indians never made common cause, but have wasted energy seeking some kind of superiority over each other.

Karl, the protagonist of the novella, does everything that I would consider right: he goes to elementary school and is the perfect scholar. He gets a scholarship to high school, where he does well, and earns a scholarship to university. Again he does well and returns home to a job commensurate with his education and talents.

I understand the frustration of the Karls of Jamaica. I grew up in a place where education was thought to be the key to every future. Everybody in my elementary school class wanted to get a scholarship – a parish scholarship for 'unprovided parishes', that is, parishes which did not have a high school within their borders. Very late in life I heard a friend and colleague berating an enemy with the words 'You are a scholarship boy. My parents paid for every bit of my education'. For the first time I noted that there was another point of view on such a fundamental matter. To my urban, middle-class friend, being a scholarship boy was low-status, while I had thought it a matter for pride. The value of education paled there before the value of the money that could pay for it.

Karl's frustration and his eventual death are the result of his dilemma which is in turn partly the result of his personal history. He is faced with a job situation which seeks to make him ineffective, a social situation which each day unearths a new surprise – something his background and upbringing would have prevented him from knowing – and a marriage that has become less than satisfying. His discomfort with his position as he reviews what he himself and his mother wished for him is described in the comment: ' . . . when you get what you want and stop wanting what you get, is fool you turn fool'. His wife Daphne survives because she accepts without question the privilege her husband's position brings, the kind of privilege she had spent her life working towards.

The question implicit in this story is whether the Jamaican society of the time in which the story is set really supports the upward mobility of the little man. Kenneth, the young man presented in the epilogue, comes at a time when this society allows the individual the right to certain choices. Kenneth accepts that right and opts out of corporate Jamaica. The retired headmaster who has taught them both comments on their differences.

The narrative provides another opportunity for describing the hard-working Jamaican woman. Karl's mother is a single mother, not, as in the case of Gran, because of the death of a husband, but because her young lover ran away from the village forever when he discovered that she was pregnant. The novella notes briefly the stereotypical disappearing father, while Aunti's own father, by contrast, is a returning resident from years on the Panama Canal, where he worked like hundreds of other Caribbean men. He provides her and her bright son Karl with the security of a home.

That father was my opportunity to draw another character who has always interested me – the Jamaican who returns after years of living and working abroad. The history of labour in Latin America includes the lives of workers (chiefly men) from all over the Caribbean seeking a better life. The evidence of these migrants remains in the tongues of black people all over that continent who speak, in addition to Spanish, Anglophone Creole languages that were transported there at the turn of the century.

The following brief extract conjures up the old man in the memory of his grandson:

> Gramps used to tell me about the glittering shops in Panama, only he called it Canal Zone, and he never said shop, he said

commissary and made me spell out that big word CO-MMI-SSA-RY. I am not sure this is what he intended, but I somehow got the impression that everything was free – you just walked around taking things from shelves and putting them in large shopping bags. And always I could see him, straining with heavy packages, grinning his wide grin, right down to the gold teeth in the far recesses of his mouth, his whole strong, shiny, black face lit up with pleasure saying, "Caramba!" as he took a bar of Baby Root from the stand. (Caramba was the special thing he said when anybody brought him something unusual or when Aunti cooked a really grand Sunday dinner.)[4]

The narrative also provides a description of the comparative lifestyles of the different classes of Jamaican society and of the beautiful Jamaican landscape against which the stories of these lives are played out. Karl grows up in a picturesque village in the hills of rural St Andrew where he lives in a humble home. As a successful corporate citizen he lives in urban St Andrew with all the trappings of financial success. Things change. Karl and Kenneth exist with perhaps a decade between. I felt the need to document the battles that a Karl would have had to fight.

Later, in *Homestretch*, I try to record the altruistic behaviour of ordinary people (returning residents this time) in a place where journalists mostly report the negatives, ignoring the positives which are there if you look for them. It is a novel about my ideals for a society which now exerts itself in the dual pursuit of money and drugs.

Notes

1. *Considering Woman* was published by the Women's Press, London, 1988. *Karl* was published first in a bilingual (Spanish/English) edition by Casa de las America, Havana in 1993 then in *Karl and Other Stories* by Longman, Harlow, 1994.
2. V. Pollard, *Considering Woman* (London: Women's Press, 1989) p. 69.
3. I owe the term to Louis Lindsay, Social Scientist at the University of the West Indies, and will continue to use it because I like it.
4. V. Pollard, *Karl and Other Stories* (Harlow, Essex: Longman, 1994) p. 17.

Works by Velma Pollard

Considering Women (stories) (1989)
Homestretch (1994)
Karl and Other Stories (1994)

3

Writing Fiction, Writing Reality

Merle Collins

In March 1984, I left my home country, Grenada, travelling via St Lucia to England. On October 19th, 1983, several people in Grenada, including political leaders and the Prime Minister Maurice Bishop, had been killed in internecine political strife. I was very much a part of what one called the political process. I believed in some kind of revolutionary change for my island home not because I had any profound theoretical knowledge of the Marxism-Leninism which the revolutionary leaders came eventually to advocate but because I had lived through the times of political opportunism; because I knew, lived and was concerned about inequities based on race, class and gender.

Eventually political leaders of about my age or a little older began to verbalize all of this, or most of this; began to put into perspective the class and race inequalities in the society; began to talk about the effects of colonialism and the need to define new parameters for education, for the economy, for social relations, in order to raise the collective self-esteem of the majority. When this happened I felt that I had found a major motivating factor for my existence. I was not in the country when the then government was overthrown on March 13th, 1979. But when I returned at the beginning of 1982, there was for me no hesitation about being part of 'the process'. What Marxism-Leninism meant for me was, in a vague way, equality of the classes, better living conditions for everybody, education available to all. And at that time I believed implicitly in altruism where the welfare of the country was concerned.

I imbued these political leaders – who, I appreciate now, were themselves travelling to an understanding of self, nation and politics – with a sagacity which was not yet theirs. When I realized they were stumbling, I still felt that they would recognize the shapes of impediments in the dark. When they fell over these and brought the whole country with them, stumbling into a bruised and bloody mess on October 19th, I was, to use a word not original but appropriate, staggered. I realized, so to speak, that we, leaders and followers, were basically all more or less in the same boat where political sagacity was concerned. And a few days later the United States, which I had no reason to believe had any interest in Grenada, staged an invasion to save the nation from murderous leaders.

I was against the invasion. But when, in those early days after the October 25th landing of American troops, friends who had supported the idea of revolutionary change asked me quietly, but what else could be done? What would happen if the Americans hadn't come? I could only say quietly, 'We would have worked it out. We would have worked it out.' And we didn't argue about it. From us, there were no angry shouts of 'Down with imperialism' or 'Up with imperialism'. I recognized my friends' ambivalence; they recognized mine. And as American troops (with a quieter, more sheepish-looking Caribbean contingent) set about consolidating the 'rescue', disposing of revolutionary billboards and forcibly sequestering the more obviously revolutionary figures, I listened with friends to the welcoming shouts of those who were openly supportive of the American presence. We shared in the silence of others – those who were unequivocally opposed, those who regretted the invasion but were still thankful that it had happened, and those who were secretly relieved, although they would not express gratitude to the USA for invading a country it obviously considered subordinate and inferior. In those days, I asked myself whether in this small-island post-independence reality, some kind of continuing colonialism was inevitable, whether the destiny of these islands would necessarily be agriculture, tourism, dependence and insularity.

What does all this have to do with the story of my work as a creative writer? That year, 1984, was the time when, with my belief in one kind of expression of truth totally crushed, my belief in the possibility of altruism in politics crumbling, I came to have more confidence about using the power of fictitious re-creation to tease out the truth.

I had been writing before, in particular writing a lot of poetry during the period of revolutionary experimentation, but my writing then was a way of seeking out the inner truths of revolutionary excitement. When I began to question political decisions, I could express quietly in writing what I wouldn't be safe or comfortable saying on a political platform. When I was enthusiastic, the best way to express that enthusiasm was in poetry. Now that was gone; my writing turned towards the politics of existence. The decision was not made as clearly as it seems now that I'm writing about it. But this, in effect, was what happened.

When I left Grenada in 1984, I had with me a number of poems that I had written and performed in Grenada during the revolutionary years. I knew that I wanted to continue writing. I felt that there was a lot that I would have to write about just to do that trite but appropriately named thing called 'getting it out of the system'. To try to understand my journey. I had no wish then to explore issues in any formal political sense. Although I did not know many details of the actual events of the political trauma of October 1983, I felt that I knew, in a deeper way, a lot of what had happened in Grenada's journey. I wanted to talk about this, but, in the spirit of the times, there seemed nothing to talk about if I did not know sensational details. I remember that when I first talked about 'having to write this', some people encouraged me, saying that I should, because they felt I knew a lot. I would have a story to tell. They were talking about a different kind of writing. In that leaving and in that wanting to tell a truth, I was carrying in my head the beginnings of *Angel*.

I have often been asked whether *Angel* is autobiography. What it is really is fiction drawing heavily on the reality of my existence, of the existence of those around me, reconstructing stories around images from the Grenada of the 1950s onwards. Using broad details rooted in lived experience, it dramatizes particular facets of existence, in an effort to understand, dynamically, how events in Grenada during the neo-colonial and post-independence period could have led to the 1980s and beyond. It focuses on the lives of people not in the headlines. It might be broadly called autobiographical. It is not straight autobiography.

While writing *Angel*, I came to understand and appreciate more fully how colonialism continues in a world that is often characterized as 'post-colonial'. I read interpretations of the Grenada situation constructed by North American and British writers, many of whom were concerned with Marxist-Leninist interpretations, with political leadership and the US–Soviet axis of influence. Reading what they wrote, I thought constantly of the many Grenadians who supported revolutionary ideas and the many who did not support them, people who gave allegiance to different political leaders because of the circumstances of their lives. I wanted to write something, not any grand political treatise, but a story about everyday lives, about expressions of revolutionary ideals which are hardly ever voiced on political platforms or in an international forum, about expressions of neocolonial ideas which were perfectly understandable when one traced how naturally they were born from the experience of colonialism. And I didn't want to shout any revolutionary slogans. The collapse of the Grenada revolution had reminded me of the value of family and friends, many of whom expressed concern for my welfare in various ways, not because they were ever in agreement with my political views, but because they were family, or because they were friends.

In London, while writing *Angel*, after a while I also started on a PhD in Government, essentially researching Grenadian political history at the Public Records Office and necessarily also reading the material that was being written about Grenada. The people whom I met at seminar groups, at various discussion groups and in social situations throughout London, in many cases, had very different experiences from the people whom I was writing about. Often, they had experiences that were vastly different from mine. As I researched, I was struck constantly by the differences between political pronouncements by leaders and the everyday lives of my characters. I thought about such issues as political leadership and class, political leadership and representation, colony and nation. As I listened, I was constantly conscious of difference and bothered by what seemed to be the impossibility of the existence of peace in one country, far less world peace.

London, where many people from once-British colonies were constantly meeting to discuss their particular circumstances of persecution because of oppositional politics, of migration for educational opportunities, for economic opportunities or simply because of wanderlust, was a perfect place for such troubling thoughts. In fact, when I left for London in 1984, knowing I wanted to write but not knowing whether I would get published, I was conscious that Caribbean writers before me had lived there and found a space for their writing. The example of Lamming, Selvon,

Una Marson and several others contributed to my hope of finding a space for writing in England. It is a fascinating comment on colonialism that so many writers whose work might be considered anti-colonial in instinct, whatever their intentions might be, go to London to write. George Lamming has written at length about the phenomenon of writers from the region wanting 'to get out' of the country of their birth in order to write.

Writing in Grenada in the revolutionary days, I was content with my audience (audience, yes, since much of my poetry was performed and/or read aloud in public places). My ideas were not only considered to be fairly well expressed in poetry, but they were also in tandem with those of the revolution and so were given space. Writers less given to performance and less given to expression of their political views, supportive or otherwise, may have felt they had little opportunity or space for development. Writing as a way of life, writing as a profession, was not a popular enterprise. There were no precedents, no known Grenadian writers who had published and promoted their work, and there was little encouragement for this activity. By 1984, I knew that I wanted to continue to write, I had begun to think that I wanted to look for opportunities for publication. This was an added problem in a situation where my political truth had vanished. London, where others had wandered before me, seemed like a good idea.

In London, I not only found details of my history resting in documents in various libraries, but discussions of issues of race, nationhood and gender lent further complicating substance to the already complicated. I decided to settle down to learn about myself. Once, at the Public Records Office at Kew, a woman (white, British, in her late fifties or early sixties perhaps) asked me curiously what I was researching. She told me that she was researching her ancestry and said, with genuine curiosity, that she had often wondered what the black people whom she saw looking through similar records were researching. I was not offended. She did not seem to me to intend offence. She was genuinely curious. I explained that in my case, I was researching my history, finding details which could help me eventually determine my ancestry. Many of the records for my own country, Grenada, were there, I said. I could trace movements of ships carrying enslaved people, of ships carrying indentured workers, of ships carrying liberated Africans. I could follow the involvement in the slave trade of merchants from Liverpool and Bristol, for example. And I could trace a lot of the political goings-on in the Caribbean up to at least the 1950s. She was amazed. And I could not help reflecting that it was this kind of lack of information both about our own stories and about the stories of each other that fosters the continuation of bigoted attitudes.

I worked towards a PhD in Government more as part of a search for answers than because of a very focused interest in academia. I had no wish to teach or even work actively in the area of politics and government. I knew that then. If I had been thinking of how the PhD would further my academic career, I would perhaps have studied literature. My main early academic interest had always been literature. I have never really been interested in the theoretical aspects of those other disciplines in which I found myself getting more involved. I have chased the content, seeking the information with a view to deeper understanding of the processes that have shaped me and the Caribbean. And fiction, recreating stories round the kind of fiction that History is, usually helps me towards that deeper understanding, and towards expressing myself, hopefully in a way less didactic than many political pronouncements. Perhaps the didacticism that may be part of political interest comes across somewhat in the shaping of my poetry, informed by oral traditions and leaning very much towards narrative commentary on particular events or situations. The novel *Angel*, my first, developed partly because of the perception that the story I wanted to tell was a long one. In response to the articles and news reports about Grenada in that 1983–84 period, characters were tumbling over themselves in my head in an effort to say something. They were responding to nearly every article, to news reports, saying things like, 'What you talking about? You know me at all?' and 'You remind me of a doctor I went to one time. He talk louder because when I didn't answer his nonsense he thought I couldn't hear.'

With this activity going on in my head, I knew that there was no way all of these people aching to say something could be accommodated in a short story. They wanted different years, different parts of their lives highlighted, they wanted to take a long walk from then to now, pointing out things along the way. That was a novel. In Grenada during that period of revolutionary excitement, I had written poetry, perhaps partly because there were the opportunities for public readings at rallies and partly because there was so much constant commentary about what was going on. My first collection of poetry focused on Grenada and most poems, written during that period in Grenada, moved from pieces reflecting excitement to ones voicing disappointment to those questioning the conflict and the invasion and expressing sadness. 'Nabel String', the first poem in that collection, was the only one written in the United States, where I was studying in that immediate pre-Grenada-revolutionary period. In it, the nabel string (umbilical cord) is pulling me back to Grenada. The last poem is 'A Song of Pain'. So the collection tells a particular part of the Grenadian story, and also, inevitably, of facets of my early poetical (and political) development. I knew, during that entire period, that I was interested in orality, in finding ways to incorporate the rhythms of Grenadian speech-patterns and proverbial expressions in my writing. I was interested, too, in the actual presentation and performance of the work.

But even before writing those poems, in fact before leaving to study in the United States, I had an early interest in the short story as a form. In my adult life, the first piece I remember writing and presenting at a public forum in Grenada was a short story, now entitled 'The Walk', and published in a 1990 collection, *Rain Darling*. 'The Walk', like 'Butterfly Born', a poem written later, tells the story of a little girl growing up in Grenada somewhere around the late 1920s or early 1930s. The child walked from almost one end of the island to the other, running important errands for her mother, who was a domestic worker living in the shadow of an estate Great House. 'The Walk', concerned with issues of class and survival, drew for its material on stories told me by my mother about her own childhood. *Now* I say it was concerned with issues of class and survival. When I wrote it, I knew only that it drew on stories told by my mother which had moved me profoundly. I was not conscious, at that time, that I wanted to talk about 'class'.

Since then, I have been writing short stories occasionally. I am now working on a collection which will probably be ready by the end of 1996. Most of these are new stories but the title story, 'The Ladies are Upstairs', was published in a 1994 Virago collection, *By the Light of the Silvery Moon*. Essentially the new collection reiterates my interest in class issues. Some of it was written in London, some conceived and born in London, and some conceived in various places and born in the United States.

The experience of being Black in London (and not specifically the experience of being Caribbean in London) kept me looking back to the Caribbean which had shaped my perceptions. Exploring facets of that experience of what is generally called 'underdevelopment' helped contextualize for me my Black London reality, helped to illuminate the marvellous fact that while Britain knew so little about blackness, some of Black Britain also knew little about the everyday conditions of existence in the Caribbean. In London, when there were discussions about health care and pensions, I thought about the presence or absence of these in parts of the region which had shaped me; when there were discussions which seemed to focus on the West Indian child's inadequate preparation for education, I thought of the British-based education system in many parts of the Caribbean. I thought of the schools which had taken on my early shaping, I thought of how important formal education was generally considered to be. With the advantage of being able to observe circumstances on both sides of the Atlantic, I marvelled that people in my homeland could be speaking so confidently of the superiority of British education and questioning the Caribbean ability to run its own examination system at a time when many British educators were very critical of the trends in British education.

In addition, London, and the constant need to explain myself before audiences in the role of 'Black writer from the Caribbean' or 'Afro-Caribbean writer' or 'Black woman writer' or 'Caribbean writer', or, heaven help us, an 'ethnic minority writer', kept me constantly looking back for stories that unravelled and explained to me the various experiences that gave me my sensibility as a human being and the events and experiences that had led me to London and this questioning. The short stories continue this reaching back, and record too some of the Britain that was impacting on my consciousness.

In my constant movement between Grenada, Britain and the United States, I continue to write about Grenada, writing about the others specifically too sometimes, but always in any event writing about my temporary home because I'm writing out of it and of the particular kind of need to know what my presence there (wherever there is) gives rise to. Perhaps the 'there' will continue to change because it is all part of a journey that is unfolding more of, and conceivably also leading me constantly back towards, the land that I came first to know as home.

Works by Merle Collins

Angel (1987)
Rain Darling (1990)
The Colour of Forgetting (1995)

4

The Development of My Art as a Fiction Writer

Vernella Fuller

I began my writing in the summer of 1990. I can credit this beginning to the writer Joan Riley who invited me to an informal women writers' workshop at her home. I went never having seriously considered taking up writing, yet I was intrigued by what was on offer. I went along intending to feed my fascination but also to hear writers read from their work. It was certainly not to contribute anything myself. Once there I was not allowed to get off as lightly as I had imagined.

I had to write my piece and, causing me even more consternation, read what I had written to the small group of seemingly seasoned writers. The comments by the host, an established writer, on the piece I had attempted, were to provide the initial impetus and encouragement for my writing. For some inexplicable reason I went home and night after night engrossed myself in the story that I had started at the workshop. At this time I did not have in mind the idea of getting the work published. I was simply absorbed by the process and found myself intrigued by my own plot and characters.

The publishing offer I was eventually to receive for *Going Back Home* surprised me in one sense. In another sense, by this stage, after nearly two years of writing, I felt a number of things were being said in this work that had not been said before, and once I had committed myself to sending it to one publisher I was determined to try to get it published. I had not, however, bargained or braced myself for the necessary redraftings, or for the input of an editor. The work had come from my head to the written page and I had barely reread it; even though as I had written I had constantly said to myself that this or that character could be developed further, or that I could further enhance the plot by adding more here or there. I did not initially listen to these voices from within, caught up as I was in this whole new world. I was to learn the hard way the important maxims that the early stages of writing are only part of the process, and that one's own satisfaction is as important a gauge, if not more important, than an editor's later opinion; if one knows one's characters well, is totally familiar with the setting, and the plot, then one should be able to defend them against any later bid to question, alter or erase.

Five years later my approach is completely different from that of those faltering experimental days. Now I see each page I write as a draft, and plan to do at least three or four before sending off work to the publisher. If it turns out that I am satisfied before this number is reached, then I am gratified. It is actually refreshing and liberating to write with the knowledge that one does not have to attain perfection in the first, or even the second draft.

I discovered too along the way that if talent is needed to be a published writer, it is only part of the equation. Of more weight are tenacity, commitment, determination and the passion to develop despite the obstacles. I have heard many writers say that they were initially motivated to write because they could not always find the story they wanted to read on the shelves. I have always found stories I wanted to read, but I feel there is some truth in what these writers say, in that the stories that I seek to tell are therefore unique and cannot be told by anyone else: I must therefore tell them.

But telling the story is only part of the minefield; there are too the idiosyncrasies of different publishers, contracts, advances, reviews, or the lack of them, and of course the readers. How will they receive what one has written? How will they use one's writing to evaluate one's worth as a person, as a writer and, in my case, as a black woman? In retrospect there was a sweet joy in the early naivety of writing a first book without all this weight on one's shoulders.

I am sometimes asked what it was that I started with in writing my first novel, *Going Back Home*. In this novel I began with the idea of second-generation black British-born women and the question of belongingness. The phrase *going back home* is a cliché in West Indian families. My father in particular spoke of *going back home* constantly. His view, like that of many others who initially vowed that they had come to England only for five years, was that home could only be in Jamaica. But I wanted to explore the question of where home is for the generation who know no other home but Britain, and how they relate to the home of their parents. In addition, the perception of black families in this society and their portrayal in literature and the mass media have always been of concern to me. I did not seem to see families similar to my own and to many others that I knew.

Of course, it is true that slavery had a tremendous impact on the black family. Slave owners were unconcerned about previous family groupings or other units that existed prior to their conquest. Their preoccupation was the capture of fit and able men, women and children. Once a desired destination was reached, it was the interest of the slave owners that remained paramount, not any relationship that had previously existed or that had been formed between the slaves on their perilous journey. A mother could be wrenched from her child, sibling from sibling, lover from lover. Indeed it was the habit of slave owners to take slave women for themselves, with no regard either for the slave women or for their own wives, who ironically were safeguarded from the supposed lasciviousness of the black man.

The profound effect of this legacy can be seen in the various manifestations of the Caribbean family, which is, however, often not *analysed* in its own peculiar historical context but in many instances is portrayed as uniquely dysfunctional. In writing *Going Back Home*, I was keen to set the story in the context of a family, but one that did not conform to the stereotype of a typical Caribbean family, but one that is nuclear and closely-knit. In one sense that structure is a rare ideal, but it is certainly not unheard of as the media and some novels would have us believe. There are two parents with children who are successful and loved, who together form a mutually supportive unit. The Browns, the parents of the main characters, Joy and Esmine, are in some ways typical of those who emigrated to Britain. They hold firmly to the traditional values of rural Jamaica, values that elevated the unity of the family, that gave specific roles to the father and the mother, and allocated to both responsibility for the well being of their children. Beatrice, the mother, speaks constantly of the family staying together, referring often to the cruelty of history that has dissipated the black family and vowing that she will not allow this to happen to her own family.

It is characteristic of many Caribbean families that they boast of or bemoan the fact that their members are scattered all over the world, especially to Europe or North America. Most families have had to come to terms with this diaspora. In the late fifties and the late sixties, as is true of the Brown family in *Going Back Home*, a number of families came to Britain both to answer the call of the mother country for labour and to seek a better life. The typical scenario was that the father came first, either with the promise or the confirmation of a job. He would have left wife, and most usually a young family, in the Caribbean with a grandmother who formed part of an extended family. The mother would follow her husband after he had secured job and accommodation. This is the situation that I portrayed in *Unlike Normal Women*. This novel, set in rural Jamaica, begins with a young girl being prepared for her journey to England. She, like two of her other siblings, had been left with her maternal grandmother when her parents emigrated to England. One by one, before their twelfth birthday, which meant adult fare, each was *sent for*, leaving an ageing and ailing grandmother. I tried to show the tremendous wrench that this necessitated, both for the child and for the grandmother who is left alone without a family. These separations have also had other profound impacts on families, for example, in making it difficult for reunited parents and children to bond after a long absence.

This is an aspect of Caribbean history that, though it is well known, has not been given much serious consideration, especially in Europe where the impact on the family is often manifest. It is an aspect of the life of many black people that is painful and so is left dormant and undiscussed, giving the impression that this is not a common experience and thus not valid as a literary topic. The introductory chapter of *Unlike Normal Women* was written to show the pain of the forced separation of children from grandmothers who had often been the only parent the children knew. A grandmother who had often raised children from their formative years saw them leave, perhaps never to return before her death.

The role of the grandmother in the family and in the community is a major theme of *Unlike Normal Women*. I wanted to show the impact older women have had on the family. In *Unlike Normal Women*, grandmothers, and old women in general, are shown in a number of guises, as matriarchs and wise women, dispensing advice and counsel, and in the roles of midwives, confidantes, and agitators. They see their families not just as those related by blood but as all those who are part of the community. Hence, perhaps, their survival and sanity despite the seemingly brutal disintegration of their families.

Another type of family portrayed in *Unlike Normal Women* is one that is fairly common in the Caribbean: one where children are raised by someone other than their parents or relatives. The setting of the novel is the late sixties when migration from Jamaica or from country to town was at fever pitch. Children were often left with grandmothers, but sometimes with unrelated guardians. This was the case with Miss Dee, one of the main protagonists of *Unlike Normal Women*. Here the family portrayed was a single independent woman, Jane, raising a child, Miss Dee, to whom she was not related.

In depicting relationships between the sexes in the two novels, I was motivated by a number of factors, many related to my own experiences or the experiences of people I have known.

One of the important focuses of my first novel *Going Back Home* was also the relationship between the parents, Joseph and Beatrice. Their relationship is one that in some senses can be defined as traditional. Yet Beatrice's experience, like that of most black women, does not reflect that of the European woman who fought for equality with men. She did not have to fight for the right to work. She has always worked, some might say too hard. She has a strong decision-making role in the family and, if anything, wields most of the power, although this does not mean the emasculation of her husband. Beatrice and Joseph have a strong, active relationship, but this coexists with the reality of conflict and unresolved differences between them. Readers, I believe, are interested in conflict and tension, if not in their total resolution: perhaps because this is the human condition.

The supportiveness of the relationship between the Browns in *Going Back Home* contrasts with that of Pastor Murray and his wife in the same novel. What defines this relationship is Pentecostal fundamentalism: Christianity is pervasive in the life of many blacks. The indoctrination of Christian religion is among the most significant and far-reaching effects of slavery and colonialism. In the case of the Murrays, the pastor sees his main vocation in life as that of service to God; all other relationships, including those with his wife and children, take a secondary role and indeed have to be subjugated to his relationship to God and his church. In a period of estrangement from his daughter, his main preoccupation when she attempts a reconciliation is that she had become a sinner, so that she has to ' . . . acknowledge (her) sins and be washed in the blood of the lamb'. Janet's mother remains in the uncomfortable and unhappy position of neutrality, her role contrasting starkly with that of the other mother, Beatrice, who is not afraid to grapple with difficult decisions, as she has to do when the family is split between those who want to remain in England and those who perceive Jamaica as home. Indeed, in their relationship with their children she and her husband strive for unity, perceiving this as the single most significant aspect of their lives, the main succour in a society that is hostile and seeks to marginalize them.

Joy's relationship with her boyfriend Lee in *Going Back Home* has attracted a great deal of comment because of its supposedly uncharacteristic nature. Joy is an independent single-minded uncompromising woman who demonstrates this both in her atti-tude to Lee and in the crucial decision she eventually makes to leave her family and go to Jamaica for good. She subordinates all other concerns to her passion for Jamaica, and her relation-ship with Lee is no exception. She sacrifices, if not happily and easily, the latter for the former. This is made clear in Joy's non-chalance compared with Lee's devotion to her; for instance, he is the one left weeping when she leaves him and England. Joy's behaviour, like that of a man who puts his career above family or a relationship with a woman, sits uncomfortably with the tradi-tional perception of women.

Joy's relationship with her sister ranges from passionate devo-tion to jealous rivalry. This relationship is, however, set in the context of a society from which Joy feels estranged and of which her sister feels very much a part. It is at times a very conflictual relationship yet it replicates the experiences of many black families in Europe. It raises questions that have plagued and continue to plague these families since the circumstances of history wrenched them from their homes. Where now is home? Where should our allegiance be? Is one a traitor if Britain is chosen as home above the home of foreparents? Dare one add credence to the cry that one cannot be black and British?

In *Unlike Normal Women* the themes of work and the role of women in society are important and pervasive. In rural Jamaica working-class women are, like men, indentured farmers, market sellers, and the controllers of businesses, contributing to the local and national economy. But the relationship between the sexes is not free from conflict and tension, which are explored in my novel in a variety of ways. It was not my intention in *Unlike Normal Women* to challenge the commonly held view that black women are in some way promiscuous, but to me sexual activity is simply one of the many choices that women make. Ironically, one of the criticisms of this story was that the plot was resolved with all the main protagonists remaining independent of men. When the story begins Vie has had one previous relationship with a man who has fathered her only child. When the relationship ended she was loath to become involved in another relationship because she did not believe that men were sane, and for 49 years she remained celibate. Not that she had totally enjoyed this period: '. . . She had ridden the waves of loneliness, frustration and yearning to be married, matched only by the more lengthy periods of grim contentment when she had gloated that she was not like other women without the resolve to be alone.' Later in her life Vie embarks on a brief guilt-ridden affair with one of her married neighbours, but then recaptures her confidence that normality in women does not have to mean marriage and children.

Vie is the antithesis of Jane, another of the protagonists of *Unlike Normal Women*. Although her relationships with men have been stormy she retains an obsessive yearning for a relationship, motivated by her desire to have children. In rural Jamaica, as is the case in most societies, children are prized and desired. In Top Mountain, the setting of the story, children are valued for themselves, but also seen as an important indication of a woman's worth. Jane has been all too aware over the years that her childlessness has isolated her from other women, with the crueller of them labelling her a mule. She too finds herself avoiding men after a particularly destructive relationship, '. . . frightened that she could not trust herself when, as was inevitable, they wronged her'. She too contrives a relationship, but in her case with the expressed intention of having a child. The bitterness of her resulting experience is exacerbated still further by the weight of the unrelenting view that she is an abnormal woman because of her childlessness. Jane's relationship with the men in her life is characterized by constant struggles for power, and her own inability to shake off the shackles of socialization and tradition. Despite her success as a businesswoman and the owner of a prized piece of land, she fails to value herself.

The portrayal of the three other main characters in *Unlike Normal Women* also interrogates the supposed normality of women. Azora, the village savant and herbalist, is a recluse. Unlike Jane, she refuses to be defined by the standards of tradition and so-called normality. In one sense she feels that her unusual height, her riding of mules and horses, and the fact that at one time she was a champion cyclist have excluded her from the society in which she was brought up because of her perceived 'manly ways'. Azora, unlike Jane, does not perceive this as problematic.

The young Miss Dee is unconventional in many senses. She is a successful businesswoman, and dares to challenge the traditional expectation that she would succumb to the advances of the wealthy absentee landlord of the Cleary family, which has a long tradition of taking concubines from her District.

These women, Aunt Vie, Azora, and Miss Dee, are vividly juxtaposed with Dora, a married woman envied by other women in the District, especially Jane, because she has a husband and children. Yet Dora is embittered and sour because of her discontentment with the life her husband has led her. She blames him, but she blames herself too for tolerating his infidelity and his disrespect of her.

Unlike Normal Women explores the concept of the supposed normality of women, in their relationships with men and with other women, and most importantly, in the roles they play in effecting lasting change. It challenges the prevalent stereotypes of normality in women and attempts to create a new paradigm of women in which they seek to construct their own definition of themselves despite the weight of tradition and history.

My third novel, *Life as a Colour*, set in the UK, is about political activism, intransigence and hypocrisy. It is the story of the relationship between the founder of a black nationalist organization and her daughter: the mother attempts to indoctrinate her daughter with her own extreme ideals of racial separation and exclusivity. It is also the story of an interracial relationship, and its impact on the lives of a black woman struggling to define herself and of a white man confident of himself and his place within society.

I am often asked about the progression of my writing since *Going Back Home*. *Life as a Colour* is potentially more controversial, yet I now have more confidence in the whole process of producing the text and defending my theme to an editor. After the publication of *Going Back Home* I was plagued by the fear that it was too simplistic and accessible. I have been far less uneasily unconscious of the reader in writing my second and third novels. That is not to say that I do not bear the reader in mind, but rather that I now have more trust in my own ideas and in my own way of presenting them.

If there was a conscious aim, implicit or explicit, in each novel, it was to show the complexity of relationships, and especially to challenge the view that black relationships are predictable and one-dimensional. It was to provoke new thinking about black women and their relationships with their men, and about black families in British and Jamaican society.

Works by Vernella Fuller

Going Back Home (1992)
Unlike Normal Women (1995)
Life as a Colour (1997)

Part II
Theoretical and Critical Responses

5

Literary Allusion in the Fiction of Jean Rhys

Thorunn Lonsdale

As a white Creole with a family history of slave-owning, Jean Rhys might be seen to sit precariously within the Caribbean literary canon. Kenneth Ramchand[1] and Evelyn O'Callaghan[2] have argued for her Caribbean identity and she remains a pivotal figure despite a continuing debate. John Hearne speaks of Rhys's best-known novel, *Wide Sargasso Sea* (1966), as representing a character 'abandoned by history'; it would be sad if Jean Rhys too were to be abandoned by history because she is not deemed sufficiently 'Caribbean'. As Denise deCaires Narain and Evelyn O'Callaghan have said, the

> privileging of the black, working-class woman, while being 'politically correct' tends to homogenize writing by regional women, encouraging fixed agendas of appropriate subjects and setting limits on just who actually qualifies to be considered 'Caribbean'.[3]

While these questions are still being hotly contested, for instance in Kamau Brathwaite's and Peter Hulme's literary quarrel in the pages of *Wasafiri*,[4] a neglected aspect of this issue is the extent to which Jean Rhys has enabled and influenced later Caribbean texts. For example, the Trinidadian writer Dionne Brand cites Rhys among her literary influences, incidentally including Rhys in a list of 'literature that is made by Black people and other people of colour'.[5] The Jamaican writer Michelle Cliff, in speaking of her own 'purpose as a writer' says of Bertha Mason in *Wide Sargasso Sea* that 'It took a Caribbean novelist, Jean Rhys, to describe Bertha from the inside, using the lens of the colonized female questioning colonization'.[6]

43

Rhys herself, throughout her work, uses other literary texts to amplify and complement her narratives, and, as Veronica Gregg observes, 'In her fiction, there is an unrelenting engagement with the literary and ideological traditions of England and Europe'.[7] Many writers from the Caribbean have confirmed the European literary heritage that the Guyanese writer Beryl Gilroy acknowledges when, in this volume, she writes, 'We had kissed Shakespeare, Byron, Charles Lamb and all the rest on their literary cheeks and whispered how much we loved them'.[8,9] As a white Creole from the Caribbean, Rhys called upon her literary heritage both to enrich her work, and to emphasize her antipathy for the 'mother' country.

Rhys's most celebrated and successful use of another text is, of course, *Wide Sargasso Sea*, which developed from her interest in the portrayal of the mad wife in Charlotte Brontë's *Jane Eyre* (1847). As she remarked,

> It might be possible to unhitch the whole thing from Charlotte Brontë's novel, but I don't want to do that. It is that particular mad Creole I want to write about, not any of the other mad Creoles.[10]

Wide Sargasso Sea is the most obvious and most extensively discussed example of Rhys's use of another text.[11] Even Rhys's choice of title may have been inspired by Ezra Pound's poem 'Portrait d'une Femme' which begins 'Your mind and you are our Sargasso Sea'.[12] However, in her other four novels and in her short stories there are many, comparatively critically neglected, intertextual references to nineteenth and twentieth century European and American literature.

In her short story 'Again the Antilles', a title which suggests return and emphasizes the reminiscent aspect of the narrative, Rhys makes intertextual links to explore and highlight heritage itself. Underscoring the interplay of literary and ethnic heritage and the potency of the written word, her protagonists' debate takes the form of published letters in the local newspaper. The unnamed narrator remembers a feud fuelled by references to literary texts which developed between the editor of the *Dominica Herald and Leeward Islands Gazette*, 'known as Papa Dom' and an estate owner, Mr Hugh Musgrave.[13] The narrator says that Papa Dom was

A born rebel, this editor: a firebrand. He hated the white people, not being quite white, and he despised the black ones, not being quite black. .... "Coloured" we West Indians call the intermediate shades, and I used to think that being coloured embittered him.[14]

Papa Dom's name suggests 'father of Dominica' and his mixed race may be intended to symbolize Dominica and the hybrid and syncretic nature of its people's development. The narrator's reference to 'we' West Indians who called the intermediate shades 'coloured' highlights difference and separation, and also demonstrates an awareness of a 'foreign' audience, since it is clear that s/he is removed from Dominica: 'I wonder if I shall ever again read the *Dominica Herald and Leeward Islands Gazette'.*[15] The narrator's attribution of Papa Dom's contrariness to resentment about his mixed race is perhaps intended to be perceived as purely subjective, and as specifically Caribbean.

The description of Mr Musgrave is more sympathetic and he is referred to as

a dear, but peppery. Twenty years of the tropics and much indulgence in spices and cocktails does have that effect. He owned a big estate, just outside the town of Roseau, cultivated limes and sugar canes and employed a great deal of labour, but he was certainly neither ferocious nor tyrannical.[16]

There is an implicit tolerance here, together with an implicit resistance to potential criticism, and an emphasis on his importance to the local economy. Coral Ann Howells suggests that 'Rhys is carefully non-judgemental about the exchange, but for all its humour it highlights language as the site of the power struggle in a colonial culture'.[17] While there is no doubt about this power struggle, it is less certain that Rhys is being 'non-judgemental' in her use of such a biased narrator.

The three-page short story begins with a portrait of Papa Dom and his house which takes up more than a page. The narrator, who appears to be reminiscing about a childhood in a now distant Dominica, but about whom little is disclosed, remembers Papa Dom as 'awe-inspiring' in his 'tall, white house with green Venetian blinds' and his 'gold-rimmed spectacles and dark clothes always – not for him the frivolity of white linen even on the hottest day'.[18] By contrast there is no physical depiction of Musgrave, which may indicate an easy acceptance of him, as opposed to an affectionate amusement at Papa Dom's adoption of a dresscode from which 'true' Englishmen never deviated.[19] He is seen to conform to the social practices of a society against which he is said to rail, so that his character articulates the conflict of his mixed race. Because Papa Dom is depicted as pretentious and resentful, the narration is weighted in favour of Musgrave, who, albeit the stereotypical white colonial and one lacking in social graces, nevertheless is a 'dear'.

The feud between the two men once in 'full swing'[20] is remembered and documented by a series of letters in Papa Dom's newspaper.[21] One of Papa Dom's letters laments the fact that Mr Musgrave is far 'removed from the ideals of true gentility' and the ideal is established through the invocation of 'a very gentle, perfect knight',[22] an ideal then wrongly attributed to Shakespeare. Not only does Papa Dom invoke the very tradition he supposedly abhors, but he does so incorrectly, thus emphasizing his own marginalized status in relation to it. But equally, Musgrave is socially discredited because he chooses to respond, even if it is 'briefly and sternly as befits an Englishman of the governing class. . . . Still he replied.'[23] The ellipsis and 'Still he replied' establishes that a 'perfect knight' would have refrained from entering into argument.

In response to Papa Dom's literary inaccuracy Musgrave 'took his opportunity'[24] and replies:

> 'The lines quoted were written, not by Shakespeare but by Chaucer, though you cannot of course be expected to know that. . . . It is indeed a saddening and a dismal thing that the names of great Englishmen should be thus taken in vain by the ignorant of another race and colour.'[25]

The narrator then adds that 'Mr Musgrave had really written "damn niggers"',[26] a phrase which Papa Dom had presumably discreetly edited, here wielding a colonist's power on behalf of the colonized. We are not told how the narrator comes by this inside knowledge.

In his reply Musgrave also quotes more extensively but incompetently from the preface to the *Canterbury Tales* and adds:

> *He never yet no vilonye had sayde*
> *In al his lyf, unto no manner of wight –*
> *He was a verray parfit, gentil knyght.*[27]

In so doing, he unwittingly uses Chaucer's words against himself. Papa Dom responds by stating that '"I do not write with works of reference in front of me, as you most certainly do"'[28] (alluding to the privilege of position and wealth) and retaliates, '"I fail to see that it matters whether it is Shakespeare, Chaucer or the Marquis of Montrose who administers from down the ages the much-needed reminder and rebuke"'.[29] His rather odd inclusion of the Marquis de Montrose, who although a poet, is remembered more for his political and battle skills and for his allegiance to Charles I in the English civil war than for his literary prowess, emphasizes the savage nature of this supposedly literary debate. This short story highlights the importance of the hegemony of literary heritage for the characters, a hegemony which Rhys explores throughout her work.

An example of Rhys's intertextual borrowing, one which serves to locate her in the literary movement of her time, and reinforces the influence of her mentor Ford Madox Ford, occurs in *Quartet* (1928). After Marya has begun her affair with Heidler, she begins to feel paralysed by her situation:

> As she lay in bed she longed for her life with Stephan as one longs for vanished youth. A gay life, a carefree life just wiped off the slate as it were. Gone! A horrible nostalgia, an ache for the past seized her.
>
> > *Nous n'irons plus au bois;*
> > *Les lauriers sont coupés . . .*
>
> Gone, and she was caught in this appalling muddle. Life was like that. Here you are, it said, and then immediately afterwards. Where are you? Her life, at any rate, had always been like that.[30]

The lines in French (We shall not go to the woods any more, the laurels have been cut[31]) are from the opening of a traditional children's song[32] and evoke the idea of a past made irretrievable by a brutal act. Although the same children's song is essentially happy and ends in renewal, Rhys uses the refrain gloomily. It is likely that Rhys is making an intertextual link with Edouard Dujardin's groundbreaking work, *Les lauriers sont coupés* (1887), the title of which he borrowed from the children's song. Dujardin's novel explores Daniel Prince's infatuation with a young actress, Lea, his self-deception, his endeavours to seduce her and his gifts of money to her. The novel is not dissimilar to much of Rhys's work, in which impecunious young women and chorus girls are depicted as sexual commodities.[33] But Lea is comparable to Rhys's more discerning chorus girls, for example Maudie or Laurie (whose name perhaps echoes Dujardin's title) in *Voyage in the Dark* (1934), who have no illusions about their value. It is Prince who is naive, and like many of Rhys's protagonists, deludes himself about the nature of a relationship. The narrative unfolds through Prince's immediate thoughts and feelings and his obsessions and pre-occupations are reminiscent of Marya's life in Paris.[34]

Dujardin's novel is most commonly celebrated for its connection with James Joyce and its influence on the narrative technique of *Ulysses* (1922) and, therefore, as a precursor of the Modernist technique with which Rhys experiments. Although *Quartet* is a third-person narrative, Marya's interior monologue intrudes throughout the text and her immediate thoughts and feelings dominate. It is worth noting that although written in 1887, Dujardin's novel did not receive much acclaim upon publication, but did so much later, primarily, it appears, for its influence on *Ulysses*.[35] The French influence on Rhys's work from her Parisian days was compounded by the elements of French culture in her homeland Dominica.

Ford's influence on Rhys's work is undeniable, and if *Quartet* is read as a roman-à-clef, then another literary 'borrowing' by Rhys can be found in Hemingway's representation of Ford as the 'fatuous' character Braddocks in *The Sun Also Rises* (1927). Hemingway was Ford's editorial assistant on the *Transatlantic Review* and William Wiser describes them as 'mismatched in most every way'.[36] Wiser notes that in *The Sun Also Rises*, Hemingway documented

> sequences of Montparnasse life in a fresh and unadorned style that would be the cornerstone of his reputation. Reactions by the living prototypes of the characters in the novel were mixed. . . . In his minor and fatuous role as Braddocks, Ford

Madox Ford must have been dismayed, but he kept his annoyance to himself.[37]

Rhys's 'borrowing' from Hemingway of the passage in which his depiction of Ford occurs confirms her own condemnation of Ford (albeit a condemnation that was to soften with hindsight). In *The Sun Also Rises* Jake takes Georgette to 'Braddocks's dancing club':

> The dancing-club was a *bal musette* in the Rue de la Montagne Sainte Geneviève. Five nights a week the working people of the Panthéon quarter danced there. One night a week it was the dancing-club. . . . When we arrived it was quite empty, except for a policeman sitting near the door, the wife of the proprietor back of the zinc bar, and the proprietor himself. . . . There were long benches, and tables ran across the room, and at the far end a dancing-floor.[38]

In *Quartet* Marya goes with Lois and Heidler (Ford) to one of Mr Rolls's 'weekly parties':

> The Bal du Printemps is a small, dingy café in the Rue Mouffetard. There is a long zinc bar where the clients can drink a peaceful apéritif after the day's work. There are painted wooden tables, long wooden benches and a small gallery where the band sits – a concertina, a flute and a violin. The couples dance in a cleared space at the end of the room. . . . Two policemen at the door supervise the proceedings . . .[39]

The quotations establish the similarities of description and the 'fresh and unadorned style', and there are numerous incidental parallels, including the fact that the rue de la Montagne Sainte Geneviève is only a few minutes walk away from the rue Mouffetard.[40] *Quartet* itself has served as an influence on or stimulus for other fictional works such as Rhys's first husband's novel *Barred* (1932), in its French form *Sous Les Verrous* (1933),[41,42] and Ford Madox Ford's *When the Wicked Man* (1931).[43]

An important aspect of intertextuality in *Quartet* is the accentuation of the marginalization of female characters. Rhys's epigraph in *Quartet* is from R.C. Dunning's poem 'The Hermit', a poem which also appeared in Ford Madox Ford's *Transatlantic Review*. It is therefore an appropriate choice because it serves to implicate

Ford Madox Ford in the text from the beginning.[44] The epigraph reads,

> . . . *Beware*
> *Of good Samaritans – walk to the right*
> *Or hide thee by the road side out of sight*
> *Or greet them with the smile that villains wear.*

It prophetically forewarns Marya not to trust the Heidlers or at least to arm herself against them. In her biography of Rhys, Carole Angier wonders if Rhys did not quote an earlier line from the poem 'Let not thy bedfellow divine thy plight' because 'it reminded Jean of how much she hid and held back from her husband',[45] alluding to the autobiographical aspect of Rhys's novel.[46] Angier links the last two lines of the quoted portion to Rhys's protagonist and suggests that 'what is false about Marya is her submission, and what is real is some hidden villainous intent'.[47] Angier explains her point by references to Marya's hostile feelings towards Lois and her subsequent repression of them, but the argument is not thoroughly convincing. Thomas Staley in his book *Jean Rhys* suggests that:

> The admonishment in the epigraph, however, is curious, for the weight of the novel is certainly directed to the last line; Marya, unable to hide, is also unable to fix the right smile, or assume the appropriate posture.[48]

While the allusion to good Samaritans clearly accuses the Heidlers, the rest of the poem is less obviously appropriate. It is possible that it was either a careless choice from a work at hand, but one which had several lines that sufficed, although that would seem unusual given Rhys's painstaking approach to her work, or, perhaps more likely, a deliberate choice to implicate Ford.

References to other fictional works to highlight gender concerns can be found in Rhys's short story 'La Grosse Fifi',[49] which has distinct similarities to Arnold Bennett's novel *The Old Wives' Tale* (1908). Rhys makes no direct reference to Bennett's work, but, whether consciously or not, she adopts Bennett's emphasis on the poignancy of every stout woman once having been a young girl. In her elaboration of this idea, Rhys 'borrows' images, themes, events, and characters from *The Old Wives' Tale*. In 'La Grosse

Fifi', Roseau and Fifi at first appear very different, both physically and in personality, the former shy, retiring, and sullen, and
the latter ebullient, provocative and boisterous, but as the story
unfolds Fifi comes to represent a prophetic vision of what Roseau
might become. Just as Bennett demands sympathy and compassion for his ageing women both in his preface and his novel, so
Rhys bestows on Fifi a 'gay and childlike soul, freed from its
gross body'.[50] Thomas Staley in his critical study of Jean Rhys's
fiction asserts that Roseau and Fifi are indeed twinned.[51]

Rhys's main borrowing occurs from the section in *The Old Wives'
Tale* which depicts Sophia's initial experiences in France. Sophia,
who has just eloped to Paris with Gerald Scales, is taken by her
new husband to the restaurant 'Sylvain' for dinner. It is here
that she learns from Gerald of the forthcoming execution by
guillotine of Rivain for the murder of Claudine Jacquinot.

'She was a tremendous-er-wrong 'un here in the forties. Made
a lot of money, and retired to her native town.'
Sophia, in spite of her efforts to maintain the rôle of a woman
who has nothing to learn, blushed.
'Then she was older than he is.'
'Thirty-five years older, if a day.'
'What did he kill her for?'
'She wouldn't give him enough money. She was his mistress
– or rather one of 'em. He wanted money for a young lady friend,
you see. He killed her and took all the jewels she was wearing.'[52]

This episode recalls Fifi's relationship with her young lover and
murderer Rivière (whose name bears a striking resemblance to
that of Jacquinot's murderer, Rivain). The references to courtesans
and gigolos in the texts are similar and when Fifi's murder is
reported in the local paper, it is reminiscent of Gerald Scales'
analysis of the motives for Claudine Jacquinot's murder.

A further similarity is the depiction of the older women Madame
Foucault and Fifi and their relationships with Sophia and Roseau
respectively. They are both caricatured in their attempts to camouflage their age, and to redistribute their weight, albeit in different
directions. In *The Old Wives' Tale* Sophia

looked curiously at Madame Foucault, who was carefully made
up and arranged for the street, in a dress of yellow tussore

with blue ornaments, bright lemon-coloured gloves, a little blue bonnet, and a little white parasol not wider when opened than her shoulders. Cheeks, lips, and eyes were heavily charged with rouge, powder, or black. And that too abundant waist had been most cunningly confined in a belt that descended beneath, instead of rising above, the lower masses of the vast torso.[53]

In 'La Grosse Fifi'

Fifi was not terrific except metaphorically, but she was stout, well corseted – her stomach carefully arranged to form part of her chest. Her hat was large and worn with a rakish sideways slant, her rouge shrieked, and the lids of her protruding eyes were painted bright blue.[54]

Under their glamorous façades, Fifi and Madame Foucault are both portrayed as slovenly and in each text the dressing gown is the emblem of an unsavoury lifestyle. As a result, in *The Old Wives' Tale* Sophia decides 'she would dress herself "properly", and never again wear a peignoir; the peignoir and all that it represented, disgusted her.'[55, 56]
The younger women Sophia and Roseau comfort their ageing friends, for whom appearance is fundamental.

'My hat?' she asked anxiously. 'Does it make me ridiculous? Is it too small? Does it make me look old?'
'No,' said Roseau, considering her carefully – 'I like it, but put the little veil down.'
Fifi obeyed.
'Ah, well,' she sighed, 'I was always ugly. When I was small my sister called me the devil's doll. Yes – always the compliments like that are what I get. Now – alas! You are sure I am not ridiculous in that hat?'
'No, no,' Roseau told her. 'You look very nice.'[57]

Fifi acknowledges that she was always ugly, but we are told of Madame Foucault that 'Her beauty had undoubtedly been dazzling'.[58] Like Roseau, Sophia reassures the ageing woman:

Madame Foucault was not rejuvenated by her toilette, but it almost procured her pardon for the crime of being over forty, fat, creased, and worn out. It was one of those defeats that are a triumph.

> 'You are very chic,' said Sophia, uttering her admiration. 'Ah!' said Madame Foucault, shrugging the shoulders of disillusion. 'Chic! what does that do?' But she was pleased.[59]

Madame Foucault and Fifi both voice their devotion to their young lovers: Madame Foucault explains to Sophia,

> No. I loved him. And then a man is a moral support, always. I loved him. It is at my age, mine, that one knows how to love. Beauty goes always, but not the temperament! Ah, that – No! . . . I loved him. I love him.[60]

Fifi says to Roseau of Rivière,

> 'But when one is caught it is not so easy. No, I adore my Pierrot. I adore that child – I would give him my last sou – and how can he love me? I am old, I am ugly. Oh, I know. Regarde moi ces yeux là!' She pointed to the caverns under her eyes – 'Et ça!' She touched her enormous chest. 'Pierrot who only loves slim women. Que voulez vous?' Fifi's shrug was wonderful! 'I love him. . . .'[61]

Although constitutionally opposed, Madame Foucault self-pitying and Fifi defiant, they look after their younger friends, who are both the victims of failed love matches. Madame Foucault nurses Sophia back to good health and Fifi watches over Roseau through her depression. As a result, the courtesans are romanticized by the heroines, although Roseau is more genuinely fond of Fifi than Sophia is of Madame Foucault. Roseau and Sophia simultaneously sympathize with, and despise, the ageing women. Fifi and Madame Foucault are caricatures of their younger selves and as such a sobering vision for Sophia and Roseau. Rhys and Bennett both dwell on these aspects in their works.

In Rhys's third novel *Voyage in the Dark* the protagonist Anna is reading Zola's *Nana* (1880) about which her chorus girl roommate, Maudie, puns '"Besides, all books are like that – just somebody stuffing you up"'.[62] The title of Zola's famous novel about a French courtesan, who dies horribly infected from smallpox, forms an anagram of Anna's name, and the reference to the novel functions as a foretelling of Anna's likely destiny. In the original version of the novel, Anna dies after an illegal abortion although in the published version her fate is ambiguous. Rhys intended Anna to die like Nana and by the inclusion of Nana in her novel, she twins the characters in much the same way as she does Fifi and Roseau in 'La Grosse Fifi'.

In *After Leaving Mr Mackenzie* (1930) Jean Rhys highlights female marginalization through a quotation from Conrad's *Almayer's Folly* (1895), a novel read by the protagonist's sister Norah:

> She thought over and over again, 'It isn't fair, it isn't fair.'
>
> She picked up the book lying on her bed-table – *Almayer's Folly* – and had begun to read:
>
> > The slave had no hope, and knew of no change. She knew of no other sky, no other water, no other forest, no other world, no other life. She had no wish, no hope, no love. . . . The absence of pain and hunger was her happiness, and when she felt unhappy she was tired, more than usual, after the day's labour.[63]

Norah is not portrayed sympathetically, but the description of slavery illuminates Norah's repressed fury at being trapped looking after her mother. It is clear that Julia's visit to her dying mother and her obvious connection to a permissive and sexually active world (insinuated in Norah's comment: 'She doesn't even look like a lady now'[64]) arouses her sister's repressed sexual yearnings:

> Then she had got up and looked at herself in the glass. She had let her nightgown slip down off her shoulders, and had a look at herself. She was tall and straight and slim and young – well, fairly young.[65]

This image can be linked to another passage in Conrad's novel in which the slave girl Taminah, who is the subject of the earlier quotation,'stood on the tender grass of the low bank, her robe at her feet, and looked at the reflection of her figure on the glass-like surface of the creek'.[66]

Taminah's sexual awakening is the result of a few words spoken by the trader, Dain. His words '"Who is that girl?"' and '"Do not be afraid"'[67] awaken her from her slavery-induced stupor. Taminah ultimately betrays Dain through her jealousy of his love for Nina, the mixed race daughter of the protagonist, Almayer. Significantly, it is Nina, the revered beauty, who 'always had a few friendly words for a Siamese girl [Taminah], a slave owned by Bulangi'.[68] It is likely, therefore, that Rhys chose Taminah for the intertextual link with Norah because Taminah, who received sisterly words from Nina, is jealous of her.

A link is made not only between Norah and Taminah, but between Julia and Nina. Like Nina, Julia chose to escape the social environment in which she was raised, and the one to which Norah had conformed.

'I wanted to go away with just the same feeling a boy has when he wants to run away to sea – at least, that I imagine a boy has. Only, in my adventure, men were mixed up, because of course they had to be. You understand, don't you? Do you understand that a girl might have that feeling? I wanted to get away. I wanted it like – like iron. Besides, I wasn't frightened of anything. So I did get away. I married to get away.'[69]

Nina too felt that she must escape from her environment because of the racial prejudice she had endured, and her father's aspirations for her. As with Julia, a man is the only route of escape. Speaking to her father, Nina explains:

'You wanted me to dream your dreams, to see your own visions – the visions of life amongst the white faces of those who cast me out from their midst in angry contempt. But while you spoke I listened to the voice of my own self; then this man came, and all was still; there was only the murmur of his love.'[70]

Nina chooses to identify with her mother's supposedly inferior racial and cultural heritage instead of her father's supposedly superior European background. As someone aware of the difficulties of confused cultural identification, Rhys would have had an instinctive sympathy for Conrad's marginalized character Nina. Rhys's reference to *Almayer's Folly* relates to her major preoccupations: ethnic identification and the management of difference.

A Caribbean story which depicts female and ethnic marginalization, which focuses on the written word, which confirms Ford's influence on her writing career,[71] and which uses intertextual references to unravel the story is 'The Day They Burned The Books'. The children, Eddie Sawyer and the unnamed girl narrator, who are the focus of the short story, each steal a book which prophetically announces the children's futures. The books are stolen when Eddie's mother, Mrs Sawyer, is deciding which books from her hated dead husband's library are for burning and which for selling. The European classics which the children save, Kipling's *Kim* (1901) and Maupassant's *Fort Comme La Mort* (1899), not only attest to colonial inheritance but also underscore the poignancy of the two children's positions. Eddie's plight, if he lives long enough, will be to confront his own racial inheritance much as Kim, although of white parentage (like Rhys), confronts his mixed cultural socialization. Like Julia in *After Leaving Mr Mackenzie*, and most of Rhys's protagonists, the female narrator's quest will be to find a space or place in a world where security is afforded through men. In *Fort Comme La Mort* both mother and daughter, whose names are Anne and Annette,[72] are destined to follow the same path of making good marriages to secure their futures. In the daughter's case the marriage to the Marquis de Farandal provides him with money and her with status. The story functions as a precursor to Rhys's *Wide Sargasso Sea* in which both mother and daughter are also compelled to marry.

Not only is Rhys a writer who engaged with her European literary heritage, she is also a writer who was very much influenced by her literary contemporaries in Europe, and just as she used European texts to enrich her fiction, so has her fiction enriched later Caribbean texts.[73] Sometimes the exact nature of the literary influence is hard to disentangle. In the afterword to the Virago edition of *The Orchid House* (1953) Elaine Campbell suggests that Phyllis Shand Allfrey's novel inspired Rhys to write *Wide Sargasso Sea* and Coral Ann Howells writes that '*The Orchid House* perhaps acted as a catalyst for her imaginative effort of dreaming her way back to the past as she does in her novel'.[74] The two novels do have similarities and do explore comparable themes, but while Allfrey's novel may have inspired Rhys to write *Wide Sargasso Sea*, it is more appropriate to credit the similarities to cultural familiarity rather than to any deliberate 'borrowing' on Rhys's part.[75]

Phyllis Shand Allfrey, Rhys's younger Dominican contemporary, wrote of the impact of reading *Voyage in the Dark*, a novel which has powerful Caribbean elements, long before the publication of *The Orchid House*. *The Orchid House* has a more general social and political resonance: the family is located in a world which has changed and, in particular, on an island which is changing, with its colonial superstructure in decline, and the novel is not dominated by any one character. Although *Wide Sargasso Sea* does explore notions of race, nationality, and oppression, it details the specific experience of one woman's isolation. There are also obvious differences in style: *The Orchid House* is lushly descriptive in comparison with the terse economy of *Wide Sargasso Sea*. However, both works highlight female isolation, a consistent theme in the Rhys canon, and in each the Creole mothers, Madam and Annette, are depicted raising children without the help of their husbands, and relying on their devoted black servants, Lally and Christophine. In *The Orchid House* Lally contemplates the situation:

> I stood there at the gate watching the thin little moon struggling through the clouds. It had grown to be a heavy night, the breeze had died. I was feeling heavy, too, and tired. I thought of the house, which had been a house only of women for six years. I thought that I must be different from the others of my dark skin, for I had small love for men. They made everything of a different quality and sound and smell. They would bring into a house deep voices and smoke and a feeling in the air.[76]

In each novel male characters are depicted as intrusive and disquieting to the women's worlds, and in each the arrival of male characters has negative consequences. In *Wide Sargasso Sea*, Mason, who marries Antoinette's mother Annette, does not heed his wife's warnings in relation to their black workers and consequently Pierre, Antoinette's brother, dies after the house is set alight by angry workers. Annette blames her husband for the loss of her son and her madness develops after the uprising. Mason subsequently abandons her to the care of unsympathetic and abusive carers: Annette's treatment foreshadows that of her daughter Antoinette. In *The Orchid House*, the master, returning shellshocked, is unable to become a working member of the family and community. He is an isolated character, lost and emotionally scarred by the experience of war, from which he escapes through opium. Interestingly, one of the few books available to the Rochester character at Granbois in *Wide Sargasso Sea* is Thomas De Quincey's *Confessions of an English Opium Eater* (1822).

In her critique of one of Rhys's short stories 'Let Them Call It Jazz', Coral Ann Howells concludes that '[i]t would seem that gender politics are more intricately registered in this story than racial politics, which work on a much simpler pattern of binary opposition'.[77] But although gender politics and female resistance are fundamental, racial issues are the driving force. The Guyanese writer Pauline Melville's short story 'A Disguised Land'[78] recalls Rhys's short story 'Let Them Call It Jazz' and it would seem likely that Pauline Melville was influenced by the work of her literary foremother, Jean Rhys. Both stories highlight racial and gender issues and detail the experiences of young women of colour and their alienation in London, a place they were sent to by their grandmothers, and both stories culminate in the imprisonment of the protagonists.

The hypocritical nature of the English is stressed in both stories. In 'A Disguised Land', the protagonist, Winsome, is haunted by a repeated dream in which the pleasant and kind attitudes of the English are oddly out of step with their intentions in a manner suggestive of Emily Dickinson's 'Because I could not stop for Death, he kindly stopped for me':

> She dreamed she was in England and that she had been sentenced to death. . . . Small knots of white people stood chatting like parents after a school function. They were always extremely kind to her. In one of the dreams a man drew up beside her in his car. He put his head out of the window and said helpfully:
> 'Hop in and I'll give you a lift to the gallows'. . . .
> 'No, I jus' walk there. Tank you.' Her fear seemed inappropriate amongst such pleasantly relaxed people. A taboo caught her tongue and forbade her to say how she felt.[79]

In Jean Rhys's 'Let Them Call It Jazz' Selina Davis is equally confused by the cruel comments disguised in kind tones uttered by her neighbour:

> That evening the woman is by the hedge, and when I pass her she says in very sweet quiet voice, '*Must* you stay? *Can't* you go?'[80]

Rhys and Melville emphasize, therefore, how malicious content, when disguised in polite tones, destabilizes their protagonists.

Selina and Winsome both end up in prison, Winsome through a life of petty crime and Selina for disturbing the peace and breaking a window, and both are silenced and abandoned by a judicial system which fails to recognize them.

Once in prison, however, the two protagonists' instincts for survival are revealed. Resistance is possible after Winsome and Selina obtain affirmation from other women: for Selina, another inmate sings the Holloway song and it reawakens her desire to live and for Winsome, the black hospital cleaner talks of the strength of black woman. However, both writers emphasize that although their marginalized heroines have manifested some resistance and an ability to survive, the system will continue to work against them. This is evident in the refusal to allow Selina to return to collect her powder compact when she leaves prison and later through the appropriation of her song. In 'A Disguised Land', Winsome's newsworthiness is of limited interest and, after the initial screening, her story is eliminated from later news bulletins. Both metaphorically return to the Caribbean in search of warmth and support. Selina returns through her singing: 'when I sing all the misery goes from my heart. Sometimes I make up songs . . . other times I sing the old ones like *Tantalizin'* or *Don't Trouble Me Now'*,[81] the latter being a song that reminds Selina of her 'grandmother for that is one of her songs'.[82] 'A Disguised land' ends with Winsome dreaming of her burial in a land which is 'unfamiliar', but which is reminiscent of the Jamaican landscape. Ironically, it is these connections with another location that provide the impetus for the protagonists to recognize and subsequently collude with their marginalized positions. Selina's song may have been taken from her and she may no longer sing, but she realizes that its meaning has not: 'let them play it wrong. That won't make no difference to the song I heard'.[83] Equally, Winsome's burial journey in her final dream suggests an acknowledgement of the reality of her situation and perhaps an acceptance of her earlier displacement to England from Jamaica.

The most striking example of Rhys's enrichment of contemporary Caribbean fiction is the Jamaican writer Elean Thomas's novel *The Last Room* (1991), which details the history of a Jamaican woman and her daughter. *The Last Room*[84] reworks *Wide Sargasso Sea*, which itself reworks *Jane Eyre*, which in turn reworks concepts of male patriarchy. Charlotte Brontë's *Jane Eyre* was itself an innovative and radical text, but Rhys reveals the way in which the marginalized Jane in turn marginalized others.

Rhys's novel intrudes throughout *The Last Room*. The openings of each provides the historical and social setting of the adolescent protagonist and the disruption caused by the death of a father.[85] *Wide Sargasso Sea* and *The Last Room* both begin in Jamaica, include widowed mothers, their re-marriages to opportunist new husbands, treacherous stepbrothers, wise black obeah women who act as surrogate mothers after the abandonment by the biological mother, and journeys to England which end in madness and seclusion. The black protagonist of *The Last Room*, Valerie Putus Barton, travels to England to join her husband, Fitzie Mason, and to finish the education which was interrupted by her pregnancy, and the birth of her daughter Icy, who is left behind. However, Valerie's expectations of England are contrasted with her actual experience in ways more obviously reminiscent of Anna's in *Voyage in the Dark* or Selina Davis' in 'Let Them Call It Jazz'. Antoinette in *Wide Sargasso Sea* lost her illusions before leaving for England, although she maintains that the ship lost its way and that she never reached England, thus echoing Christophine's words '"You think there is such a place?"'[86] But the overriding influence in *The Last Room* is that of *Wide Sargasso Sea*. Throughout Rhys's work, and in *The Last Room*, innocence is violently disrupted by the attitudes of the English. For Valerie, racist treatment by her white English nursing colleagues culminates in her rape by the hospital administrator. The rape, although different from the last sexual encounter between Antoinette and her husband, also acts as the catalyst for madness. The betrayal by a white man in a position of authority induces Valerie to leave Fitzie and go to Birmingham, where she effectively hides away in a room at the top of the house and where her story unfolds through her schizophrenic dialogue with voices from her past. In 1963, three years before its publication, Rhys wrote that in an earlier version of *Wide Sargasso Sea*,

The book began with a dream and ended with a dream (though I didn't get the last dream right for a long time). All the rest was to be a long monologue. Antoinette in her prison room remembers, loves, hates, raves, talks to imaginary people, hears imaginary voices answering and overhears meaningless conversations outside.[87]

This is curiously similar to much of *The Last Room* in which Valerie is haunted by voices.

In the final dream sequence in *Wide Sargasso Sea*, Antoinette sees, but does not recognize herself, and watches the fire spread before she jumps into her past.

> It was then that I saw her – the ghost. The woman with streaming hair. She was surrounded by a gilt frame but I knew her. I dropped the candle I was carrying and it caught the end of a tablecloth and I saw flames shoot up. As I ran or perhaps floated or flew I called help me Christophine help me and looking behind me I saw that I had been helped.[88]

In *The Last Room* the arrival in England of her daughter Icy makes Valerie fear fire:

> Alone in the world, with only God to call on. . . . Is this the time that the Eckna is going to catch the oilskin tablecloth afire? Perhaps I should look to see if the oilskin is burning. I wish they would turn off that music. If I look if the Eckna catch the oilskin, I will have to leave it . . . her . . . on the landing. Shut the door. The voice in bodily form say she is my daughter.[89]

Valerie is trapped between Icy and the stove and has to decide which way to 'jump'. Just as Antoinette appeals to an imaginary Christophine for help, it is an imagined Granny Lou who tells Valerie to welcome her daughter: 'Cum, mi likkle mudder. Tek her up. Tek her up before she dead in front yu door'.[90] Like Antoinette, who has her name changed to Bertha, Valerie has had her name changed from Putus: the Rhys protagonist and the Thomas protagonist converge in their third naming as Mason. Elean Thomas also expands on the comment made by Antoinette's mother Annette in the opening pages of *Wide Sargasso Sea*. After her horse has been poisoned, Annette refers to the family as 'marooned', a word Rhys must have chosen for its particular ironic significance in the context of the Caribbean. The white Creole family is marooned, or cast away, after emancipation, whereas previously the term referred to the escaped black slaves who founded free colonies;[91] it is this aspect that is emphasized in *The Last Room*.

It is however in contemporary Caribbean poetry that Rhys's influence is most dominant. The Jamaican poet and short story writer Olive Senior also plays on the word 'marooned' in her poem 'Meditation on Red', a contemplation of Rhys's life in England. The line 'Marooned / in the grey / you decided / to garden'[92] ostensibly refers to Rhys's attempts to grow colourful flowers, but has a wider reference to Rhys's antipathy to England. The poem draws heavily on letters written by Rhys after she moved to her last home, 'Cheriton Fitz Paine', Devon, in 1960. The poem's opening 'You, voyager / in the dark / land-locked / at Land Boat Bungalows no. 6', is an allusion both to Rhys's third novel *Voyage in the Dark* and to her last home in Devon. Implicit in the mention of a traveller in the dark locked in by land is the absence of water, namely the 'Wide Sargasso'[94] alluded to later in the poem. Senior also comments on the '"Christmas cracker dress"',[95] a red dress linked to Rhys's paranoia about the local community, a dress which functions as a metaphor for the Caribbean and which first appears in Rhys's own letter to her daughter in 1961:

> I am better now, or nearly, and Max, who has been in hospital for rest and a check up, is home again. I bought a bright red dress to celebrate – at Exeter – a cheap Christmas cracker dress, and, do you know although I've never worn it (as it is too cold) – the entire village knows.
> I think they must be witches and warlocks. The dress is hanging in my wardrobe unseen and yet they gossip – 'That Mrs Hamer bought a *red dress*!' So you will see the sort of place it is.[96]

The red dress in the closet also recalls Antoinette's red dress in *Wide Sargasso Sea*:

> As soon as I turned the key I saw it hanging, the colour of fire and sunset. The colour of flamboyant flowers. 'If you are buried under a flamboyant tree . . . your soul is lifted up when it flowers. . . .'
> The scent that came from the dress was very faint at first, then it grew stronger. The smell of vetivert and frangipanni, of cinnamon and dust and lime trees when they are flowering. The smell of the sun and the smell of the rain.[97]

Senior associates the pessimistic Rhys of the letters with the rages 'which long ago came from the attic' of *Wide Sargasso Sea* and then steps into the poem as a fellow writer and says:

Right now / I'm as divided / as you were / by that sea. / But I'll / be able to / find my way / home again / for that craft / you launched / is so seaworthy / tighter / than you'd ever been / dark voyagers / like me / can feel free / to sail / That fire / you lit / our beacon / to safe harbour / in the islands.[98]

The poem's opening, 'You, voyager / in the dark'[99] is inverted in the phrase 'dark voyagers / like me' and stresses Senior's racial difference from Rhys, but the poem is a gracious tribute to Rhys as literary foremother.

In his poem 'Jean Rhys', the St Lucian poet Derek Walcott emphasizes Rhys's relationship to the colonial age, but does not deny her significance as Caribbean writer. Walcott's poem draws on Rhys's childhood in Dominica and on *Wide Sargasso Sea*, to which he is clearly paying tribute. Walcott's poem begins with a description of 'faint photographs / mottled with chemicals'[100] which are the vestiges of a time past, and he comments ironically that through discoloration 'bone-collared gentlemen / with spiked moustaches / and their wives embayed in the wickerwork / arm-chairs' look 'coloured'.[101] The poem ends with a return to the opening lines in which the stylized and mannered 'world / when grace was common as malaria'[102] is linked directly to England. The child, described earlier 'sitting on a lion footed couch', is now described with 'her right hand married to *Jane Eyre*',[103] an image of Jean Rhys the child of colonialism, her writing married to a nineteenth century English classic.

Another Caribbean writer for whom Jean Rhys is an important figure is the Jamaican poet Lorna Goodison. Her poem 'A Jean Rhys Lady' uses bestial and fire imagery to portray a crazed woman's dreams, those of Antoinette, and, at the same time, a writer's attempts to escape into 'luminal / liquid sleep'.[104] The refusal of dreams and creative impulses to be exorcized by drugs or alcohol is also suggested in 'A Jean Rhys Lady'. Thoughts refuse to be repressed so are 'gathered' and 'swallowed' but they return 'fanning the flames in / her head'.[105] Not only does Goodison's poem allude to Rhys's turbulent life, but it interweaves images from *Wide Sargasso Sea*. Goodison incorporates images of 'some strange wild animal'[106] from *Jane Eyre* and a woman unable to sleep for whom embers become flames. Equally, in addition to the suggestion of a writer's torment, images of Antoinette are recalled with the 'coals glowing' and the 'flames in / her head'.[107]

They recall the passages in *Wide Sargasso Sea* which deal with Antoinette's imprisonment, the cold in England and the import- ance of fire as an association with the warmth of home:

> At last Grace Poole, the woman who looks after me, lights a fire with paper and sticks and lumps of coal. She kneels to blow it with bellows. The paper shrivels, the sticks crackle and spit, the coal smoulders and glowers. In the end flames shoot up and they are beautiful.... When she is snoring I get up and I have tasted the drink without colour in the bottle. The first time I did this I wanted to spit it out but managed to swallow it. When I got back into bed I could remember more and think again. I was not so cold.[108]

Goodison's 'coals glowing' and 'flames in / her head' not only refer to the writer's imagination, but equally to Antoinette's last dream of fire which precipitates the novel's denouement. Although violent, this poem, like Olive Senior's 'Meditation on Red', pays tribute to the power of Rhys's images in *Wide Sargasso Sea*. In a 1991 interview, it was suggested to Lorna Goodison that

> Obviously, you consider Jean Rhys important, or you feel strongly about her. But in the first poem [A Jean Rhys Lady] the images of claws, flames, drunkenness, representing violent or destructive features are in sharp contrast to the second poem, a lullaby about sleep.[109]

Goodison's response makes no reference to 'A Jean Rhys Lady', but of her second poem, 'Lullaby for Jean Rhys', she says,

> 'Lullaby' was just before Jean Rhys's death. It's the same kind of thing that would make me do the 'Jamaica 1980' poem. It's just a dreamer's attempt to make something right in a world over which I have no control.[110]

Of her poem 'Jamaica 1980' she says,

> There were actually over 800 people killed in the election of that year. These are human beings. Somebody should talk about them.... I think that after 1980, we should have had some public grieving, some ceremony, or monument to the fact that over 800 people died. We never really did.[111]

It might be inferred, therefore, that at some level a 'Lullaby For Jean Rhys' constitutes a public grieving for Rhys. Senior demonstrates a similar compassion for Rhys. Goodison's poem begins with the capital letters 'SLEEP IT OFF LADY',[112] the lead title of Rhys's last published collection of short stories (1976), the story about Mrs Verney, who is left to die, presumed drunk, by a 'bovine looking' local schoolgirl: '"Sleep it off lady,' said this horrible child, skipping away'.[113] In Goodison's poem, however, the phrase is gentle and soothing and is reworked at the end into 'Sleep now Miss Rhys'. Her description of the nurse unites images of Christophine from *Wide Sargasso Sea*, and Cinderella's fairy godmother, and a personification of the Caribbean. With compassionate intuition Goodison unites the story of Antoinette with Rhys's own, and provides images of what both had lacked, namely love and healthy intimacy. The imagery of Goodison's poem is drawn directly from Antoinette's nightmare at the convent:

> I am wearing a long dress and thin slippers, so I walk with difficulty, following the man who is with me and holding up the skirt of my dress. It is white and beautiful and I don't wish to get it soiled. I follow him, sick with fear but I make no effort to save myself; if anyone were to try to save me, I would refuse. This must happen. Now we have reached the forest. We are under the tall dark trees and there is no wind. 'Here?' He turns and looks at me, his face black with hatred, and when I see this I begin to cry. He smiles slyly. 'Not here, not yet,' he says, and I follow him, weeping. Now I do not try to hold up my dress, it trails in the dirt, my beautiful dress.[114]

Kenneth Ramchand has said of this passage that it 'is used to point the work towards the relationship between Antoinette and her husband'[115] and as such it prefigures the outcome of their union. Goodison adapts its imagery to offer up a more hopeful scenario in 'a dreamer's attempt to make something right'. The Jamaican poets Jean Binta Breeze and Anthony McNeill also pay tribute to Rhys. Jean Binta Breeze's 'Red Rebel Song' draws on images of fire, madness and rage, and the refrain unites the images with an allusion to the title of Rhys's novel: 'jus a raw fire madness / a clinging to de green / a sargasso sea'.[116] Her song of 'siddung eena attic'[117] implies a desire to move on from the oppressions described by Rhys. Anthony McNeill's 'The White Shell' blesses 'Jean Rhys / of Parisian nightmare',[118] for her writing.

His title alludes to the way her fiction 'remembers the sea', to the fragile emptiness of her heroines, and to the surprising discovery of Rhys as a truly Caribbean writer. While intertextuality clearly demonstrates the importance of her European heritage and experience, she has, in her turn, served as a 'beacon to safe harbour' for many contemporary writers from the Caribbean.

Notes

1. K. Ramchand, *An Introduction to the Study of West Indian Literature* (Sunbury-on-Thames, Middlesex: Nelson and Sons, 1976) pp. 91–7.
2. E. O'Callaghan, *Woman Version: Theoretical Approaches to West Indian Fiction by Women* (London: Macmillan, 1993) pp. 29–35.
3. D. deCaires Narain and E. O'Callaghan in 'Anglophone Caribbean Women Writers' in *Into the Nineties* eds A. Rutherford, L. Jensen and S. Chew (Armidale, NSW: Dangaroo Press, 1994) p. 626.
4. See Wasafiri Nos 20, 22 and 23.
5. Carol Morrell (ed.), *Grammar of Dissent: Poetry and Prose by Claire Harris, M. Nourbese Philip, Dionne Brand* (Fredericton, NB: Goose Lane, 1994) p. 170.
6. P. Mariani (ed.), *Critical Fictions: The Politics of Imaginative Writing* (Seattle: Bay Press, 1991) p. 67.
7. V.M. Gregg, 'Ideology and Autobiography in the Jean Rhys oeuvre' in A. Rutherford (ed.), *From Commonwealth to Post-Colonial* (Sydney, NSW: Dangaroo Press, 1992) p. 409.
8. See B. Gilroy's 'Reflections' (Chapter 1).
9. A less benign view is offered by Judie Newman in *The Ballistic Bard* which highlights the importance of the 'imperial' text and its function in the process of colonization. see J. Newman, *The Ballistic Bard: Postcolonial Fictions* (London: Arnold, 1996) p. 4.
10. F. Wyndham and D. Melly (eds), *Jean Rhys Letters, 1931–66* (London: André Deutsch, 1984) p. 153.
11. See, for example, E.R. Baer, 'The Sisterhood of Jane Eyre and Antoinette Cosway' in E. Abel, M. Hirsh and E. Langland (eds), *The Voyage In: Fictions of Female Development* (Hanover and London: University Press of New England, 1983); S. Branson, 'Magicked by the Place: Shadow and Substance in *Wide Sargasso Sea*', *Jean Rhys Review*, 3:2 19–28; K. Brathwaite, 'A Post-Cautionary Tale of the Helen of our Wars', *Wasafiri*, 22 (Autumn 1995) 69–78; M.L. Emery, 'The Politics of Form: Jean Rhys's Social Vision in Voyage in the Dark and *Wide Sargasso Sea*', *Twentieth Century Literature*, 28:4 (Winter 1982) 418–30; M. Fayad, 'Unquiet Ghosts: The Struggle for Representation in Rhys's *Wide Sargasso Sea*', *Modern Fiction Studies*, 34:3 (Autumn 1988) 437–52; M. Ferguson, 'Sending the Younger Son Across the Wide Sargasso Sea: The New Colonizer Arrives', *Jean*

Rhys Review, 6:1 2–16; N.J. Casey Fulton, 'Jean Rhys's *Wide Sargasso Sea*: *Exterminating the White Cockroach'*, *Revista / Review Interamericana*, 4 (1974) 340–9; V. Gregg, 'Symbolic Imagery and Mirroring Techniques in *Wide Sargasso Sea*' in P. Frickey (ed.) *Critical Perspectives on Jean Rhys* (Washington DC: Three Continents Press, 1990) pp. 158–65; W. Harris, 'Carnival of Psyche: Jean Rhys's *Wide Sargasso Sea*' *Kunapipi*, II:2 (1980) 142–50; J. Hearne, 'The Wide Sargasso Sea: A West Indian Reflection' in P. Frickey (ed.) *Critical Perspectives on Jean Rhys* (Washington DC: Three Continents Press, 1990) pp. 186–93; P. Hulme, 'The Locked Heart: The Creole Family Romance of *Wide Sargasso Sea* – An Historical and Biographical Analysis', *Jean Rhys Review*, 6:1 20–36; P. Hulme, 'The Place of *Wide Sargasso Sea*', *Wasafiri*, 20 (autumn 1994) 5–11; P. Hulme, 'A Response to Kamau Brathwaite', *Wasafiri*, 23 (Spring 1996) 49–50; F. Johnson, 'The Male Gaze and the Struggle Against Patriarchy in *Jane Eyre* and *Wide Sargasso Sea*', *Jean Rhys Review*, 5:1–2 22–30; A. Koenen, 'The Fantastic as Feminine Mode', *Jean Rhys Review*, 4:1 15–27; L. Lawson, 'Mirror and Madness: A Lacanian Analysis of the Feminine Subject in *Wide Sargasso Sea*', *Jean Rhys Review*, 4:2 19–27; T. Loe, 'Patterns of the Zombie in Jean Rhys's *Wide Sargasso Sea*', *World Literature Written in English*, 31:1 (Spring 1991) 34–42; W. Look Lai, 'The Road to Thornfield Hall', review in *New World Quarterly*, IV:2 (1968) 17–27; A. Luengo '*Wide Sargasso Sea* and the Gothic Mode' in P. Frickey (ed.) *Critical Perspectives on Jean Rhys* (Washington DC: Three Continents Press, 1990) pp. 166–77; J. Newman, 'I Walked with a Zombie, Jean Rhys, *Wide Sargasso Sea*' in J. Newman, *The Ballistic Bard: Postcolonial Fictions* (London: Arnold, 1996); J.C. Oates, 'Romance and Anti-Romance from Brontë's *Jane Eyre* to Rhys's *Wide Sargasso Sea*', *The Virginia Quarterly Review*, LXI (1985) 44–58; D. Porter, 'Of Heroines and Victims: Jean Rhys and *Jane Eyre*', *The Massachusetts Review*, Autumn (1976) 540–52; K. Ramchand, 'Terrified Consciousness', *The Journal of Commonwealth Literature*, 7 (July 1970) 8–19; K. Ramchand, '*Wide Sargasso Sea*' in P. Frickey (ed.) *Critical Perspectives on Jean Rhys* (Washington DC: Three Continents Press, 1990) pp. 194–205; R. Scharfman, 'Mirroring and Mothering in Simone Schwarz-Bart's *Pluie et vent sur Télumée Miracle* and Jean Rhys's *Wide Sargasso Sea*', *Yale French Studies*, 62 (1981) 88–106; G.C. Spivak, 'Three Women's Texts and a Critique of Imperialism', *Critical Inquiry*, 12:1 (Autumn 1985) 243–61; J. Thieme, '"Apparitions of Disaster": Brontëan Parallels in *Wide Sargasso Sea* and *Guerrillas*', *Journal of Commonwealth Literature*, 24:1 (1979) 116–32; M. Thorpe, 'The Other Side: *Wide Sargasso Sea* and *Jane Eyre*' in P. Frickey (ed.) *Critical Perspectives on Jean Rhys* (Washington DC: Three Continents Press, 1990) pp. 78–185. See references to *Wide Sargasso Sea* in critical studies of Jean Rhys's fiction including: H. Carr, *Jean Rhys* (Plymouth: Northcote House, 1996); A. Davidson, *Jean Rhys* (New York: Frederick Ungar, 1985); M.L. Emery, *Jean Rhys at 'World's End': Novels of Colonial and Sexual Exile* (Austin, Texas: University of Texas Press, 1990); V. Gregg, *Jean Rhys's Historical Imagination: Reading and Writing the Creole* (Chapel Hill and London: University of North Carolina Press, 1995); N. Harrison, *Jean Rhys and the Novel as Women's Text* (Chapel Hill and London: University of North Carolina, 1988); C. Howells, *Jean Rhys* (London: Harvester Wheatsheaf, 1991); L. James, *Jean Rhys* (London: Longman, 1978); P. Le Gallez, *The Rhys Woman* London: Macmillan, 1990); H. Nebeker, *Jean Rhys, Woman in Passage: A Critical Study* (Montreal: Eden Press, 1981); T. O'Connor, *Jean Rhys's West Indian Novels* (New York: New York University Press, 1986); T.F. Staley, *Jean Rhys: A Critical Study* (London and Basingstoke: Macmillan, 1979); P. Wolfe, *Jean Rhys* (Boston: Twayne, 1980). See biography, C. Angier, *Jean Rhys: Life and Work* (London: André Deutsch, 1990).

12. It is likely that she was aware of the poem given Pound's close association with Ford.

13. See Coral Ann Howells's important critique of this short story in C. Howells, *Jean Rhys* (London: Harvester Wheatsheaf, 1991).

14. J. Rhys, 'Again the Antilles' in *Tigers Are Better-Looking with a selection from the Left Bank* (London: André Deutsch, 1968) p. 177.

15. Ibid., p. 180.

16. Ibid., p. 178.

17. C. Howells, *Jean Rhys* (London: Harvester Wheatsheaf, 1991) p. 38.

18. J. Rhys, 'Again the Antilles', p. 177.

19. See Jean Rhys's short story 'Pioneers, Oh, Pioneers' for further representations of Englishmen in the Caribbean and my article 'Reconstructing Dominica: Jean Rhys's "Pioneers, Oh, Pioneers"' in *Journal of the Short Story*, 26 (Spring 1996) 75–86. (See also for literary allusions to Walt Whitman and Willa Cather.)

20. J. Rhys, 'Again the Antilles', p. 178.

21. Rhys uses the device of letters in newspapers in a number of her stories which in itself further confirms the importance of the written word and its relationship to other texts for Rhys. Examples include 'Pioneers, Oh, Pioneers', 'Tigers Are Better-Looking' and 'Fishy Waters'.

22. J. Rhys, 'Again the Antilles', p. 179.

23. Ibid., p. 178.

24. Ibid., p. 179.

25. Ibid.

26. Ibid.

27. Ibid.

28. Ibid., p. 180.

29. Ibid.

30. J. Rhys, *Quartet* 1928 (London: Penguin, 1988) pp. 70–1.

31. Dujardin's novel of the same name has been translated into English as *The Bays are Sere*, but the laurels have been cut would seem more appropriate.

32. The song is printed in *Le livre d'or de la chanson française: De Clément Marot à Georges Brassens*. Tome II (Paris: Les Editions Ouvrières, 1972) pp. 112–13.

33. Although Rhys's novels are about chorus girls, they invariably involve

elements of prostitution. In *Smile Please: an unfinished autobiography* (London: André Deutsch, 1979) p. 63. Rhys says 'I liked books about prostitutes, there were a good many then, and vividly recollect a novel called *The Sands of Pleasure* written by a man named Filson Young. . . . It was about an Englishman's love affair with an expensive demi-mondaine in Paris.'

34. It is worth noting that restaurants and meals are important to the landscape of Rhys's work. In Dujardin's novel, Daniel Prince has dinner at the Café Oriental before keeping his rendez-vous with Lea. In *Quartet*, during her first meeting with the Heidlers, Lois explains that 'H.J. and I have quite made up our minds that eating is the greatest pleasure in life' and later in August's restaurant after the Heidlers invite Marya to live with them 'Monsieur August placed a large sole on the table, glanced at Heidler with light blue, very ironical eyes, and departed.' Daniel Prince also orders sole and spends much of his time admiring 'une assez jolie femme', belittling her bald male companion 'ce monsieur parait stupide' and fantasizing about how he might make contact with her. The female character and her companion recall Marya and Heidler or Julia Martin and Mr Mackenzie at Maitre Albert's restaurant. In both works attention is paid to descriptions of the staff, their attitudes, the surroundings, the general ambience of restaurants in Paris and the association of food and sexual appetite. This association is found on various occasions in Rhys's work including *Voyage in the Dark*. Arnold Davidson notes that after Anna's first dinner with Walter when 'he kisses her, she senses that he is assaying her in much the same fashion that he earlier sniffed the cork of the wine they would consume, and she 'hated him' for so obviously reducing her to a connoisseur's dessert'.

35. It was not until the early 1920s, the time when Rhys was living in Paris, knew Ford and would have had her greatest exposure to literary circles, that Joyce's use of interior monologue was attributed to Dujardin. An important review of Dujardin's *Les lauriers sont coupés*, which stemmed from Valéry Larbaud's comparison of the text with *Ulysses* appeared in *Les Nouvelles Littéraires* in 1925, three years before the publication of *Quartet*. The review substantiated many of the points Larbaud wrote in the 1924 edition of Dujardin's novel.

> I noted that *Les Lauriers sont coupés*, although totally different in style and spirit from James Joyce's work, had in fact to be considered as one of the sources for the form of *Ulysses*. But I was above all astounded to think that such a book, of such obvious literary worth, and which contained a completely new and attractive literary technique, full of all sorts of possibilities, capable of renewing the novel form or of replacing it entirely, had gone unnoticed for so many years. (from notes and commentary to the translated edition of E. Dujardin, *Les lauriers sont coupés* (1987). London: Libris, 1991, p. 95).

36. W. Wiser, *The Crazy Years: Paris in the Twenties* (London: Thames and Hudson, 1990) p. 59.
37. Ibid., p. 152.
38. E. Hemingway, *The Sun Also Rises* in *The Essential Hemingway* 1947 (London: Grafton, 1977) pp. 19–20.
39. J. Rhys, *Quartet*, pp. 54–5.
40. See also I. Thompson, 'The Left Bank Apéritifs of Jean Rhys and Ernest Hemingway' in *The Georgia Review*, XXXV:1 (Spring 1981) 94–106, and N. Hemond Brown 'Aspects of the Short Story: A Comparison of Jean Rhys's "The Sound of the River" with Ernest Hemingway's "Hill Like White Elephants"' in *Jean Rhys Review*, 1:1 (Fall, 1986) 2–12.
41. The writer Edouard de Nève was the pseudonym of Rhys's first husband Jean Lenglet.
42. See M. Van Kappers definitive study 'A Gloomy Child and Its Devoted Grandmother: Jean Rhys, *Barred*, *Sous les verrous*, and *In de Strik*' in ed. D. MacDermott, *Autobiographical and Biographical Writing in the Commonwealth* (Barcelona: AUSA, 1984).
43. See M. Kappers-den Hollander's article 'Measure for Measure: *Quartet* and *When the Wicked Man*' in *Jean Rhys Review*, 2:2 (Spring 1988) 2–17.
44. Rhys published her first short story in Ford's magazine *Transatlantic Review*.
45. C. Angier, *Jean Rhys: Life and Work* (London: André Deutsch, 1990) p. 196.
46. *Quartet* is generally read as a fictionalized account of Rhys's affair with Ford Madox Ford in Paris.
47. C. Angier, *Jean Rhys: Life and Work* (London: André Deutsch, 1990) p. 196.
48. T.F. Staley, *Jean Rhys: A Critical Study* (London and Basingstoke: Macmillan, 1979) p. 39.
49. Coral Ann Howells links the title character, Fifi, with Maupassant's short story 'Mademoiselle Fifi' and considers the importance of the intertextual connection.
50. J. Rhys, 'La Grosse Fifi' in *Tigers Are Better-Looking with a selection from the Left Bank* (London: André Deutsch, 1968) p. 201.
51. 'Having adopted a narrative of Fifi's experiences rendered through Roseau, who is only beginning to endure what seems to be the long series of disastrous relationships with men, Rhys ties Roseau and Fifi through a series of identifications. Fifi is Roseau's doppel ganger, and the power of the story resides in Roseau's implicit recognition that her life is somehow anticipated by Fifi, for their souls possess similar shapes.' T.F. Staley, *Jean Rhys: A Critical Study* (London and Basingstoke: Macmillan, 1979) p. 31.
52. A. Bennett, *The Old Wives' Tale* 1908 (London: Hodder and Stoughton, 1911) pp. 312–13.
53. Ibid., pp. 368–9.
54. J. Rhys, 'La Grosse Fifi', p. 186.
55. A. Bennett, *The Old Wives' Tale* 1908 (London: Hodder and Stoughton, 1911) p. 374.

56. At the end of *Good Morning, Midnight* dressing gowns are also representative of sordid lifestyles.
57. J. Rhys, 'La Grosse Fifi', p. 198.
58. A. Bennett, *The Old Wives' Tale* 1908 (London: Hodder and Stoughton, 1911) p. 314.
59. Ibid., p. 369.
60. Ibid., p. 378.
61. J. Rhys, 'La Grosse Fifi', p. 192.
62. J. Rhys, *Voyage in the Dark* 1934 (Harmondsworth, Middlesex: Penguin, 1987) p. 9.
63. J. Rhys, *After Leaving Mr Mackenzie* 1930 (Harmondsworth, Middlesex: Penguin, 1987) pp. 74–5.
64. Ibid., p. 53.
65. Ibid., p. 75.
66. J. Conrad, *Almayer's Folly* 1895 (Harmondsworth, Middlesex: Penguin, 1981) p. 94.
67. Ibid., pp. 93–4.
68. Ibid., p. 33.
69. J. Rhys, *After Leaving Mr Mackenzie*, pp. 39–40.
70. J. Conrad, *Almayer's Folly* 1895 (Harmondsworth, Middlesex: Penguin, 1981) p. 145.
71. Rhys commented on how Ford pressed her to read Maupassant and other French authors.
72. See chapters 5 and 6 and note 3 to chapter 6 in H. Carr, *Jean Rhys* (Plymouth: Northcote House).
73. Laura Niesen de Abruna has linked Rhys's *Voyage in the Dark* to Jamaica Kincaid's *Annie John* in her article 'Family Connections: Mother and Mother Country in the Fiction of Jean Rhys and Jamaica Kincaid' in S. Nasta (ed.), *Motherlands: Black Women's Writing from Africa, the Caribbean and South Asia* (London: The Women's Press, 1991) pp. 257–89) and Louis James considers the similarities between the short stories of Olive Senior and Jean Rhys in his article 'The Other Side of the Mirror: the Short Stories of Jean Rhys and Olive Senior'. in J. Bardolph (ed.), *Short Fiction in the New Literatures in English: Proceedings of the Nice Conference of the European Association for Commonwealth Literature and Language Studies* (Nice: Faculté des Lettres et Sciences Humaines de Nice, 1988) pp. 90–4.
74. C.A. Howells, *Jean Rhys* (London: Harvester Wheatsheaf, 1991) p. 105.
75. See also E. O'Callaghan, *Woman Version* (pp. 29–35) and K. Ramchand, 'Terrified Consciousness', *The Journal of Commonwealth Literature*, 7 (July 1969) 8–19 for further comparisons of these works.
76. P.S. Allfrey, *The Orchid House* 1953 (London: Virago, 1990) p. 25.
77. C.A. Howells, *Jean Rhys* (London: Harvester Wheatsheaf, 1991) p. 128.
78. See Sarah Lawson Welsh's critique of 'A Disguised Land' in 'Pauline Melville's Shape-Shifting Fictions'.
79. P. Melville, *Shape-shifter* 1990 (London: Picador, 1991) p. 41.
80. J. Rhys, 'Let Them Call It Jazz' in *Tigers Are Better-Looking with a selection from the Left Bank* (London: André Deutsch, 1968) p. 54.

81. Ibid., pp. 49–50.
82. Ibid., p. 58.
83. Ibid., p. 67.
84. See B. Lalla, *Defining Jamaican Fiction: marronage and the discourse of survival* (Tuscaloosa, Alabama: The University of Alabama Press, 1996) for analysis of *The Last Room*.
85. In *The Last Room* the father is alive in the opening chapters.
86. J. Rhys, *Wide Sargasso Sea* (London: André Deutsch, 1966) p. 111.
87. F. Wyndham and D. Melly (eds), *Jean Rhys Letters, 1931–1966* (London: André Deutsch, 1984) p. 233.
88. J. Rhys, *Wide Sargasso Sea*, pp. 188–9.
89. E. Thomas, *The Last Room* 1991 (London: Virago, 1992) p. 129.
90. Ibid., p. 144.
91. In *The Last Room* Elean Thomas develops the history of the maroons through the story of Grannie Lou, Putus's great-grandmother and her equivalent of Christophine in *Wide Sargasso Sea*. Grannie Lou had left one of the 'free villages' founded by Grandy Nanny and had

> struck a path over to St Catherine, where they had some relations already settled. As far as they were concerned, all the land belonged to the Arawak Indians, who were the original Jamaicans, and since they had been killed off by the Spanish and, later, the British, Grannie Lou and Kayam felt that they were the proper inheritors of the Arawaks' land. (p. 65.)

Not only does Thomas amplify the maroon's history, she also includes the island's original settlers, the Arawaks, in much the same way that Anna in *Voyage in the Dark* and the narrator of Rhys's short story 'Temps Perdi' allude to the Caribs in Dominica.

92. O. Senior, 'Meditation on Red' in *Gardening in the Tropics* 1994 (Newcastle upon Tyne: Bloodaxe Books Limited, 1995) p. 46.
93. Ibid., p. 44.
94. Ibid., p. 49.
95. Ibid., p. 47.
96. F. Wyndham and D. Melly (eds), *Jean Rhys Letters, 1931–1966* (London: André Deutsch, 1984) p. 209.
97. J. Rhys, *Wide Sargasso Sea*, p. 185.
98. O. Senior, 'Meditation on Red' in *Gardening in the Tropics* 1994 (Newcastle upon Tyne: Bloodaxe Books Limited, 1995) pp. 51–2.
99. Ibid, p. 44.
100. D. Walcott, 'Jean Rhys' in *Collected Poems, 1948– 1984*, 1986 (New York: Farrar Straus and Giroux, 1992) p. 427.
101. Ibid.
102. Ibid., p. 429.
103. Ibid.
104. L. Goodison, 'A Jean Rhys Lady' in *Tamarind Season* (Jamaica: Institute of Jamaica, 1980) p. 20.
105. Ibid.

106. C. Brontë, *Jane Eyre* 1847 (Harmondsworth, Middlesex: Penguin, 1966) p. 321.
107. L. Goodison, 'A Jean Rhys Lady' in *Tamarind Season* (Jamaica: Institute of Jamaica, 1980) p. 20.
108. J. Rhys, *Wide Sargasso Sea*, pp. 178–9.
109. F. Birbalsingh, (ed.), *Frontiers of Caribbean Literature in English* (London: Macmillan Education Limited, 1996) p. 155.
110. Ibid.
111. Ibid., pp. 154–5.
112. L. Goodison, 'Lullaby For Jean Rhys' in *I Am Becoming My Mother* 1986 (London: New Beacon Books, 1995) p. 37.
113. J. Rhys, *Sleep It Off Lady* (London: André Deutsch, 1976) p. 171
114. Rhys, *Wide Sargasso Sea*, pp. 59–60.
115. K. Ramchand, 'Terrified Consciousness', *The Journal of Commonwealth Literature*, 7 (July 1969) 17.
116. J. B. Breeze, 'Red Rebel Song' in *Spring Cleaning* (London: Virago, 1992) p. 2.
117. Ibid., p. 6.
118. A. McNeill, 'The White Shell' in *Jamaica Journal*, 22.3 (August 1989) 59.

Bibliography

Allfrey, P.S. *The Orchid House* (1953) London: Virago, 1990.
Angier, C. *Jean Rhys: Life and Work*. London: André Deutsch, 1990.
Bennett, A. *The Old Wives' Tale* (1908) London: Hodder and Stoughton, 1911.
Breeze, J.B. 'Red Rebel Song' in *Spring Cleaning*. London: Virago, 1992.
Birbalsingh, F (ed.), *Frontiers of Caribbean Literature in English*. London: Macmillan Education Limited, 1996.
Carr, H. *Jean Rhys*. Plymouth: Northcote House, 1996.
Conrad, J. *Almayer's Folly* (1895) Harmondsworth, Middlesex: Penguin, 1981.
deCaires Narain, D. and E. O'Callaghan in 'Anglophone Caribbean Women Writers' in (eds) A. Rutherford, L. Jensen and S. Chew *Into the Nineties*. Armidale, NSW: Dangaroo Press, 1994.
Dujardin, E. *Les lauriers sont coupés* (1887) London: Libris, 1991.
Goodison, L. 'A Jean Rhys Lady' in *Tamarind Season*. Jamaica: Institute of Jamaica, 1980.
——. 'Lullaby For Jean Rhys' in *I Am Becoming My Mother* (1986) London: New Beacon Books, 1995.
Gregg, V.M. 'Ideology and Autobiography in the Jean Rhys oeuvre' in (ed.) A. Rutherford *From Commonwealth to Post-Colonial*. Sydney, NSW: Dangaroo Press, 1992.
Hemingway, E. *The Sun Also Rises* (1927) in *The Essential Hemingway* (1947) London: Grafton, 1977.
Howells, C. *Jean Rhys*. London: Harvester Wheatsheaf, 1991.

74   *Caribbean Women Writers*

McNeill, A. 'The White Shell' in *Jamaica Journal*, 22.3 (August 1989) 59.
Mariani, P. (ed.), *Critical Fictions: The Politics of Imaginative Writing*. Seattle: Bay Press, 1991.
Melville, P. *Shape-shifter* (1990) London: Picador, 1991.
Morrell, C (ed.), *Grammar of Dissent: Poetry and Prose by Claire Harris, M. Nourbese Philip, Dionne Brand*. Fredericton, NB: Goose Lane, 1994.
Newman, J. *The Ballistic Bard: Postcolonial Fictions*. London: Arnold, 1996.
O'Callaghan, E. *Woman Version: Theoretical Approaches to West Indian Fiction by Women*. London: Macmillan, 1993.
Rhys, J. *Quartet* (1928) London: Penguin, 1988.
——. *After Leaving Mr Mackenzie* (1930) Harmondsworth, Middlesex: Penguin, 1987.
——. *Voyage in the Dark* (1934) Harmondsworth, Middlesex: Penguin, 1987.
——. *Good Morning, Midnight* (1939) London: Penguin, 1969.
——. *Wide Sargasso Sea*. London: André Deutsch, 1966.
——. *Tigers Are Better-Looking with a selection from the Left Bank*. London: André Deutsch, 1968.
——. *Sleep It Off Lady*, London: André Deutsch, 1976.
——. *Smile Please: an Unfinished Autobiography*. London: André Deutsch, 1979
Ramchand, K. 'Terrified Consciousness', *The Journal of Commonwealth Literature*, 7 (July 1969) 8–19.
Staley, T.F. *Jean Rhys: A Critical Study*. London and Basingstoke: Macmillan, 1979.
Senior, O. 'Meditation on Red' in *Gardening in the Tropics* (1994) Newcastle upon Tyne: Bloodaxe Books Limited, 1995.
Thomas, E. *The Last Room* (1991) London: Virago, 1992.
Walcott, D. 'Jean Rhys' in *Collected Poems, 1948–1984* (1986) New York: Farrar Straus and Giroux, 1992.
Wyndham F. and D. Melly (eds). *Jean Rhys Letters, 1931–66*. London: André Deutsch, 1984.

6

Perceptions of Place: Geopolitical and Cultural Positioning in Paule Marshall's Novels

Heidi Slettedahl Macpherson

The acknowledged tension between community and individual in the fiction of Paule Marshall extends beyond the perimeters of any imagined country. Indeed, Marshall's use of fictionalized, composite island backdrops moves her representation of Caribbean identity beyond specific geography while still acknowledging the geopolitical space accorded representations of the Caribbean. In her 1991 novel, *Daughters*, Marshall symbolically names her composite island Triunion, and in this name links not only the three colonial powers said to have engaged in historical struggle over the island – France, England, and Spain – but also the African-American and Caribbean identities of her main protagonist, Ursa Beatrice Mackenzie. Thus, Marshall symbolically deconstructs any sort of binary opposition implied by the juxtapositioning of American and Caribbean, while simultaneously exploring how the tension between individual and community is mediated through these representations. Focusing primarily on *Daughters*, this chapter will trace Marshall's manipulation of the individual-community struggle which is apparent from her first novel, *Brown Girl, Brownstones* (1959), through her most recent, and explore how this struggle is represented through contestations of place.

In *Brown Girl, Brownstones*, perhaps Marshall's best known novel, the tension between the individual and the community is captured concretely in the figure of Selina Boyce, daughter of the Barbadian-identified Deighton Boyce and the American-identified (though equally Barbadian-born) Silla Boyce. In this early, semi-autobiographical text, Marshall locates Caribbean geography firmly in the actual island of Barbados, yet this physical reality remains figured only as a memory or as a destination never reached. For Deighton Boyce, Barbados is the source of his fantasies of restful ease; his recollections of the island are tinged with utopian memories of childhood games. In these configurations, white people are seen as benign, rich tourists for whom he performed diving tricks; Deighton's recollections do not admit any resemblance between his childish actions and the performances expected of him in America. Indeed, it is only when he attempts – in his own faulty way – to get a job in New York that Deighton connects his treatment by white employers to the treatment that he received by whites back in 'Bimshire': '"They does scorn yuh 'cause yuh skin black"'.[1] Yet Barbados, for Deighton, remains configured as '"poor-poor but sweet enough"'.[2]

In contrast, Silla Boyce envisions Barbados as the site of childhood suffering and the source of adult ignorance and passivity, a place where '"[t]he rum shop and the church join together"'[3] in order to keep the Barbadians down. Instead of childhood games, Silla recalls childhood labour, and any memories she has of the country of her birth are focused on images of 'the sun on her back and the whip cutting her legs'.[4] Just as Deighton refuses to connect his childhood experiences scrambling for the white tourists' coins with his adult scrambling for a job, so, too, does Silla disconnect her childhood labour in Barbados from her adult labour in New York. For Deighton, this is a means of keeping 'Bimshire' pure and unsullied, whereas for Silla this refusal to connect the two places marks an attempt to create in New York the haven that her husband finds in Barbados. As a result, neither character is able to see beyond these restricting formulations. As their daughter, Selina, recognizes, 'her father carried those gay days in his irresponsible smile, while the mother's formidable aspect was the culmination of all that she had suffered'.[5]

Barbados as a site of struggle is also represented by a piece of land that Deighton inherits and which Silla manages to sell through deception. In crushing Deighton's dream of a house back 'home', Silla ensures that Deighton will retaliate; he squanders the money raised by the sale of the land on extravagant gifts rather than using it, as Silla wished, for a down payment on their rented brownstone. Deighton's behaviour is a signal that he will not be forced into behaviour acceptable to the Barbadian-American community, which buys into the myth of the American dream and sees the acquisition of property as the first step in establishing a proper place in America. Indeed, even Deighton's method of arriving in America offers a clear indication of his relationship to the place: bound for Cuba, he simply jumped ship and landed in America.[6] As unofficial alien resident, Deighton signals not only his outsider status – '"As far as the record goes I ain even in this country since I did enter illegally . . . I don't even exist as far as these people here go"'[7] – but also his unwillingness to align himself with America in any public way.

By refusing to align himself in this way, however, Deighton ironically excludes himself from the Bajan community, too. This exclusion is signalled graphically when Deighton attempts to join in the celebration of 'Gatha Steed's daughter's wedding after his betrayal of Silla. Silla and her daughters are dancing in the midst of a crowd, all of whom refuse to greet Deighton: 'But they had seen him by now and they closed protectively around Silla and Ina; someone pulled Selina back. Then, like the men at the bar, the dancers turned in one body and danced with their backs to him'.[8] Significantly, the song to which they are dancing is accompanied by the words, '"Small Island, go back where you really come from!"'[9]

This exclusion marks the end of Deighton's vitality. Shortly afterwards, he is injured in an accident at work that renders his arm useless and prevents him from working. In his convalescence, he encounters Father Peace and gives himself up to a religious community which accepts his lack of ambition. First emotionally distancing himself from his family, and then physically moving away, Deighton provokes Silla's wrath. Her revenge is to denounce him to the authorities and force his repatriation to Barbados, the land of his dreams. Frightened of its reality, especially since he cannot fulfill his desire to return as a successful man, Deighton commits suicide by jumping overboard in sight of Barbados rather than return to the land of his birth. Having jumped ship to enter America, he jumps ship in order to avoid re-entering Barbados.

With Deighton's death the spectre of Barbados retreats from the text, as Silla embraces America with more vehemence than before and as Selina struggles against the forces that make up the Bajan community. Only at the end of the novel, when Selina learns that, despite her efforts, she will always be aligned with West Indians in the minds of white people, does Selina recognize her own connection both to the Barbadian community that her mother represents and the Barbados of her parents' birth. With this knowledge comes a desire to visit Barbados and strengthen her newly-recognized cultural connection. While her method of getting to Barbados – she plans to get a job on a cruise ship and disappear into Barbados once there[10] – contains undertones of her father's journey, it also echoes her mother's journey in some ways. She is the same age that her mother was when Silla came to America as her 'own woman',[11] and like Silla, will be making her journey alone.

The final image of the novel – Selina throwing away one of the silver bracelets that marks her connection to Barbados, yet retaining the other – suggests that her connections will always be two ways. By choosing to go to Barbados, she recognizes that she has a choice. Unlike her mother's journey, Selina's journey does not necessarily have to end in one final destination. Barbados can be merely one of Selina's many stops along the way. Susan Willis argues that this final image connects with 'Marshall's role as a writer, whose task has been to articulate both the difficulties of being in two worlds at once and the need to unite the Afro-American cultures of North America and the Caribbean'.[12] Indeed, in interviews, Marshall herself foregrounds her composite identities as African-American and West Indian. Maintaining that she does not make any explicit distinctions, preferring to think that '"All o' we is one"',[13] Marshall also reveals that she likes to think of her work as '"a kind of bridge that joins the two great wings of the black diaspora in this part of the world"'.[14]

Marshall's next novel is set entirely on the fictional Caribbean island of Bourne. In *The Chosen Place, the Timeless People* (1969), the dream-like formulations of *Brown Girl, Brownstones* are replaced by physical descriptions of the Caribbean. According to Barbara Christian, Marshall's second novel 'encompasses the theme of the first – becoming – and moves it to a sociopolitical and mythological sphere'.[15] Furthermore, Christian argues that this second novel in some ways shows a progression from the first, as Marshall's 'emphasis moves from the way the world affects an individual psyche to how our many psyches create a world'.[16] To this end, *The Chosen Place, the Timeless People* does not hinge on one central consciousness, but examines Bourne Island – and specifically a portion of it called Bournehills – through a number of different characters: the committed anthropologist Saul, who despite himself will never be more than an outsider, his wife Harriet, who feels intimidated by the few connections forged between herself and the Bournehills residents, Allen Fuso, Saul's assistant, who as a homosexual is doubly an outsider, Vere, a Bournehills resident who returns to the island after working away from it for a number of years, and finally, and perhaps most importantly, Merle, a self-appointed leader in Bournehills whose ambiguous position in relation to Bournehills is represented in the contradictions which surround her.

The reader first encounters Merle on a washed-out road in Bournehills, in a battered car which has been 'deliberately abused, wilfully desecrated'.[17] The car, significantly, is assumed to have once belonged to a colonial governor. Through the car, Merle is connected in some way both to positions of present and past authority. Merle herself is portrayed as a cacophony of contradictions, most clearly expressed in her customary apparel, in which parts of her outfit war against each other, from her West African dress to her European earrings to her West Indian bracelets. The narrator insists that this 'somewhat bizarre outfit' is meant to express 'a diversity and a disunity within herself, and her attempt, unconscious probably, to reconcile these opposing parts, to make of them a whole'.[18] Merle perhaps stands as an objective correlative for Bourne Island as a whole; by driving an ex-colonial car, Merle suggests the Caribbean island's historical past; by figuring the car as deliberately misused, the narrator suggests the colonial powers' treatment of the island. Finally, by positioning this contradictory character at the wheel of the car, the narrator suggests that Merle's ambiguous relationship to the various aspects of herself and her past is emblematic of Bourne Island's own uncertain position.

Merle is introduced before the geography of the island itself, and this reinforces the connections between character and landscape. Indeed, other characters themselves eventually make this connection: Saul's anthropological focus, which ironically makes possible his mental conflation of his Bournehills project and some of his former projects, is seriously flawed by his inability to view the island as a specific, rooted, geopolitical space. The island merges with Merle in his mind: 'in his desire to know and embrace

Bournehills, it was inevitable, indeed necessary, that he first know and embrace Merle'.[19]

Not only does the description of Merle precede the description of the island, but the perspective used is significantly different as well; detailed attention is paid to Merle's appearance, whereas the island is first described through the windows of an aeroplane. This distancing technique, which reinforces the idea of an outsider perspective, also allows a variety of perspectives to be explored and juxtaposed. The island is first described as 'another indifferently shaped green knoll at the will of a mindless sea, one more in a line of steppingstones that might have been placed there long ago by some giant race to span the distance between the Americas, North and South'.[20] This characterization permits Bourne Island to become, in Barbara Christian's words, 'a prototype of other Caribbean islands',[21] for it clearly indicates the Eurocentric perception of the Caribbean as 'a gateway to the New World'.[22] What is significant about this perception, however, is that it is that of Vere, a Bournehills native who is returning to his country of birth after working in the United States. This suggests the powerful influence that the United States exerts, and sets up an outsider/insider opposition even within one character.

First indicating the way in which Bourne Island resembles other Caribbean islands, the narrator, who both takes up Vere's position and stands outside it in a seemingly objective way, then addresses its difference: 'the island below had broken rank and stood off by itself to the right, almost out in the Atlantic'.[23] This difference is all the more relevant considering that Vere's return is in some ways expressed as a homecoming, albeit an ambiguous one. Vere's 'accomplishments' – such as they were – that took place outside of this island are now figured as 'nothing suddenly in the face of that dark steepled hill and the village obscured at its foot'.[24] Vere sees his return as 'fixed and inevitable',[25] and this realization troubles him.

In contrast to Vere and his aerial examination of the island, Allen Fuso concentrates on appraising his fellow passengers; having already lived on the island, he claims it in an offhand sort of way that does not seem to need any gaze to buttress or establish it. Saul Amron, the character who will attempt – and fail – to claim the island more clearly than the other visiting characters, sleeps rather than attempting to define the island visually or metaphorically before he has actually encountered it. This task is left to his wife Harriet, who defines Bourne Island – and eventually its residents – as Other. The sense of othering is particularly acute in Harriet's reactions to Bournehills, the section of the island designated to receive the most attention from the visiting anthropologists. Harriet divides it off in her mind quite clearly from the rest of the island: 'It struck her as being another world altogether, one that stood in profound contradistinction to the pleasant reassuring green plain directly below; and she wondered, gazing intently out toward those scarred hills, how an island as small as this could sustain such a dangerous division'.²⁶

For both the Amrons, Bournehills comes to represent something other than it is. For Harriet, Bournehills, even initially, represents less a geographical entity than 'some mysterious and obscured region of the mind which ordinary consciousness did not dare admit to light. Suddenly, for a single unnerving moment, she had the sensation of being borne backward in time rather than forward in space'.²⁷

By contrast, Saul seeks – equally unsuccessfully – to define himself as part of Bournehills. Yet for a variety of reasons, Bournehills still occupies a space not quite real for Saul, and this is apparent from his very first appraisal of the area: 'because of the thick haze which made the landscape waver and lose shape before the eye, and the sunlight spilling down like molten steel from the lip of the sun, the entire place looked almost illusory, unreal, a trick played by the eye'.²⁸ Using physical, 'scientific' reasons for this impression – the haze – Saul is able to deny the àctual force of this impression. However, the reason that the place looks illusory and unreal has less to do with weather than with the fact that for Saul, the place is unreal because he sees it as representative rather than actual: 'It was suddenly, to his mind, every place that had been wantonly used, its substance stripped away, and then abandoned'.²⁹ Bournehills therefore becomes merely one of many and its characteristics those of the victimized: the image is a disturbingly sexualized one. It is not by accident that this vision is linked to a white man, and comes from a high vantage point, a ridge, connecting Saul's view with Harriet's when she looked out of her aeroplane window the previous day. Despite being ostensibly closer to Bournehills than Harriet, Saul cannot see the place clearly. Even when Saul comes to know Bournehills better, the sense of unreality never quite disappears: ' . . . he would be struck by the feeling, too fleeting to grasp, that he had stumbled upon a world that was real, inescapably real, yet at the same time somehow unreal; of the present but even more so of the past'.[30]

In some ways, Harriet's deliberate distancing and othering of Bournehills is a more legitimate response than Saul's attempts at inclusion. Although as a scientist, Saul recognizes that his position as observer precludes a position of participant, at the same time, his desire to ameliorate his sense of displacement never quite leaves him. Even as he sees this position as inevitable, he desires a different position. His inevitable displacement results less from his position as anthropologist working in developing countries than as a result of his own sense of being the Other. Connecting Saul's Jewishness with his attempts at reconciliation, Marshall explores the dynamics of geopolitical positioning from more than one perspective. In *The Chosen Place, the Timeless People*, Marshall explores the ways in which outsiders express their own sense of 'otherness' through projection. Allen's sense of otherness through his latent homosexuality and Saul's through his Jewish heritage are displaced on to the island.

If the 'place' of the novel's title is variously represented, so, too, is the island's 'timelessness' most clearly represented in the central historical moment which is repeated in various ways throughout the text. In pageants and arguments, the Bournehills natives celebrate a historical slave revolt led by Cuffee Ned. Their fierce hold on the past is reinforced by physical reminders: an area called Pyre Hill, the site of the revolt, still bears the scars of the occasion: 'The hill appeared to have been almost totally destroyed by some recent fire. It might have only just stopped burning. . . . The ground, you were certain, would still be hot underfoot'.[31] The physical space has inscribed upon it the emotional resonances which bind the Bournehills residents to each other. Merle names them as '"an odd, half-mad people"'[32] for whom that past holds a greater power than the present, but by the end of the novel, Merle herself has recognized that understanding comes through sifting through the events of the past. For Merle, this equates with going to Africa, not to search for her ethnic roots, but to search for her branches, her daughter and her estranged husband. She must go back and explore the reasons for her marriage break up, and through that movement, move forward.

If Merle is searching for branches, the protagonist of Marshall's next novel must first explore her roots. Like Saul and Harriet, Avey Johnson of *Praisesong for the Widow* (1983) is a visitor to a Caribbean island. Unlike the Amrons, however, Avey manages to forge connections with her past which transform her present. It is through recognizing her connections to the Caribbean that Avey Johnson is able to integrate several aspects of herself. But, as Carole Boyce Davies says of the novel, 'Thematically, however, it is set in Africa, in that it examines the continuations of African culture in the New World and their connection to the parent'.[33]

Marshall's use of African motifs is by no means unique. As Velma Pollard notes, the African connection has long been a familiar aspect of African American writing.[34] However, what Pollard does note as unusual in Marshall's writing is her linking not only of Africa and America, but of Africa, America, and the Caribbean, both in its Anglophone and Francophone manifestations.[35] In *Praisesong for the Widow*, the geography of the Caribbean is less important than its society and culture, and these link clearly with an African past. America, by contrast, becomes figured as a site where people are unable to 'call their nation'.[36] Avey does not even initially recognize her nation, which is the source of her unsettling physical symptoms and dreams, and she looks at Grenada only with a tourist's eyes, picking out the sandy beaches, the pier and the rum shop as if they metonymically stand for the Caribbean.

The novel opens with this middle-aged, middle-class widow, Avey Johnson, deciding, inexplicably, to leave her Caribbean cruise and return home to New York. Stopping off in Grenada, initially just for the night, Avey becomes progressively more disoriented. She is met on the pier by people who greet her as if they know her. Spirited away from the hubbub to a remote, antiseptic hotel, she spends the night dreaming of the past. The text then becomes riddled with references to babyhood. She wakes to the 'faint but familiar' odour of a baby who needs to be changed,[37] which she only later recognizes as her own odour after sleeping in her clothes. Stripping herself of her soiled clothes, she is 'as slow and clumsy as a two-year-old just learning how to undress itself'.[38] Leaving the hotel, she does not at first recognize her own name, and she accidentally leaves her watch behind:[39] as figurative child, she would be unable to 'tell the time' anyway. But more importantly, in order to begin her journey towards her nation, Avey must leave behind all reminders of her sheltered life, even her con-stricting clothes.

Ann Armstrong Scarboro locates six aspects of Avey's 'para-digm for self-renewal', including 'interaction with a mentor'.[40] Avey's mentor is Lebert Johnson, an 'out-islander' who, after learn-ing that Avey cannot 'call her nation', invites her to join him on the annual excursion to Carriacou. In her extreme disorientation, for which Marshall provides a physical explanation in Avey's heat exhaustion, she submits. Lebert's name, as well as his role in Avey's journey, connects him with Legba, the African deity who is represented both as a 'trickster' and as the 'guardian of the cross-roads where all ways meet'.[41] Eugenia Collier argues that Lebert, 'in his implied role as Legba, contains many linkages: Africa and the Diaspora; the carnate and the spirit worlds; the present generation, the ancestors, and the yet unborn'.[42]

Although Lebert is the most vivid expression of diasporic connections, the text also foregrounds other connections between Avey's experiences, the New World, and Africa. For example, three different types of journey are alluded to in the text: Avey's middle-class cruise on a ship called 'Bianca Pride', her childhood boat trips up the Hudson to Bear Mountain, and the journey to Carriacou, which is connected with the Middle Passage and which begins Avey's purification process. The Bianca Pride cruise is presented immediately as a retreat into whiteness; as Christian indicates, it is not accidental that the ship has the word 'white' inscribed within its name, nor that Avey's home is in White Plains.[43] Avey's youngest and most political daughter, Marion, finds her mother's choice of vacation inexplicable: '"Why go on some mean-ingless cruise with a bunch of white folks, anyway . . .?"'.[44] On Avey's last day on board ship, she constantly has her solitude invaded by other passengers, whose faces loom 'abnormally large and white'.[45] When she comes face to face with her own reflec-tion, she does not recognize it.[46] Clearly, by taking on the trap-pings of the middle class, Avey has lost part of her identity.

The excursion to Carriacou is figured as a connection between Avey's childhood and the Caribbean. Her 'matronly handbag', for example, is refigured as 'a little girl's pocketbook of white patent leather'.[47] The excursion is linked not just to Avey's personal experiences, but also, explicitly, with the out-islanders' ancestors' first arrival in the Caribbean, in the hulls of slave ships.

Bonds between the out-islanders and herself are further established through the process of 'purification' which follows Avey's purging sessions. Lebert's daughter, Rosalie Parvay, takes charge of cleaning Avey once she has arrived on the island and slept through her shame of soiling herself. Again, Avey is figured as a baby[48] yet, it is through her enforced child-like state that she matures in some ways. This is indicated by the clear reference to orgasmic release which accompanies her bathing: 'All the tendons, nerves and muscles which strung her together had been struck a powerful chord, and the reverberation could be heard in the remotest corners of her body'.[49]

Avey's 'psychological reintegration' begins here, and is fully established by the end of the evening, when she first watches and then joins in the ritualistic dancing. Keith Sandiford argues that *Praisesong for the Widow* 'reaffirms authorial faith in the efficacy of cultural survivals, whether as discrete individual beliefs or collective ritual practices'.[50] This is made clear in the way in which Avey responds to the music around her, which connects back to her childhood memories of her Great Aunt Cuney, and even further back to the ancestors whom she did not know. As a result of this response, Avey, reclaiming the name Avatara, vows to return home and change her own and her descendants' perceptions of place.

The Caribbean as the site of this renewal is important in that it is part of the New World, yet also firmly connected to Africa through ritual. The island of Carriacou remains 'more a mirage rather than an actual place. Something conjured up perhaps to satisfy a longing and need'.[51] Images of Bourne Island in Marshall's earlier novel were in some ways quite specific, though the island itself was fictional. Marshall clearly identified some geographical landmarks on Bourne Island, painting a picture of the island through reference to outsiders' points of view, although Hortense Spillers does maintain that the reader sees Bourne Island, and specifically Bournehills, 'as a continuum of geopolitical and cultural movements'.[52] In *Praisesong for the Widow*, however, Marshall sidesteps the issue of geographical precision by siting her text within the realm of the mythic and imaginary rather than of the explicitly real. Sandiford argues that in this novel, Marshall opposes the mythic and the historic, and as a result, 'the central character consciously apprehends the dilemma of a personal choice as a confrontation between the claims of history and the claims of myth'.[53] By contrast, Eva Lennox Birch maintains that '*Praisesong* is a compelling and tightly constructed novel in which form and meaning fuse into a poetic *whole*, marking a *unified* resolution of the thematic concerns explored singly in Marshall's earlier fiction'.[54] These thematic concerns include the place of the individual in relation to the community, and the source of identity markers. Susan Willis argues that in *Praisesong for the Widow*, '. . . Marshall lifts her character out of a purely personal experience and makes her life's story our means of access to the history of black people in the New World'.[55]

It does seem, then, that Marshall's novels trace a movement from a point of view which is the result of hybridity, to multiple, flawed points of view, to a cultural point of view expressed through a single character but connecting with larger issues. Missy Dehn Kubitschek argues that, increasingly, Marshall's characters 'become aware of overarching similarities between themselves and others from separate but contemporaneous cultures. These unities expand in both space (outward from the individual through family and wider community to culture) and time (backward from the individual through historical generations to the mythic past)'.[56]

Marshall's latest novel, *Daughters*, reformulates these concerns yet again. Here Marshall explores the relationship between Caribbean and African American identities through another hybrid character, Ursa Beatrice Mackenzie, but she also provides two geographic locations. The daughter of a Caribbean politician and his American-born wife Estelle, Ursa lives in New York and rarely visits her Caribbean childhood home. In an interview with Melody Graulich and Lisa Sisco, Marshall notes the importance of placing on to the 'literary map' the 'dual community, West Indian and African American' that provided nurture for her,[57] and stresses the need to honour her 'dual tradition' as a writer.[58]

The novel is divided into four 'books'. The first book, 'Little Girl of All the Daughters', is mostly set in New York, just after Ursa undergoes an abortion. Only one chapter is placed outside New York, the second chapter, devoted to Estelle, Ursa's American mother, indicating this character's ambiguous position, located in Triunion, but closely connected to the country of her birth. The chapter focuses on Estelle's inability to maintain her pregnancies; as the chapter opens, Estelle has experienced yet another 'slide', or miscarriage. Indeed, she only successfully bears one child, Ursa Beatrice, named after both of her grandmothers. The second chapter ends with Ursa's birth, contrasting with Ursa's abortion of her own child.

Pregnancy becomes a recurring motif in the novel; several of the female characters are defined in relation to their attitudes towards birth. The Mackenzies' long-time servant Celestine has no children of her own, but raises other children with love; Ursa imagines that Celestine would have wanted her to have the child she aborted and give it to Celestine to raise.[59] Primus Mackenzie's 'keep-miss' Astral Forde is introduced on her way to have an abortion, and, perhaps as the result of this, she remains childless. By contrast, Astral's only female friend, Malvern, has an abundance of children, which contributes to her poverty; Malvern is the only character to fit the stereotype of the over-fertile third-world woman. The other mother-figure of the novel, Ursa's close friend Viney, chooses artificial insemination and single parenthood, establishing her as modern and first-world.

The second book of the novel, 'Constellation', is set entirely on Triunion; through the structure of the novel, Marshall thus seems to set up a binary opposition between the United States and Triunion. Yet the third book, 'Polestar', disrupts this pattern by moving back and forth between the two countries. The final book, 'Tin Cans and Graveyard Bones', is once again placed entirely in Triunion, and includes much physical description of the island. Marshall called the fictionalized island of Triunion '[p]ure invention',[60] yet then qualified the statement by suggesting that 'bits and pieces of a topographical and cultural nature were borrowed from a number of islands to fashion it. They include Haiti and its next-door neighbor, the Dominican Republic, as well as several of the English-speaking islands'.[61] By placing Triunion under three separate colonial powers – and foregrounding the nature of their divisive claims which led to twenty-three wars in two hundred years[62] – Marshall hoped to portray the 'weakness that comes from disunity'.[63]

Marshall assigns the villages of Triunion distinctively ethnic names, including 'Priory Village', 'Roselle', 'Hightown', 'Concepcion', and 'Pointe Bapiste',[64] thus establishing the island's colonial heritage. The characters also think in distinctive idioms; Celestine is identified as belonging to a French part of the island not only through her name, but through the way that her viewpoint is expressed in a mixture of English with French phrases such as *'oui'*, *'mes amis'*, and *'blanche neg'*.

Identification of character with place is signalled through the way that characters associate understanding, or the lack of it, with particular places. For example, despite living for decades in Triunion, Estelle is referred to as '"the wife the PM went and find in America"'.[65] Astral Forde believes that she understands Primus Mackenzie, 'the PM', better than his wife because of their shared geographical beginnings: 'They were both from the same little two-by-four place, after all, and knew how things were done here, were said here: the unspoken that lay not only behind the words spoken but in a look, the wave of a hand, a cut-eye, a suck-teeth'.[66]

Other indicators of identity include clothes, hairstyle and accent. For example, Estelle's accent inscribes American identity, and this factor is utilized, if not exploited, by Primus and his fellow politicians. Estelle resents the implication that her accent is a means of forging ties between Triunion and visiting Americans who represent investment for Triunion, just as her daughter Ursa resents the way that her accent is used to misrepresent her:

> Others you would call Folks with a capital F would catch the island lilt in her voice she couldn't even hear any more and without stopping to listen to the strains of New England, New York and the mean streets of Hartford's North End would immediately color her immigrant, alien, islander without a green card, not realizing they were lopping off more than half her life. People who were supposed to be Folks thinking pushy, arrogant, different, difficult; thinking small island go back where you come from, thinking monkey chaser, some of them, when they detected the faint lilt.[67]

It is significant that Ursa represents herself as tripartite in American terms, for this reinforces the tripartite identity of Triunion. Moreover, it stresses the way in which the American black communities are just as divisive as those in the Caribbean. Marshall feels that, like their southern neighbours, these communities 'fall prey to the seduction and domination of their former colonial masters because of disunity'.[68] Indeed, the text repeatedly stresses the similarities between the African American communities in the United States and the communities that make up Triunion; these similarities are addressed by the two characters who straddle national boundaries. Both Ursa Mackenzie and her mother Estelle are American born, but whereas Estelle chooses to live in Triunion, and by the end of the novel has given up visiting the country of her birth, Ursa is committed to living in New York and finds it difficult to visit Triunion.

Estelle's connections between Triunion and the United States are made explicit halfway through the text in a letter home: 'But I've really come to see things here and in the States in pretty much the same light. There's the same work to be done. I drive past Armory Hill, the big slum we have here, and I could be driving through all the Harlems in the States'.[69]

This realization comes to her daughter Ursa much later, and almost in reverse. Ursa's connections to Triunion follow a line from identification to disillusionment and distancing, and finally to reconciliation. Initially, Triunion is a source of pleasant childhood memories for Ursa, and she uses the island as an escape from life in New York; when she is forced to confront the negative aspects of Triunion through the eyes of her friend Viney she flees the country. Interestingly, this withdrawal from Triunion impedes her ability to appreciate the good aspects of the country, something Viney is still able to do.

After encountering poverty and drug abuse victims in a Triunion city, the characters retreat to the beach where Viney 'tried with her long arms to embrace it all: the wide white-sand beach that went on for over a mile on either side of where she stood, the deep grove of palm, grape and almond trees that bordered it, and the sea that mirrored the flawless sky overhead. Water so clear you could see the micalike gold dust sprinkled in the sand at the bottom as you swam out to the reefs'.[70] In embracing it 'all', Viney seems to acknowledge that the island can contain and be accepted despite containing negative as well as positive aspects. This description of the beach in many ways mirrors a travel brochure depiction of the Caribbean, but Marshall undercuts this easy 'paradise' association by providing in the next paragraph an emblem of the island's historical past. Viney faces, though she cannot see, the 'Monument of Heroes', an area dedicated to Will Cudjoe and Congo Jane, co-conspirators who led a slave revolt. Congo Jane, based loosely on the historical Nanny of Nanny Town, who in the eighteenth century founded the Maroon colony in Jamaica,[71] provides a historical focus for Marshall's discussions of identity and community.

Will Cudjoe and Congo Jane commemorated in statues which

are significantly placed out of easy reach or sight, are the subject
of Ursa's unwritten master's thesis on the good relationships
between black men and women under slavery, a topic denied
her by her white male professor. By reformulating her rejected
senior dissertation into a master's topic, Ursa acknowledges the
importance of these figures to her. Marshall has indicated that,
for her, history is

> an antidote to the lies, and I'm interested in discovering and
> in unearthing what was positive and inspiring about our experi-
> ence in the hemisphere – our will to survive and to overcome.
> We have the unique opportunity to create, to reinvent ourselves.
> Since so much that's been said about us – all those negative
> and unflattering portrayals – was designed to serve the fantasies
> and motives of the larger society and had little to do with us,
> we can declare it all null and void, all that stuff, and fashion a
> self for ourselves that's more truthful and more complex. And
> I think that knowing and understanding history is an essential
> part of that endeavor. And that's why there's always the
> emphasis or the concern with the past in my work.[72]

Viney can embrace both the travel-brochure beaches and the historical past of Triunion, while in some ways escaping the negative aspects of the island. Ursa, however, finds that rejection is
her only method of coping not only with Triunion's problems
but with her sense that her father may be partly to blame for
them. It is only when Ursa can recognize what Estelle has long
known, that the problems of Triunion and the problems of the
United States in some ways mirror each other, that she can return
to Triunion and hope to effect positive change.

The turning point for Ursa comes as she visits Midland City,
the site of a previous freelance study, and sees the person she
initially saw as radical politician being co-opted by the system
which strips away his radical potential and turns him into yet
another spokesman for a 'progress' which is determined by outside needs. This confrontation with the past occurs just before
Ursa receives news of her father's own involvement in a dubi-
ous 'development' project, and it is the combination of these two
events which forces Ursa's return to Triunion.

Triunion acts then as a site of conflict, but also as a site of
reconciliation, and through this novel Marshall makes her clear-

est attempt to reconcile the perhaps divisive aspects of her own cultural identity. Calling *Daughters* a '"meditation on language"', Marshall insists that in this novel she was able to '"honor all the voices and the different variations on the English language [she] heard growing up in Brooklyn"'.[73] Furthermore, she insists that *Daughters* '"is about people, politics, culture, history, race, racism, morality, marriage, children, friendship, love, sex, the triumph and sometimes defeat of the human spirit, as well as a few other things I threw in for good measure"'.[74] Marshall's words are obviously tinged with humour, and they represent fairly clearly the realization that *Daughters* cannot be neatly summed up with a few well-chosen words. But if *Daughters* resists an easy label, it does offer compelling representations of geocultural identity as multiple and diffuse. In this way, Marshall has moved from her early depictions of the community-individual conflict as expressed through the divisive elements of the Boyce family in *Brown Girl, Brownstones* to a much more complex representation. Selina Boyce and Ursa Beatrice Mackenzie are both American born, but their identity conflicts, while connected, are also in some ways unique. If *Brown Girl, Brownstones* is in some ways a *bildungsroman*, *Daughters*, which through its title foregrounds Ursa's relationships with her parents, moves beyond the depiction of one character's identity to the exploration of cultural identity and cultural conflicts.

Marshall's recurring use of the Caribbean as a setting, and her multiple ways of figuring geography (as dream, as site of conflict, as site of projected fantasies, as site of mythic connections, as contested political space) suggest a political motivation. Marshall inserts the Caribbean into African-American literature in order to challenge any monolithic view of black culture. Graulich and Sisco connect the fact that Marshall is the daughter of Caribbean immigrants with her literary aims of creating 'characters and plots that wander back and forth – literally or imaginatively – between the States and the islands, attending to the distant echoes of Africa'.[75] In this formulation, Marshall's characters 'possess a dual citizenship' and this double identity 'feeds their imagination and inflects their speech'.[76] Given Marshall's preoccupations with double identity and otherness, it is interesting to reflect on the ways that the author herself has been characterized in terms which either foreground her immigrant heritage or firmly place her in an American context.

The 1962 London edition of Marshall's collection of short

novellas, *Soul Clap Hands and Sing*, introduces Marshall as a 'first generation American' who was 'born of Barbadian parents.'[77] By contrast, the 1983 Feminist Press paperback edition of *Reena* [sic] *and Other Stories* omits any mention of her Caribbean heritage. The 1984 Vintage edition of *The Chosen Place, the Timeless People* mentions her Brooklyn birth and also notes that Marshall 'has spent considerable time living in various of the Caribbean islands',[78] whereas the 1992 Serpent's Tail paperback edition of *Daughters* mentions no Caribbean connection, reporting only that Marshall was '[b]orn and raised in Brooklyn, New York'.[79] The 1994 edition of the novel which established Marshall's reputation, *Brown Girl, Brownstones*, does make the Caribbean connection, noting that Marshall's parents 'emigrated from Barbados during the First World War'.[80] However, Marshall herself is claimed as 'one of *America*'s finest contemporary Black writers';[81] the overriding identifier becomes Marshall's blackness, despite the overt emphasis she places on the tensions between the Caribbean and the United States in her fiction.

If one of Marshall's aims is to encompass both the American and the Caribbean aspects of her identity, why do most of the notes rely on only one aspect of her identity or clearly prioritize one if both are mentioned? Given the overt emphasis placed on reconciliation in *Daughters*, it is surprising to find the Caribbean erased from Marshall's biography. Does reconciliation permit or even assume such erasure? It is an erasure which serves as a stark reminder of the struggles that Marshall faces in asserting a Caribbean African American identity. The three aspects of this identity can be juxtaposed and compared, but perhaps not fully integrated, and, as a result, Marshall's characters remain hybrids whose ambiguous positions cannot be fully defined or contained. Multiple and contradictory, they inhabit geographical spaces variously imagined and variously described.

Notes

1. P. Marshall, *Brown Girl, Brownstones* (London: Virago, 1994) p. 83.
2. Ibid., p. 11.
3. Ibid., p. 70.
4. Ibid., p. 45.
5. Ibid., p. 46.

6. Ibid., p. 33.
7. Ibid., p. 66.
8. Ibid., p. 150.
9. Ibid.
10. Ibid., p. 279.
11. Ibid., p. 307.
12. S. Willis, *Specifying: Black Women Writing the American Experience* (London: Routledge, 1990) p. 53.
13. D. Cumber Dance, 'An Interview With Paule Marshall', *Southern Review*, 28:1 (1992) 7.
14. Ibid., p. 14.
15. B. Christian, *Black Women Novelists: the Development of a Tradition, 1892–1976* (Westport, Conn.: Greenwood, 1980) p. 135.
16. Ibid.
17. P. Marshall, *The Chosen Place, the Timeless People* (New York: Random House, 1984) p. 4.
18. Ibid., p. 5.
19. Ibid., p. 410.
20. Ibid., p. 13.
21. B. Christian, *Black Women Novelists: The Development of a Tradition, 1892–1976* (Westport, Conn.: Greenwood, 1980) p. 112.
22. Ibid., p. 112.
23. P. Marshall, *The Chosen Place, the Timeless People*, p. 13.
24. Ibid., p. 14.
25. Ibid.
26. Ibid., p. 21.
27. Ibid.
28. Ibid., p. 99.
29. Ibid., p. 100.
30. Ibid., p. 216.
31. Ibid., p. 101.
32. Ibid., p. 102.
33. C. Boyce Davies, 'Black Woman's Journey into Self: A Womanist Reading of Paule Marshall's *Praisesong for the Widow*', *Matatu: Journal for African Culture and Society*, 1:1 (1987) 21.
34. V. Pollard, 'Cultural Connections in Paule Marshall's *Praise Song* [sic] *for the Widow*, *World Literature in English*, 25:2 (1985) 296.
35. Ibid.
36. P. Marshall, *Praisesong for the Widow* (London: Virago, 1983) p. 175.
37. Ibid., p. 149.
38. Ibid., p. 151.
39. Ibid., p. 152.
40. A. Scarboro, 'The Healing Process: a Paradigm for Self-Renewal in Paule Marshall's *Praisesong for the Widow* and Camara Laye's *Le Regard du roi*', *Modern Language Studies*, 19:1 (1989) 28.
41. E. Collier, 'The Closing of the Circle: Movement from Division to Wholeness in Paule Marshall's Fiction' in M. Evans (ed.), *Black Women Writers (1950–1980): A Critical Evaluation* (Garden City, NY: Anchor, 1984) p. 312.

42. Ibid.
43. B. Christian, 'Ritualistic Process and the Structure of Paule Marshall's *Praisesong for the Widow*' in M. Evans (ed.), *Black Women Writers (1950–1980): A Critical Evaluation* (Garden City, NY: Anchor, 1984) pp. 75–6.
44. P. Marshall, *Praisesong for the Widow*, p. 13.
45. Ibid., p. 54.
46. Ibid., pp. 48–9.
47. Ibid., p. 197.
48. Ibid., p. 217.
49. Ibid., p. 224.
50. K. Sandiford, 'Paule Marshall's *Praisesong for the Widow*: the Reluctant Heiress, or Whose Life is it Anyway?', *Black American Literature Forum*, 20:4 (1986) 371.
51. P. Marshall, *Praisesong for the Widow*, p. 254.
52. H. Spillers, '*Chosen Place, Timeless People*: Some Figurations on the New World' in M. Pryse and H. Spillers (eds), *Conjuring: Black Women, Fiction, and Literary Tradition* (Bloomington: Indiana University Press, 1985) p. 155.
53. K. Sandiford, 'Paule Marshall's *Praisesong for the Widow*: the Reluctant Heiress, or Whose Life is it Anyway?', *Black American Literature Forum*, 20:4 (1986) 372.
54. E. Lennox Birch, *Black American Women's Writing: A Quilt of Many Colour* (Hemel Hempstead: Harvester Wheatsheaf, 1994) p. 111, emphasis mine.
55. S. Willis, *Specifying: Black Women Writing the American Experience* (London: Routledge, 1990) p. 59.
56. M. Dehn Kubitschek, 'Paule Marshall's Women on Quest', *Black American Literature Forum*, 21: 1–2 (1987) 44–5.
57. M. Graulich and L. Sisco, 'Meditations on Language and the Self: a Conversation with Paule Marshall', *NWSA Journal*, 4:3 (1992) 286.
58. Ibid., p. 298.
59. P. Marshall, *Daughters* (London: Serpent's Tail, 1992) p. 18.
60. D. Cumber Dance, 'An Interview With Paule Marshall', *Southern Review*, 28:1 (1992) 4.
61. Ibid.
62. P. Marshall, *Daughters*, p. 27.
63. D. Cumber Dance, 'An Interview with Paule Marshall', *Southern Review*, 28:1 (1992) 5.
64. P. Marshall, *Daughters*, pp. 23–4.
65. Ibid., p. 128.
66. Ibid., p. 188.
67. Ibid., p. 86.
68. D. Cumber Dance, 'An Interview with Paule Marshall', *Southern Review*, 28:1 (1992) 5.
69. P. Marshall, *Daughters*, p. 224.
70. Ibid., p. 109.
71. D. Cumber Dance, 'An Interview with Paule Marshall', *Southern Review*, 28:1 (1992) 6.

72. Ibid. pp. 5–6.
73. M. Graulich and L. Sisco, 'Meditations on Language and the Self: a Conversation with Paule Marshall', *NWSA Journal*, 4:3 (1992) 286.
74. D. Cumber Dance, 'An Interview with Paule Marshall', *Southern Review*, 28:1 (1992) 2.
75. M. Graulich and L. Sisco, 'Meditations on Language and the Self: A Conversation with Paule Marshall', *NWSA Journal*, 4:3 (1992) 282.
76. Ibid.
77. P. Marshall, *Soul Clap Hands and Sing* (London: W. H. Allen, 1962), not paginated explicitly, but can be determined as page 179.
78. P. Marshall, *The Chosen Place, the Timeless People* (London: Vintage, 1984), not paginated.
79. P. Marshall, *Daughters* (London: Serpent's Tail, 1992), not paginated.
80. P. Marshall, *Brown Girl, Brownstones* (London: Virago, 1994), not paginated.
81. Ibid., not paginated, emphasis mine.

Bibliography

Boyce Davies, C. 'Black Woman's Journey into Self: a Womanist Reading of Paule Marshall's *Praisesong for the Widow*', *Matatu: Journal for African Culture and Society*, 1:1 (1987) 19–34.
Christian, B. *Black Women Novelists: the Development of a Tradition, 1892–1976*. Westport, Conn.: Greenwood, 1980.
——. 'Ritualistic Process and the Structure of Paule Marshall's *Praisesong for the Widow*' in M. Evans (ed.). *Black Women Writers (1950–1980): A Critical Evaluation*. Garden City, NY: Anchor, 1984, 74–83.
Collier, E. 'The Closing of the Circle: Movement from Division to Wholeness in Paule Marshall's Fiction' in M. Evans (ed.). *Black Women Writers (1950–1980): a Critical Evaluation*. Garden City, NY: Anchor, 1984, pp. 295–315.
Cumber Dance, D. 'An Interview with Paule Marshall', *Southern Review*, 28:1 (1992) 1–20.
Dehn Kubitschek. M. 'Paule Marshall's Women on Quest', *Black American Literature Forum*, 21: 1–2 (1987) 43–60.
Graulich, M. and L. Sisco. 'Meditations on Language and the Self: a Conversation with Paule Marshall', *NWSA Journal* 4:3 (1992) 282–302.
Lennox Birch, E. *Black American Women's Writing: a Quilt of Many Colours*. Hemel Hempstead: Harvester Wheatsheaf, 1994.
Marshall, P. *Brown Girl, Brownstones*. London: Virago, 1994.
——. *The Chosen Place, the Timeless People*. New York: Random House, 1984.
——. *Daughters*. London, Serpent's Tail, 1992.
——. *Praisesong for the Widow*. London: Virago, 1983.
——. *Reena and Other Stories*. New York: Feminist Press, 1983.
——. *Soul Clap Hands and Sing*. London: W.H. Allen, 1962.
Pollard, V. 'Cultural Connections in Paule Marshall's *Praise Song* [sic] *for the Widow*', *World Literature in English*, 25:2 (1985) 285–98.

Sandiford, K. 'Paule Marshall's *Praisesong for the Widow*: the Reluctant Heiress, or Whose Life is it Anyway?', *Black American Literature Forum*, 20:4 (1986) 371–92.

Scarboro, A. 'The Healing Process: a Paradigm for Self-Renewal in Paule Marshall's *Praisesong for the Widow* and Camara Laye's *Le Regard du roi*', *Modern Language Studies*, 19:1 (1989) 28–36.

Spillers, H. '*Chosen Place, Timeless People*: Some Figurations on the New World' in M. Pryse and H. Spillers (eds). *Conjuring: Black Women, Fiction, and Literary Tradition*. Bloomington: Indiana University Press, 1985, pp. 151–75.

Willis, S. *Specifying: Black Women Writing the American Experience*. London: Routledge, 1990.

7

The Body of the Woman in the Body of the Text: the Novels of Erna Brodber

Denise deCaires Narain

Erna Brodber has written three novels to date;[1] the first of these, *Jane and Louisa Will Soon Come Home*, was published in 1980, *Myal* in 1988 and *Louisiana* in 1994. Her prolific output is very much a part of the 'boom' in Caribbean women's writing from the 1980s onwards and places her centrally in relation to what is now becoming a well-established Caribbean woman's literary tradition. Brodber's novels are notoriously 'difficult' to read and this 'difficulty factor' is perhaps exaggerated because of the predominant trend in Caribbean fiction for some form of realism to be the chosen mode of representation. While Caribbean women writers, as a group, have been described as taking more risks with style than their male counterparts, Brodber is certainly the most obviously experimental of these women writers. In this respect, her work has been compared to that of Wilson Harris, often inducing the same kind of (often bemused) respect. I begin with this acknowledgement of 'the difficulty factor' in Brodber's texts because, in the context of other Caribbean women's fiction, it is the most immediately striking feature of each of her three novels, but also because the arrangement of 'the body of the text' has implications for the focus on 'the body of woman' in the texts which I want to discuss here. It is also pertinent to mention the difficulty of reading Brodber at the outset because her writing makes demands on the reader that require a particularly flexible critical response. It strikes me as contradictory that many readings of Brodber hinge upon an invocation of precisely those binarisms which her novels have so painstakingly deconstructed, confirming my sense of critical practice, in post-colonial contexts, often appearing to lag behind creative literary practice. I acknowledge, then, that my own chronological reading of Brodber's texts may imply an inappropriately teleological approach; nevertheless, what follows offers a focus on the woman's body and female sexuality as it is handled in Brodber's three novels, and attempts to place this focus within several of the intersecting critical spaces in which the gendered body has been interrogated, and to explore the implications of this focus on sexuality for a discussion of textuality.

The body has become increasingly important as the site of a series of contested inscriptions and readings. In the context of feminist criticisms woman's body has been perceived as one of the most dramatic – and contradictory – sites of the struggle against patriarchy:

> Misogynist thought has commonly found a convenient self-justification for women's secondary social positions by containing them within bodies that are represented, even constructed, as frail, imperfect, unruly, and unreliable, subject to various intrusions which are not under conscious control. Female sexuality and women's powers of reproduction are the defining (cultural) characteristics of women, and, at the same time, these very functions render women vulnerable, in need of protection or special treatment, as variously prescribed by patriarchy.[2]

Feminists have strongly resisted this notion of 'biology as destiny', pointing up the ways in which the social and cultural meanings inscribed on woman's body have constructed her as weak and inferior, conflating 'her' with nature and nurture while 'he' represents culture. Western feminists have, as a result, been anxious to retrieve the woman's body from such limited roles and part of this process, most clearly articulated by various French feminists, has been an insistence on re-metaphorizing the female body as a powerful site of multiple possibilities, stressing the centrality of the mother's body while de-emphasizing the (almighty) phallus and insisting that woman's diffuse and unbounded sexuality be read as an exciting source of polyvocality. Black feminists have intervened strongly in this debate to argue that Western feminist accounts of the body have not recognized the ways in which, for the black woman, the body is a raced and gendered terrain; Barbara Smith argues:

> Black women have traditionally been reluctant to talk about sex with their daughters. "Keep your dress down and your drawers up," is a homily of this reticence. At the very same time, all Black women have been viewed as sexual animals by the society as a whole and at times by Black men as well. [. . .] Sexual repression, coupled with blatant sexual exploitation, has contributed to a complex psychological mix.[3]

The taboos, then, on representing the body may, for black women, become even more intensely felt, and inhibit the degree to which a celebratory 'writing of the body' may be possible. I would argue that there is still very little in Caribbean women's fiction, although slightly more in Caribbean women's poetry, which focuses explicitly on woman as a sexual being; instead, Caribbean woman tends to be defined as the capable, strong mother. Dionne Brand argues that there is still a silence about representing the black woman as a sexual agent and that Caribbean women writers tend to hide behind a focus on mother-daughter relationships; Brand describes 'big mothers' as 'overwhelming our texts' so that the discussion focuses on 'sex without the sexuality'.[4]

Post-colonial feminists have also stressed the centrality of the woman's body as symbolic fodder in inspiring the colonizing 'mission', and, later, in providing nationalist patriarchs with an eroticized and feminized landscape to 'rescue' from the colonizers. This conflation of woman with the land has interesting implications when the issue of language is added to the discussion, when women are perceived as safeguarding the 'mother tongue', and mothertongue and motherland become conflated so that women and women's language occupy a pure, original – 'untouchable' – symbolic space. It is at this juncture that 'the post-colonial' and 'the feminist' intersect. Both approaches stress the need to both describe and de-scribe imperial and patriarchal discourses by challenging the 'truths' of colonial accounts of the native other at the level of thematics, but also by mobilizing a range of textual strategies which dramatize the importance of challenging colonial literary aesthetics. W.D. Ashcroft, in an essay titled 'Intersecting Marginalities: Post-colonialism and Feminism', argues that:

the most profound similarity is probably the extent to which both 'woman' and 'post-colonial' exist outside representation itself.

Both post-colonialism and feminism, in response to this 'out-siderness', stress the need to retrieve the lost mother – the former in the repeated recuperations of 'Mother Africa' and the latter in the desire to re-member and reconnect with the maternal body. In both cases, the ways in which this 'mother' is seen to be textually recuperable is via an emphasis on 'orality':

> Isn't the final goal of writing to articulate the body? [. . .] We need languages that regenerate us, warm us, give birth to us, that lead us to act and not to flee. [. . .] In order to reconnect the book with the body and with pleasure, we must disin-tellectualize writing. [. . .] For me the most important thing is to work on orality.[5]

This quotation is from Chatal Chawaf in *New French Feminisms*, but its tenor is evocative of many passages in Edward Kamau Brathwaite's *A History of the Voice*.[6]

What I want to explore now is the way in which Brodber's difficult and polyphonic textual strategies invite connections to be made with 'écriture feminine' and with the kinds of practices seen as necessary to de-scribe colonial discourse while, at the same time, her texts are redolent with ambivalences and contra-dictions which undermine any categorization of her. In 'Fiction in the Scientific Procedure',[7] Brodber gives an interesting account of the process by which she came to be a writer. She describes being bored with the fiction of 'objectivity' required of her in her social science research and, to counter this boredom, begin-ning to keep a written record of her feelings and speculations prior to interviewing her informants, 'This activity was to me like vomiting and defecating, and I flushed away the effort.' Later in the same piece the physicality of writing is stressed again when she talks of the racism endemic in Jamaica upon her return there:

> The enemy was a ghost that talked through black faces. It was maddening, and to keep my sanity I talked on paper, review-ing from time to time what I had written before. I was now keeping my nonacademic writing for therapeutic purposes.[8]

This image of her writing as 'vomiting and defecating' and as a kind of 'talking on paper' is a very suggestive one in the context of 'writing the body', foregrounding the materiality of writing as well as emphasizing the centrality of the voice in this approach to writing – the text is conceived as a conduit for the speaking voice, an emphasis which reaches its most pronounced articulation in *Louisiana*. Brodber's description of the particular origins of her first novel are also suggestive; she says that she wrote *Jane and Louisa Will Soon Come Home* as a 'case study' to provide her undergraduate psychology students with data relevant to their Caribbean context. This description suggests a hybridizing impulse 'behind' the genesis of the text, even if, as Brodber acknowledges, it has been read exclusively as a novel rather than as a case study. This desire to challenge conventional generic boundaries is clearly a recognizably feminist or post-colonial strategy. The deconstructive thrust of Brodber's approach is consolidated almost immediately in *Jane and Louisa Will Soon Come Home* when the reader confronts the suspended titles of chapters listed on the contents page; fragments of a Jamaican children's ring game – from which the novel derives its title – are used as headings for sections of the text, stressing a sense of the novel as continuous, circular process rather than as static product, and insisting on a strong connection to the oral as central to the novel's form. The first section, 'Voices', indicates Brodber's preferred mode of communicating with the reader: rather than inviting the reader to make sense of the text via the conventional literary device of character, Brodber presents us with a cacophony of voices. These voices are presented in fragments, speakers are often not identified by name, speech marks are not used and, generally, Brodber forces the reader to construct a sense of a gallery of recognizable subject positions, rather than individuated, 'familiar' characters. The effect of this practice of privileging the voice and refusing realist conventions of character is to imbue the text with a sense of disembodiedness. So that it is the voices of the community which we hear:

> . . . the voice belongs to the family group dead and alive. We walk by their leave, for planted in the soil, we must walk over them to get where we are going.[9]

The incorporation of Anancy stories which are not framed by any authorial commentary positions the reader as listener, stressing, again, links with oral and popular culture forms.

In other instances, it is the body language of members of the community which is used as a way of inscribing the printed text with the palpable movement of the body. One of the most obvious examples of this would be the lovingly – and minutely – described dance of Mass Stanley and Miss Rose, where the reader is given, literally, a step-by-step account of this 'event':

> Watch them leaning stiff like starch. O Mass Stanley! Look how him fling him foot from the knee and stick it off like him slim. O Mass Stanley. Again. Quiet there. Again. Watch Mass Stanley foot! Second figure now.
> Rock the lady. Rock the lady on your toes. Walk like you going somewhere and yet is only behind her and around to come right back to your space. With one hand behind your back, kick the knee and stick out the heel. O Mass Stanley, toe it.[10]

The body of the text, like the intricate formation of the dance described above, progresses via a series of tightly orchestrated manoeuvres. It is not a seamless flow of continuous, chronological narrative; rather, it moves in fits and starts, is polyphonic, and makes use of a range of layouts and typography which suggest that 'meanings' can only be gleaned if the reader reads, listens and sees using a similarly multi-faceted approach – a kaleidoscopic or prismatic model of interpretation. This kind of textual practice is precisely the kind advocated by proponents of 'écriture feminine' and practised by post-colonial writers such as Kamau Brathwaite.

What interests me is the way in which, in tandem with this writing the body, there is also a relentless writing about the body – the results of each mode suggesting a tension between them. *Jane and Louisa Will Soon Come Home* charts the breakdown and tentative steps towards recovery of the 'main protagonist', Nellie, who is damaged by a patriarchal colonial value system which negates black Jamaican culture, and by a patriarchal 'black brotherhood' which effectively silences her. At the meetings of this latter group, the ritualistic incantation of ideological positions makes any meaningful communication impossible, and Nellie's involvement in taking the minutes is depicted as sterile. The doll which Baba carves for her out of pear seeds as he sits in on the meetings – and which disintegrates as he places it in her lap – becomes the evocative symbol of her own disintegration:

My minutes as I knew and needed no one to tell me, had run me into a cracked up doll.[11]

It is Baba who then shows her the way towards reintegration by guiding her out of the sterility of political dogmas which silence her, and which consumed Nellie's ex-lover Robin, and reconnecting her with the voices of her community – he 'rebirths' her into her own language, 'I was no longer alone. Baba had settled me in with my people.'[12] Earlier in the text, Nellie had recognized her need for such a 'midwife':

> I was willing to learn their ways but someone had to show me, to born me. . . . Someone had to help me test my feet outside the kumbla.[13]

Brodber's use of Baba as a kind of redeemer figure is interesting in several ways: first, as indicated above, because she presents him as 'borning' Nellie, and because she describes him as a physical presence in the text in ways in which no other 'character' is described:

> Baba was waiting for me. Straight and tall in a long white gown. He was the bride. His hair neatly plaited (as usual) and his beard obviously brushed. [. . .] The man exuded the clean astringent atmosphere of lime. It was as if he had been cured, scrubbed, cleansed in lime. What a beauty![14]

This description also stages a neat reversal of woman as the object of the male gaze. In fact, Baba's ability to 'rescue' Nellie hinges upon his difference from conventional notions of the virile, conquering hero, so that when she offers herself to him sexually, he responds:

> – Sweetheart – he tenderly, so tenderly said, – I know you want to give yourself but I fear that you offer yourself because you don't want you. That's no gift love, even if we did need gifts. That's something you throw on a scrap-heap. We won't forage for a thing in a scrap-heap. We need a walking-talking human being –[15]

It is at this point in the text that Nellie, frustrated with Baba's all-knowingness, finds her voice:

You understand this damned shameless rasta-man who is to tell me that he wants to watch me grow. You understand this r . . .-c . . .t of a hungry man from nowhere who is to watch and observe me. What the hell he think he is. Man don't let me . . . I had been talking aloud. Is that me? with such expressions. Am I a fishwife?[16]

So it is through a reconnection with community via a reconnection with language that Baba borns Nellie. Here, too, Brodber offers a 'double-take' on the increasingly orthodox view, in contemporary Caribbean cultural debates, of woman as the 'true' repository of the 'true' mother tongue: Creole, 'the mudder-language'. Simultaneously, Brodber also offers a double-take on 'the' West Indian male, though in the process of recuperating him as a revamped 'Prince Charming',[17] Brodber prunes away any signifiers of sexual potency, which suggests that this de-sexing (or textual neutering) may be a necessary narrative economy.

The stress on Baba's spirituality, and the concomitant denial of any predatory sexuality, points up one of the ways in which Brodber's narrative project holds back – or doesn't go all the way – in its attempts to articulate the body into the text. If one bears in mind Carolyn Cooper's argument that oral discourse in the context of the Jamaican oral and scribal continuum works to disrupt the 'uptightness' of scribal forms such as the novel with its sexy slackness, then Brodber's use of 'the oral' clearly works against the grain of Cooper's thesis.[18]

In *Jane and Louisa Will Soon Come Home*, Brodber's representation of female sexuality is relentlessly negative; far from any associations of fecundity or plenitude, female sexuality is seen to trap women in endless cycles of unwanted pregnancies. The very first section of the novel refers to the way in which Nellie's mother's life is ruined because of her 'fall' into early and frequent motherhood: 'Yes now. The chile life spoil. Lord take the case!'.[19] Relationships with mothers and maternal substitutes throughout the text are circumscribed by this narrative of biology as destiny, with repeated warnings against pregnancy echoing through the text. The prohibitions on contact with boys begin the minute Nellie hits puberty:

But Papa looks at me from head to toe, focuses on my middle and says with strange solemnity: – My. But you have shot up –

And my balloon stinks with shame. Something breaks and there is no warmth no more. So I am different. Something is wrong with me.[20]

This association of the womb with shame and disease reaches its most intense expression in the penultimate section of the novel, 'The Pill', in which a series of powerfully angry images of the black womb are piled one on top of the other:

> Black sperms disintegrating black wombs, making hollow women and name-less pointless children. [. . .] So the black womb is a maw. [. . .] The black womb sucks grief and anger and shame but it does not spit. It absorbs them into its body. Take an antidote. Silence it. Best pretend it doesn't exist. Give it a cap of darkness, take a pill. [. . .] What a life! What an abominable scrap heap thing is this thing womb.[21]

In this description the 'black womb' is configured pessimistically as a 'scrap heap thing' precisely because of the multiplicity of signifieds associated with it in the Jamaican cultural context – it becomes the dumping ground for all of society's frustrations. *Jane and Louisa Will Soon Come Home* does end with an image of pregnancy – Nellie dreams she is pregnant with a fish – but this image of fecundity is rendered ambivalent by the fact that the fish is stuck and she's unable to deliver it. Earlier in the novel, when Nellie starts her period, far from being the cause of celebration – as implied in notions of 'writing the body' – female fertility is described as the 'hidey-hidey thing' which gives her a strange power (like the image above of the womb as a devouring 'maw') but it is a power that does not develop into any kind of agency, rather it separates her from everybody else:

> . . . I was getting much stranger than they and much more rotten. [. . .] 'It' cut them off from everybody. 'It' spoilt your life if you weren't careful! [. . .] A chute without dimension, a hollow without name or face, a hollow that pulled innocent girls in, an instrument as hollow and one-sided as a drum, and like a drum, its message reverberated loud and very clear but it carried no physical form nor even image of one. That is you. That's what 'it' makes you.[22]

The act of 'reproductive sex' itself is also conveyed in images of repulsion and shame and Nellie's first sexual experience functions only as a way of affirming her womanhood in a socially legitimizing way. Her encounter with the penis – the snail-like 'mekke mekke thing' – is haunted by the mother's approbation and her imagined comments are woven into the description:

> A big woman running from a snail and you run. But you can't run! How can you? You want to be a woman; now you have a man, you'll be like everyone else. You're normal now! Vomit and bear it.
> Wearing my label called woman.
> Upon my lapel called normal.[23]

Female sexuality, then, is presented consistently as the source of trauma and shame. This 'take' on the female body is consolidated in the relationship which Nellie has with her Aunt Alice who is presented as the antithesis to Aunt Becca's hypocritical adoption of 'ladyhood':

> Aunt Alice shames her [Becca]. Aunt Alice has no husband. Aunt Alice works nowhere. She never seems to make a living. She plants nothing. She reaps nothing but only helps us now and again, helps out Aunt Becca now and again and smiles. Aunt Alice in Wonderland. Aunt Alice is so nice.[24]

It is Aunt Alice who takes Nellie 'travelling', encouraging her to transcend the limitations of the physical body and see; the 'spying glass' which Alice offers Nellie becomes a trope for the kind of prismatic or kaleidoscopic vision which is necessary as a strategy for short circuiting the narrowly ideological discourses (colonial, black nationalist, misogynist) which have combined to traumatize and alienate Nellie. Travels with Alice also allow Nellie – and the reader – to assemble the details of the family's histories in ways which help explain some of the secrets and tensions which have damaged Nellie. What distinguishes Aunt Alice from all the other mothers and mother substitutes in the text is her spinsterhood, and it is this which seems to free her to be the more playful, visionary role model who, along with Baba, can point Nellie towards healing. Her exit from the text marks both this playful role as manipulator of media and links her centrally to the ring game motif around which the text is organized:

With that, Aunt Alice who never married but spent her time visiting and helping out here and there, stuffed her projector in its case and left with one teasing glance in her age-old flirtation:

– The moving camera next time. Beware. But in any case . . . Jane and Louisa will soon come home. –[25]

The half has never been told. . . .

Jane and Louisa Will Soon Come Home begins with the warning that pregnancy will 'spoil the chile life' and ends with the dramatically ambivalent image of 'permanent' pregnancy, leaving the issue of Nellie's sexual healing suspended. *Myal* also makes woman's body the theatrical site on which a range of competing discourses and ideologies battle for supremacy. In *Jane and Louisa Will Soon Come Home* Brodber's focus on Nellie's breakdown – even as it includes references to colonial education – tends to keep the reader within the parameters of an individual, psychic landscape; in *Myal*, Brodber's focus includes a broader sociocultural landscape as she exposes the alienating effects of colonial education, and various forms of Christianity, on the community via 'spirit thievery' or 'zombification'. The 'body' of the text, in this novel, while less fragmented and 'difficult' than the first novel, makes use of similar narrative strategies to convey a sense of the embeddedness of the individual in the community and to stress the ways in which community and individual are constitutive of each other. So the text incorporates a wide range of discourses (which clearly represent a range of ways of knowing), blurring distinctions between them and refusing to privilege any one voice; as Evelyn O'Callaghan puts it:

> Readers are treated to anecdotes, songs and spells, statistics, dreams and lyrical fantasies, cosy practical wisdom, schoolbook stories and parables, and the local frame of reference undoubtedly loses some non-Jamaicans.[26]

This textual playfulness – or anarchy? – is, again, evocative of the agendas suggested by proponents of 'writing the body'. But, as with *Jane and Louisa Will Soon Come Home*, while woman's body is central to the economy of the text, it is represented as a 'dumping ground' for an infinite range of negative signifieds, rather than as the site of plenitude or jouissance.

Just as *Jane and Louisa Will Soon Come Home* attempts to inscribe orality into the text in its frequent intertextual links with oral forms, so *Myal* also aims to 'oralize' the novel form. Brodber focuses on the way in which colonialism, especially in the form of Christianity, attempts to take away the spirit of a people, reducing them to zombies, and it is the printed word, in *Myal*, which becomes the most potent symbol of colonial domination. This is presented early on in the text when Ella – the main protagonist – is seen and heard reciting Kipling's 'The White Man's Burden', an enunciative 'event' which accumulates tragic significance as the text progresses and the ironies of Ella's recitation become increasingly evident. The spectacle of the colonized subject ventriloquizing the colonizer's 'truths' about her own 'otherness' in that common practice of colonial education, 'reciting by heart', is exploited by Brodber as a way of visually and aurally pointing up Ella's zombification.[27] By the end of the text, Ella is able, in her role as a school teacher, to recognize the damaging effects of such representations, and to destabilize its effects by choosing to read against the grain of colonial texts and to appropriate meanings for herself. The text concludes with the farmyard storybook characters' powerful assertion of this refusal of their allotted narrative identities:

> My people have been separated from themselves White Hen, by several means, one of them being the printed word and the ideas it carries. Now we have two people who are about to see through that. [. . .] People who are familiar with the print and the language of the print. [. . .] . . . we have people who can and are willing to correct images from the inside, destroy what should be destroyed, replace it with what it should be replaced and put us back together, give us back ourselves. . . .[28]

The process by which Ella progresses from hollow ventriloquist to empowered pedagogue is a painfully messy one. Of mixed Irish-Jamaican parentage, Ella hovers in a kind of racial limbo, both in and out of place in the community of Grove Town; indeed she is described by Maydene, the pastor's wife who fosters Ella, as 'flying'. Ella's alabaster skin and straight hair set her apart from the community, for whom her body acts as a conduit for a range of superstitions, jealousies and anxieties. She is also the result and embodiment of exploitative sexual relationships between black women and itinerant white men. This colonially-inherited pattern is repeated in the relationship Ella forms with Selwyn Langley, the American she eventually marries, who exoticizes and feeds off Ella's mulatto status, recognizing that Ella's 'in-betweenness' makes her particularly vulnerable. Brodber, in the following passage, powerfully consolidates the sense of Ella's body as a repository for a hierarchy of images; images of Grove Town people were at 'the bottom' while characters from books (Peter Pan and company) are at 'the top section'. Ella succumbs to Selwyn's seductive attention and persistent questioning and he manages to penetrate 'down' to the story of Grove Town and to drain Ella of it:

> With her hymen and a couple of months of marriage gone, there was a clean, clear passage from Ella's head through her middle and right down to outside. [. . .] Selwyn's pushing had made a clean passage through which he had fallen into that group of Grove Town people.[29]

Selwyn's probing lures Ella into telling stories of her life in Grove Town which, in the process of the telling, reconnects her with that community. However, Selwyn's probing becomes akin to a violent penetration and betrayal (or rape) when Ella sees how he violates her story by transforming it into minstrelsy: 'The Biggest Coon Show ever'; this is a betrayal which the reader sees coming before the naive Ella does. It is at this point that Ella's body bloats in a grotesque phantom pregnancy and she is sent back to Grove Town to recover. Reconnected with community, her exorcism is painfully corporeal and the whole of Grove Town is privy to the smell as the poisons drain from her body, reminiscent of Nellie's breakdown in *Jane and Louisa Will Soon Come Home*, caused because she was 'choked on foreign':

> Cook say it was like twenty thousand dead bull frog, the scent that escape from that chile's body. That had to be the hand of man, Cook say to herself. Then what come out of her! Colour grey, Cook say. Cook say she marvel that a body coulda hold so much stuff. Coulda stand pon it spy Cuba, Cook say.[30]

Running in parallel with Ella's story is that of Anita, of similar age to Ella, but a black Jamaican, whose young body is possessed by Mass Levi, desperate for a cure for his impotence. His attempt to drain her of her vitality is ultimately thwarted, but not before her home is stoned regularly and her body, too, bears the imprint of his attempt to 'thieve her spirit'. What Brodber dramatizes in *Myal* with the use of Anita's and Ella's bodies is a playing out of the variety of ways in which cultural alienation is imposed on the whole community; their bodies become the stage upon which the whole community's zombification is enacted and exorcised, and it is indigenous forms of spiritual healing which provide the cure. The centrality given to Ella's phantom pregnancy suggests its function as a cathartic extension and dramatic playing out of the role of the womb as 'a terrible scrap-heap thing', and of male-female sexual relationships as violently exploitative. But, unlike the image of deferred delivery with which *Jane and Louisa Will Soon Come Home* ends, *Myal* ends with Ella about to make her debut as 'deliverer of the word' in a series of seminars, proposed by Reverend Brassington, to educate the community about zombification. It is this notion of woman as powerful deliverer of the word which is extended in *Louisiana*.

The body of the text in *Louisiana* is much more fragmented and fractured than in *Myal*, equalling *Jane and Louisa* in the kinds of difficulties with which it confronts the reader. So, once more, the text is littered with a range of voices: snatches of conversations, sayings, proverbs, songs, jazz rhythms, 'spiritualisms' and so on, but, in this text, the constant traffic in voices includes an even more rapid shifting between 'real' voices, 'spirit voices' and the voices on the recording machine. Here, Brodber's canvas is much broader than in the earlier novels as her protagonist, also named Ella, is located as an anthropological researcher in the southern state of Louisiana in the 1930s. Mammy, Ella's primary informant, dies before Ella has finished her research project, which involves using the new technology of the tape recorder to record her interviews. As Ella attempts to marshal her 'evidence' into systematic order, Mammy and her spirit-friend Lowly/Louise mysteriously communicate with Ella via the tape recorder ('The venerable sisters had married themselves to me – given birth to me, – they would say.'[31]). As Cooper puts it:

> Brodber uses the technology of tape-recording in this novel as a metaphor for complex processes of cross-cultural, transcendental communication. In a brilliantly anagrammatic trope the *physics* of sound reproduction becomes the *psychic* medium

through which the spirits of the dead communicate with the living, and the academic is challenged to really listen to her informant.[32]

Ella becomes increasingly receptive to these voices and, in the process, recuperates her own personal history and reconnects with her 'bitty old island' and her Jamaican heritage. Simultaneously, her role as conduit for the community's ancestral past is consolidated as Ella increasingly becomes the focal point for the community – operating as a spiritualist cum group therapist. Her acceptance of her new role and her engagement with '[c]elestial ethnography'[33] is most dramatically displayed when she's in Madam Marie's parlour (Madam is her 'tutor in spiritualism') where the community, which includes a large proportion of West Indian men, often meet up to sing songs and engage in informal reconstructions of their past. One of the West Indian men starts to sing 'Sammy dead' – the refrain of which has punctuated the whole text – and Ella is 'possessed' by the song; a possession which is described as an invasion of her body but one which, unlike the exploitative penetration and possession perpetrated on Ella and Anita in *Myal*, fills her with multiple possibilities for seeing and hearing her own, and their, stories:

> He/they didn't get far. I felt my head grow big, as if someone thought it was a balloon and was blowing air into it. My shoulders rocked like a little paper boat trying to balance itself in the sea. You need feet to help you balance. Mine had grown stiff and my body slid from my chair to the floor, fluttering like a decapitated fowl. And I spoke. I was seeing things as if on a rolling screen, a movie screen.[34]

The balloon image here is inflated with possibilities, unlike the balloon in *Jane and Louisa Will Soon Come Home* which stinks with shame. Interestingly, too, in *Louisiana*, men act as intermediary figures, facilitating the women's ability to find their own voices. In *Jane and Louisa* Baba reconnects Nellie with the language of her people; in *Myal* Reverend Brassington points Ella towards a more enabling way of reading colonialist texts; in *Louisiana*, as one of Madam's visitors puts it, '"She wouldn't do it for us. It took some West Indian men to get her over"'.[35] Brodber is careful, then, to suggest in her text that Ella 'qualifies' to represent the community because she has internalized not just Mammy's and Lowly's voices, but those of the West Indian men as well. Interestingly, too, it is these men who represent the motherland/ Jamaica for Ella.

As Ella internalizes more and more of the voices of the community and of the community's ancestry, there is an interesting shift in terms of her physical presence in the text. Where at the start of the text she is presented as both the fastidiously, but mistakenly, 'correct' researcher and the 'little woman', pressing her hair, wearing slacks and fantasizing and joking about her role with Reuben (her lover):

> The beautiful lady inside and out, preparing her beautiful hearth for her beautiful lover, changes and powders the sheets. Southern fried chicken! Frying smells in a love nest![36]

By the end of the text, Ella acknowledges the way her appearance has changed as her role has shifted:

> Other changes have been taking place. They are relatively small things. My hair for instance. I no longer press. I don't know if this represents spiritual or intellectual movement or just plain convenience but there it is: my hair is natural and untouched. And I wrap it. [. . .] I am also now very observable in the streets. [. . .] With my headdress and my long dress, I know I present a dignity rather like hers [Madam Marie's] and an aura which turns heads.[37]

Ella also becomes a vegetarian and, throughout the remainder of the text, there are frequent images of her in her long flowing gowns as a 'vegetarian seer'; this emphatically 'spiritual' identity is underscored by the fact that she is, despite being married to Reuben for several years, childless. It appears, then, that Ella's role as 'mother' of the community denies her the role of biological mother. In a passage towards the end of the novel, Ella becomes the body politic:

> I am the link between the shores washed by the Caribbean sea, a hole, yet I am what joins your left hand to your right. I join the world of the living and the word of the spirits. [. . .] I am Louisiana. I wear a solid pendant with a hole through its

centre. I look through this hole and I can see things. Still I am Mrs Ella Kohl, married to a half-caste Congolese reared in Antwerp by a fairy godfather. I wear long loose fitting white dresses in summer and long black robes over them in winter. I am Louisiana. I give people their history. I serve God and the venerable sisters.[38]

In taking on her role as seer, Ella's sexual presence is de-emphasized and her body represented as the asexual vessel through which the community can find expression and healing. Interestingly, too, Ella's ability to transcend the constraints of physicality is underscored by her ability to demystify and control the symbolic value attached to the tape-recording machine. Early on in the text, the tape-recorder had symbolized the physical presence of Mammy and Lowly, so that Ella would talk to it when she was dusting it:

Without planning it, we were demystifying the poor old thing. It was this process that finally led me to opening the recording machine gently and reverently as if I was cleaning my baby daughter's private region.[39]

By the end of the text, Ella disposes of the tape-recorder on a rubbish tip and replaces it with a round pendant with a hole through the middle:

As a matter of fact since I named myself Louisiana the sisters have not conducted conversation with me via the machine. I like to feel that there is some promotion in that for me. They have been making contact with me via the pendant that I designed and which Reuben got a jeweller to execute. Much better.[40]

The shift in symbols represents Ella's ability to assert some control over her 'calling', but it is interesting that both symbols are articulated in ways suggestive of female sexuality. The hole in the middle of the pendant is suggestive of both Ella's 'sex' and of her childlessness, but neither image gels with the kind of overflowing of boundaries associated with 'écriture feminine' or with the assertion of the body language and rhythms associated with a Creole ethos (as advocated in Brathwaite's notion of 'nation language'); instead, this image suggests an increasingly abstract, or disembodied, symbolizing of the community's 'voice'.

In *Louisiana*, Brodber suggests that the woman's body operates as vessel or vehicle for the powerful delivery of the word which can 'reborn' the black diasporic community. In the framing of Ella's story, a preface from the editors which outlines a mystery about the arrival of Ella's story at 'The Black World Press', Brodber seems to invite parallels to be drawn between Ella as spirit medium and the black woman writer and the text as conduit and cultural medium; it suggests parallels, too, with the ways in which writers such as Alice Walker have presented themselves as writer cum conjure-woman.

I would argue, then, that there is a shift in Brodber's texts away from the messy corporeality of the female body towards a more abstracted, or disembodied, notion of the female body. This shift in the way the body of woman is represented in the body of her texts is central also to the moral focus of Brodber's oeuvre: a moral focus which, in terms of the thematics of her texts, suggests an eschewal of sexual pleasure in favour of 'the spiritual', even as the aesthetics of her novels assert powerfully the sexual pleasures of the text. In pointing up this tension between the thematics and aesthetics of sexuality and textuality in Brodber's novels, it is not my intention to discredit her work but, rather, to explore the gendered implications of her textual choices and to suggest that my reading of her novels might also operate as a way of foregrounding some of the limitations and contradictions of 'écriture feminine' itself.

Notes

1. E. Brodber, *Jane and Louisa Will Soon Come Home* (London: New Beacon, 1980); *Myal* (London: New Beacon, 1988); *Louisiana* (London: New Beacon, 1994).
2. E. Grosz, *Volatile Bodies* (Bloomington & Indianapolis: Indiana University Press, 1994) pp. 13–14.
3. Quoted in J. Flax, *Thinking Fragments: Psychoanalysis, Feminism & Postmodernism in the Contemporary West* (Berkeley & Los Angeles: University of California Press, 1990) p. 175.
4. D. Brand, *Bread Out of Stone* (Toronto: Coach House Press, 1994) pp. 15–49.
5. E. Marks & I. deCourtivron, *New French Feminisms* (Hemel Hempstead: Harvester, 1981) pp. 177–8.

6. E.K. Brathwaite, *Roots* (Michigan: Ann Arbor, 1993) pp. 259–304.
7. E. Brodber, 'Fiction in the Scientific Procedure' in S. Cudjoe (ed.), *Caribbean Women Writers* (Wellesley: Calaloux Publications, 1990) pp. 164–8.
8. Ibid., p. 165.
9. E. Brodber, *Jane and Louisa Will Soon Come Home* (London: New Beacon, 1980) p. 12.
10. Ibid., p. 101.
11. Ibid., p. 61.
12. Ibid., p. 77.
13. Ibid., p. 70.
14. Ibid., p. 63
15. Ibid., p. 71.
16. Ibid., p. 71.
17. Ibid., p. 72.
18. C. Cooper, *Noises in the Blood* (London: Macmillan, 1993).
19. E. Brodber, *Jane and Louisa Will Soon Come Home*, p. 8.
20. Ibid., p. 23.
21. Ibid., pp. 142–3.
22. Ibid., pp. 119–20.
23. Ibid., pp. 28–9.
24. Ibid., p. 92.
25. Ibid., p. 133.
26. E. O'Callaghan, *Woman Version: Theoretical Approaches to West Indian Fiction by Women* (London: Macmillan, 1993) p. 78.
27. Helen Tiffin does an interesting reading of this aspect of Brodber's text in 'Cold Hearts and (Foreign) Tongues: Recitation and the Reclamation of the Female Body in the Works of Erna Brodber and Jamaica Kincaid' in *Callaloo*, Fall V 16 (4) (1993) 909–21.
28. E. Brodber, *Myal* (London: New Beacon, 1988) pp. 109–10.
29. Ibid., pp. 80–1.
30. Ibid., p. 94.
31. E. Brodber, *Louisiana* (London: New Beacon, 1994) p. 32.
32. C. Cooper, 'Science and Higher Science: Transmigration in Erna Brodber's *Louisiana*', paper delivered to the International Conference on Caribbean Women Writers held at Wellesley College in March 1995, p. 4.
33. E. Brodber, *Louisiana*, p. 61.
34. Ibid., p. 88.
35. Ibid., p. 97.
36. Ibid., p. 27.
37. Ibid., pp. 98–9.
38. Ibid., pp. 124–5.
39. Ibid., p. 50.
40. Ibid., p. 131.

Bibliography

Brand, D. *Bread Out of Stone*. Toronto: Coach House Press, 1994.
Brathwaite, E.K. *Roots*. Michigan: Ann Arbor, 1993.
Brodber, E. 'Fiction in the Scientific Procedure' in S. Cudjoe (ed.). *Caribbean Women Writers*. Wellesley: Calaloux Publications, 1990.
———. *Jane and Louisa Will Soon Come Home*. London: New Beacon, 1980.
———. *Myal*. London: New Beacon, 1988.
———. *Louisiana*. London: New Beacon, 1994.
Cooper, C. *Noises in the Blood*. London: Macmillan, 1993.
———. 'Science and Higher Science: Transmigration in Erna Brodber's *Louisiana*', paper delivered at the International Conference on Caribbean Women Writers held at Wellesley College in March 1995.
Flax, J. *Thinking Fragments: Psychoanalysis, Feminism and Postmodernism in the Contemporary West*. Berkeley and Los Angeles: University of California Press, 1990.
Grosz, E. *Volatile Bodies*. Bloomington and Indianapolis: Indiana University Press, 1994.
Marks, E. and I. deCourtivron. *New French Feminisms*. Hemel Hempstead: Harvester, 1981.
O'Callaghan, E. *Woman Version: Theoretical Approaches to West Indian Fiction by Women*. London: Macmillan, 1993.
Tiffin, H. 'Cold Hearts and (Foreign Tongues: Recitation and the Reclamation of the Female Body in the Works of Erna Brodber and Jamaica Kincaid' in *Callaloo*, Fall V 16 (4) 1993.

8

The Short Fiction of Olive Senior

Alison Donnell

Borrowed images
willed our skins pale
muffled our laughter
lowered our voices
let out our hems
dekinked our hair
denied our sex in gym tunics and bloomers
harnessed our voices to madrigals
and genteel airs
yoked our minds to declensions in Latin
and the language of Shakespeare

> Told us nothing about ourselves
> There was nothing about us at all
>   ('Colonial Girls' School')[1]

In her poem, 'Colonial Girls' School', Olive Senior finely satirizes the way in which the colonial education system in Jamaica promoted alienating icons of physical beauty, irrelevant versions of historical understanding, and disempowering geographies of belonging. The poem turns on the refrain 'Nothing about us at all'. In Senior's short stories the subjects in the schoolroom, and the populations of Jamaica, more widely, are given back the bodies, the voices, the pasts and the island home which the colonial cultural apparatus had wilfully tried to deny them. It is this act of reconnecting the lives of the diverse and shifting populations of Jamaica to literature which most crucially informs Senior's three collections of short stories: *Summer Lightning* (1986), *Arrival of the*

Snake-Woman (1989) and *Discerner of Hearts* (1995). However, Senior's work is not merely motivated by an oppositional stance to colonial inscriptions, for not only does she write against the erroneous and damaging versions of Jamaican selves which have been scripted and imported by colonial, and, importantly, neo-colonial cultures, but she also recuperates for a written archive the lives of those who remained excluded, unknown and significantly unknowable by those 'outsiders' who had been granted the power to tell. Indeed, as one of the few creative writers who remained in the Caribbean even after her work received critical acclaim, although she now divides her time between Jamaica and Toronto, Senior has acknowledged her commitment to 'a literature that is being written from the inside out instead of the outside looking in'.[2]

Nevertheless, the power of 'outside' meaning cannot be underestimated in material terms and it is significant that Senior achieved sudden recognition within the literary world when she was awarded the Commonwealth Writers' Prize for *Summer Lightning* in the year of its foundation, 1987. This acknowledgement from the centre did not, however, mark the beginning of Senior's literary career. She had already published a number of short stories in Jamaica during the 1970s and had been awarded local recognition and praise, along with Jamaica's own prize for outstanding creative work – winning two Musgrave medals. Nevertheless, it is a notable fact that a gesture of acclaim from the metropolitan centre is often a prerequisite for Caribbean writers to achieve a large audience and to secure an international publisher.

Although Senior's work can be helpfully located within the tradition of Anglophone Caribbean Literature and within a context of late 1970s and 1980s women's writing from the Caribbean, it is my aim to demonstrate that her work would be limited by a narrow consideration of the major themes and tropes which have informed both of these traditions to date. Indeed, if many of Senior's short stories revisit the dominant tropes and motifs of the established, one might wish to venture 'canonical', Caribbean literary tradition, then they often look back with an ironic glance and seek gently to realign the axis of interest.

Senior's work demonstrates a sustained interest in the complex and difficult task of the negotiating of identities, particularly cultural identities, for all groups within the Caribbean. The stories in all three of Senior's short story collections offer affectionate and informed snapshots of the lives of those who might be considered to be on the margins of the already peripheral (in global terms) Jamaican society. The old, the young, the poor, and particularly those whose subjectivities fall between designated identities, can be found at the centre of her narratives. The detail and the emotional concentration of her work communicate a strong belief that these lives are interesting and worthwhile in their own right and not simply because they offer up experiences which are expedient *exempla* for contemporary cultural and political metanarratives, which, whether imperialist or post-colonial, by their very nature use the particular to feed the general. However, this is not to suggest that her work does not engage with the wider political problematics underlying and overlapping individual experience, but rather that the stories wonderfully demonstrate the fact that oppressive ideological systems need to be understood within a context of everyday human meaning and that ideology-critique can be most powerfully enacted at the level of the personal.

Perhaps the most obvious area of intersection between Senior's work and that of many other Caribbean writers is the writing of childhood and the concern with the child's experience and perception of the world, a focus which is particularly striking in *Summer Lightning*. In this first volume the child protagonists seem to divide between the vulnerable and the voluble. These tales capture both the bewilderment and the excitement of the child's experience, often locating a single moment which provokes a shift of consciousness and an awareness of the irretrievable loss of the world as it was before. Both 'Love Orange' and 'The Boy Who Loved Ice Cream' portray a child's consciousness, creative and alert, but tragically implicated in systems of meaning which s/he cannot understand (and in this way bear useful comparison to the short stories of Jean Rhys). In 'The Boy Who Loved Ice Cream', a deep sense of bewilderment consumes Benjy, a child stranded in an adult universe of rivalry, jealousy and betrayal, who is unable to satisfy his most intense longing, for an ice-cream: 'The very words conveyed to him the sound of everything in his life that he had always wanted, always longed for, but could not give a name to'.[3] However, when the day of the fair arrives, the buying of the ice-cream by his father is constantly deferred until the boy reaches the peak of his frustration. The simple nature of Benjy's boyish desire is contrasted with the complicated and

tangled adult world of those around him. At the very moment
of gratification, he is snatched by his father (who suspects his
mother of an affair and Benjy of being someone else's child) and
the ice-cream falls from his hand. The devastation of this moment
is carefully represented through the unpunctuated and highly
subjective narrative. This technique serves to communicate the
alarming lack of orientation and the confusion of the child who
is unable to decipher the meanings behind the gestures and sights
he witnesses:

> Mama is standing she is apart from all the people talking to a
> strange man in a purple shirt and Papa is moving so fast Benjy's
> feet are almost off the ground and Benjy is crying Papa Papa
> and everything is happening so quickly he doesn't know the
> point at which he loses the ice cream and half the cone . . .
> and he cannot understand why Papa . . . is shouting and why
> Mama isn't laughing with the man anymore . . . and he cannot
> understand why the sky which a minute ago was pink and
> mauve just like the ice cream is now swimming in his vision
> like one swollen blanket of rain.[4]

The bizarre, almost documentary style which governs the narration of even the final image, a vision determined from within
and blurred by his tears, is suggestive of the boy's inability to
connect and to interpret the signs of the world he inhabits.

'Love Orange', which offers a retrospective reflection on childhood, opens with a powerful statement of child's logic which
links the abstract to the concrete with confidence: 'Somewhere
between the repetition of Sunday School lessons and the broken
doll which the lady sent me one Christmas I lost what it was to
be happy'.[5] The disappointment and shock at finding that the
plaster blue-eyed doll she had so longed for was deformed is
only compensated for by the love-orange which she constantly
conjures for protection in a world populated by disfigurement
and death. However, having rejected the doll, the conventional
object of girlish play, the orange, invested with all her love and
carefully guarded for fear of loss or rash generosity, is a security
device and a key to make-believe worlds both more profound
and more obtuse than the adult world can accept. When her
grandmother is dying the young protagonist decides to relinquish
the whole of her orange in the hope that she may recover, but it

is a gesture from a world of childhood hopes which not only fails to communicate the enormity of her love for her grandmother but which moreover forces a recognition of a reality in which death and pain cannot be wished away: 'But she kept on dying and I knew then that the orange had no potency, that love could not create miracles'.[6] In learning that the gift of love is both more complex and more demanding than she had thought and that the death of loved ones cannot always be deferred, the young narrator accepts the loss of childhood and of a secure future which can never be recaptured: 'In leaving my grandmother's house, the dark tunnel of my childhood, I slammed the car door hard on my fingers and as my hand closed over the breaking bones, felt nothing.'[7]

The gentle prizing open of ignored life archives to reveal impassioned and crucial 'moments of being' lived outside a dominant culture is the guiding motif of this first collection. However, the intense portraits of the child's emotional life which many of these stories offer could be seen to lack cultural specificity, to be interesting accounts of a child's experience of the adult world, but ultimately unchallenging in their status as Caribbean texts. However, in these early stories Senior begins to establish the practice of validating a world of being and of feeling which exists outside the conflicts and emotions associated with colonialism, conflicts and emotions which are too readily assumed to be the overriding preoccupation of the colonial subject's life.

It is crucial to an understanding of Senior's stories to read these moments when a consciousness is preoccupied with a family relationship, or with an imagined taste, or with the clothes of a stranger, as small gestures of refocusing, capable of displacing the huge colonial fantasy preoccupied with and constituted by the experience of colonization. Although it may appear to be an incidental narrative fact, the narrative marginalization of the doll with blue eyes – which clearly signifies that the young girl's consciousness has internalized the dominant culture of colonial idolatry – in favour of the main drama of the unfolding family relationships and the young girl's loss of innocence, could be read as a strategic rejection of themes which continue to anchor and centre experience on the legacies of colonial conflict. Furthermore, although these affectionate accounts of childhood may not easily be read within the context of radical prose, it is perhaps important to acknowledge that nothing is more radical than the act of giving subjectivity to those who have previously been regarded as insignificant and inappropriate 'subjects'.

The fact that in Senior's fictional world the child's perspective is treated seriously, and does not merely function as an allegory of the national, or as a strategic domain through which the more blatantly politicized issues expected of post-colonial writing can be made digestible for the general reading public, perhaps points to a difference in approach between Senior and her mainly male antecedents. Many of the earlier childhood narratives were structured by the classic formula of the *bildungsroman*, with the child's development and passage to maturity and independence mirroring that of the emergent island nation, a formula which Frederick Jameson has named 'national allegory' and identified as paradigmatic of Third World literature.[8] In these narratives the child carried the burden of being 'representative', and therefore was often constrained by a rather formulaic series of experiences and responses often connected to their interaction with colonial culture.

Although the interface between the world of the child and the world of the colony is also explored in *Summer Lightning*, it is often the resistance and empowerment of the child which is foregrounded. In 'Confirmation Day' the interior monologue of a young woman about to be confirmed is presented as a series of overlapping and repeated observations, as if the child is rehearsing a personal litany as she struggles to prime herself for the moment of confirmation and to make sense of the spiritual dimension of her imminent experience. Aware that there are no words which are equivalent to the 'meaning' she will experience, her mind retraces the paradoxically familiar although 'other worldly' images of holiness and of fear:

> [N]ow we are in another time another church and the smell of incense mingles with the smell of the church and the smell is the smell of the aged. What happens to the young after their Confirmation Day? I used to wonder. Once I knew a girl who had been baptised and she had caught pneumonia and died so maybe becoming a child of God and dying were the same thing. But now the smell of starch belongs to the world of the young who never return to church after their Confirmation Day because of the terrible reality of Him.[9]

The strangeness of ritual to the uninitiated is wonderfully evoked by the fine detailing of the child's sensory apprehension. Yet, despite these anxieties the story ends with the moment of confirmation for the young girl, which is also undoubtedly a moment of redemption. But while it is a conventional act of spiritual grace in her grandmother's eyes, it is a more secular epiphany for the young woman, who has been delivered from the unknowable realm of spiritual experience to the safe and knowable world of her rural community: 'But once outside those doors I see the Bishop's car as nothing but a small black beetle in a vast green world. . . . I know instinctively that not the reeds in the river nor the wine nor the blood of Christ nor the book of Common Prayer can conquer me'.[10] The story affirms the ability of the girl's consciousness to participate in but make different meanings from a ritual in which the self is traditionally humbled in an act of consensual sacrifice. Nevertheless, the flashing Sprite sign which punctuates the story is a foreboding alter-icon of an age in which 'consumer' is a more comfortable identity-tag than 'believer', and a sign of the other equally powerful and potentially consuming dogma of capitalism.

This same process through which children are empowered by the very rituals designed to make them submissive informs the delightfully and powerfully humorous 'Do Angels Wear Brassieres?' Probably the most irreverent and knowing of Senior's child protagonists, Beccka in this story certainly has more in common with Jamaica Kincaid's female protagonists Annie and Lucy than with Lamming's G. Beccka is cheeky, inquisitive, intelligent and energetically resistant to her aunt's attempts to rear her 'properly'; she is the antithesis of the colonial feminine ideal outlined by Erna Brodber as: 'delicate, diffident, tender, pleasing, tactful, suffering and at home'.[11] Although her night-time act of rebellion is the seemingly innocent, if not pious, study of the Bible by torchlight, her intent 'to try and find flaw and question she can best them with'[12] indicates her more serious quest to counter the textual authority of the Bible, and those who use its words to socialize and silence her and her aptitude for verbal rebellion. The story hinges on the much awaited visit of the Archdeacon to Auntie Mary's house and the terrified anticipation of what Beccka might do or say in the presence of this hallowed guest. However, when the occasion arises, her mother and aunt are so pleasantly surprised by her good behaviour that they leave young Beccka alone with the Archdeacon. Seizing the opportunity to exercise her penetrating knowledge, Beccka begins a Biblical banter which the Archdeacon finds amusing, if a little inappropriate, but which is a source of mortification and domestic disaster to her female guardians who overhear the most memorable of her questions, 'Do angels wear brassieres?'

Moreover, it is not only in her seemingly playful though irreverent questions to the Archdeacon that Beccka communicates her resistance to the order and values of the dominant culture. Despite her success in winning a scholarship to the school of her aunt's choice (even Auntie Mary, the chief victim of Beccka's tricks and transgressions, has to acknowledge that '"this is really a gifted child"'[13]), she does not wish to pursue the conventional life-narrative of the intelligent Caribbean child. Rather, she dreams of a life with the circus, and of a future in which she may fulfil her 'make-believe' version of womanhood, which encompasses the three biggest sins for a woman to commit – going out to a nightclub, drinking alcohol and dancing all night! As this story shows, the locales of dominant colonial authority (the church, the aspiring home, and the school), may have remained constant in twentieth-century Caribbean literary representations, but the strategies and the successes of the children who reconfigure their place within the hegemonic social order suggest a shift in emphasis from the writing against oppressive structures to the writing in of resistant subjects.

It is also significant that self-empowerment in Senior's stories often involves an acknowledgement of those cultural resources and alternative ways of knowing which were marginalized or undervalued within a conventional 'colonial' education. The young boy turns to Bro Justice the Rastafarian in 'Summer Lightning' when threatened by sexual abuse, Theresa turns to the 'discerner of hearts' and traditional healer in the story of that name in order to secure the happiness of Cissy and her child, and Lenora in 'Ballad' turns to the resources of an oral culture, when 'teacher' forbids her to write an elegy for Miss Rilla, a 'notorious' local woman and surrogate mother to Lenora. These acts of resistance, which all take place outside the spaces of colonial culture and beyond the gaze of cultural custodians such as guardians, parents and teachers, provide an insight into acts of agency and defiance which could not necessarily be seen by the colonial eye and which further deprivilege it.

This emphasis is particularly important to the title story of Senior's second collection *Arrival of the Snake-Woman* which centres on the impact of 'strange arrivants' in a rural district of Jamaica.[14] In this story the 'snake-woman', a beautiful and exotic prize won by SonSon in a game of straws, and brought to the community as a silent bride, is seemingly divested of her cultural identity:

> I don't think that anyone ever knew her Indian name or anything about her. . . . It was as if, crossing over the mountains to start a new life, or perhaps even earlier when she crossed the seas, she had left behind all that reminded her of the old, shed her identity and her history, became transformed into whatever we would make of her, our Miss Coolie.[15]

However, our narrator's notion of her plastic and acquiescent identity calls for further analysis. If this fascinating woman is constructed as 'Miss Coolie' to 'the boys', she represents the absolute spiritual other to Parson Bedlow: 'replacing rum drinking, fornication, smoking, cursing, lying, wife-beating, idleness, backsliding, taking the Lord's name in vain and some other sins we had never heard before'.[16] Despite this hostile identification, which characterizes her treatment in the community, Miss Coolie appears untroubled and continues her Indian cooking and cultivation, only abandoning her jewellery, an obvious signifier of Indianness, because it was impractical given her manual work. Indeed, Miss Coolie remains indifferent to the identifications and machinations of the Parson until her son, Biya, needs the medical attention that only he can provide. However, in a crucial episode of cultural arrogance Parson Bedlow turns her away and she has to travel to the Bay to seek a cure for her son. Despite this rejection Miss Coolie is once again driven to the Parson on behalf of her son, this time for his place at the school, and this time she is welcomed into the flock as she wears the garb of conformity and acquiescence, a seemingly 'docile' Foulcauldian body: 'She is dressed for Sunday now like the other women all in white – long starched petticoats and skirt, a long-sleeved, high-neck blouse and white headwrap that totally hides her hair'.[17]

Nevertheless, the garments of submission cannot guarantee a conquered consciousness, and as the story draws to a close it becomes evident that Miss Coolie's cultural compromise was only a costume. She had not converted at the level of belief, and moreover she had not abandoned her culture or history as those around her assumed, but only suspended this constituent of her identity until it could be comfortably reassumed:

She has reverted to wearing saris again . . . put back on her
bangles, her rings, earrings and her nose ring; put a red spot
on her forehead to show she is a married lady. . . . And she
gave all her daughters Indian names. . . .'[18]

The snake-woman's actions, like those of the child protagonists
above, testify to a mode of resistance which survives because it
can be silent and invisible and endures at the level of consciousness despite the necessity of working within dominant cultural
imperatives.

Indeed, for Aunt Lily in 'Lily, Lily', accepting the role of post-
mistress, designed to constrain the possibilities for self-determination
since female government officials were not allowed to marry or
cohabit, is a means through which to achieve a level of independence whilst dissembling consent to a patriarchal colonial order.
These acts of strategic submission are not only significant resistant strategies which present moments of empowerment that
destabilize the orders of power and of agency upon which colonial cultures depend, but they are also mechanisms by which
those who live in colonial and neo-colonial cultures manage to
survive and, importantly, to remain.

Within a context in which diasporic writing and writings of
diaspora form nearly the entire canon, it seems important to
address Senior's continued interest in those Caribbean peoples
who have stayed. This focus could even be perceived as writing
against the grain of those dominant narratives of exile circulated
within Caribbean Literature during its so-called 'boom' years of
the 1950s and often written by men who had themselves travelled, usually on the scholarship trail, to the metropolitan motherland of London. Senior's heroines, and heroes, are not exceptionally
gifted in the old way – bright beyond their community with a
compulsion to learn and to leave – and indeed this is often a
path which they reject or from which the narrator chooses to
divert our attention.[19] While many of her stories, like the major
cultural and historical narratives of the Caribbean region itself,
depend on arrivals and exiles, the texts do not trace the pilgrim-
age to the metropolitan centre and away from Jamaica, or at least
from rural communities, but rather concentrate on those journeys
which take place within the island, and on those individuals who
return.

'Ascot' in *Summer Lightning* is the first of Senior's stories to map out the trajectory of exile and return. Ascot is singled out not by aptitude for learning, but by the fact that he 'come out with fair skin and straight nose',[20] and perhaps more pointedly by his one driving ambition 'to dress up in white clothes and drive a big white car'.[21] Yet when Ascot leaves for the States, the narrative does not follow him but remains with the young female narrator in Jamaica, and his 'foreign' life is merely documented by three extremely brief and (unintentionally) comic letters recording his relative success in achieving his ambition:

> Dear Ma wel i am her in New York is Big plase and they have plenty car I am going to get one yr loving son Ascot. . . . Dear mother wel here I am in Connecticut. . . . I driveing car two year now but is not wite yr loving son Ascot. . . . Dear Mother Chicago is Big plais I drevein wite car for a wite man but he don make me where wite is black uniform so I mite leave yr loving son Ascot.[22]

As these letters reveal, Ascot has not grown or developed as a result of his journey but remains arrested in his 'white' fantasy, and it is this lack of personal development which becomes both more apparent and more painful when he eventually returns to his island home with the trappings of fulfilment. It would seem that in order to possess his dreams, Ascot has dispossessed his history. In a disturbing gesture of surrogacy, Ascot makes a desperate attempt to deny his own mother and stepfather and adopt 'Aunt Essie' and 'Uncle Jackie' as his parents. Yet his attempt to reconstruct a childhood past from the vantage point of his whitewashed life ultimately fails when Miss Clemmie, his real mother, shatters all illusions in a single utterance: '"Yes'm Hascot is de heldes but is not de same fader"'.[23] This declaration, which cuts across Ascot's pretensions of education, of wealth and of parentage, situates his identity in a context to which he no longer consents to belong, and one which he hastily leaves again. For the poor rural community, Ascot's material elevation may be a source of pride, but his disavowal of his family and his cultural origins is a source of anger for the child narrator, and it is the narrator, not Ascot, who is at the centre of this story.

This same interest in those who return from 'foreign' and also in the community which is left behind informs 'The Case Against the Queen' in *Discerner of Hearts*. For the Uncle of this story, who had left Jamaica as a young man bound for England and a promising future as a medic which would embody all his parents' dreams, return to the rural and close-knit community entails both the shattering of his parents' public illusion and the difficult process of his own re-belonging. This process is seemingly obstructed by his 'madness', signified by his wearing of a three-piece suit and bowler hat in the 'tropics', and his trunk full of letters to the Queen, as well as his attendant indifference towards the life at 'home'. However, while he is constructed by those around as having lost his mind, as he confides to Girlie, our narrator, it is actually his heart which he has lost: '"... I don't have a heart any more. That's a mechanical contrivance they put inside of me. . . . It was advantage-taking to the highest degree. I wrote to the Queen about it"'.[24] His failure to appreciate the technology of his pacemaker and his extreme naïvety in corresponding with the colonial monarch are clear signals of his failure to understand both medicine and the Motherland, despite years of residency and of study. However, his missing heart more pointedly suggests that as a diasporic subject the Uncle has lost his emotional centre, and it is significant that even after his return, he remains a body housing a subjectivity in exile. Like Erna Brodber's *Jane and Louisa Will Soon Come Home*, this story presents a returner significantly damaged by the cultural dislocation and emotional alienation of migration. However unlike Nellie, Brodber's protagonist, Uncle is unable to reconnect to the cultural resources which might heal him, until his parents die and he is released from the burden of their expectations – the surprising source of his emotional death. The implication that the Uncle had been exiled into another world even before he left his community, indeed by the collective aspirations of his community for success abroad, raises interesting questions concerning the construction of cultural identities within colonial and postcolonial societies.

Moreover, the very fact that a journey between different worlds can be a guiding motif in *Arrival of the Snake-Woman*, a collection of stories all set in Jamaica, clearly indicates Senior's interest in different cultural geographies and 'migrations of the subject'.[25] This is particularly evident in 'Arrival of the Snake-Woman' itself, which weaves into its structure not only the tale of Miss Coolie's arrival and her quiet, gradual movement to the centre of the community, but also that of the Parson and his wife, and which yet retains its commitment to documenting the lives of the resident population, addressing their ability to embrace the arrivants as much as the arrivants' strategies for accommodating themselves. The explanatory and reflective ending of this long 'short story' explicitly draws attention to the way in which those who come, those who leave and those who come back generate the constant flux which keeps the rural community alive even for those, indeed most of all for those who never leave:

> Her arrival represented a loosening of the bonds that had previously bound her, that bind all of us to our homes. Cut free from her past, she was thus free of the duties and obligations that tie us so tightly to one another, sometimes in a stranglehold. She became a free agent with a flexibility that enabled her to ... "do business" with family, friend, or the white men that came to buy produce from her. Miss Coolie, in short, is our embodiment of the spirit of the new age, an age in which sentiment has been replaced by pragmatism and superstition by materialism.[26]

The cultural shift towards materialism and pragmatism may be seen as a lamentable sign of Jamaica's capitulation to the globalizing forces of late capitalism as the story brings us into the second half of the twentieth century. However, as part of the affectionate portrait which Ishmael constructs of this woman, we are encouraged to perceive the positive qualities which this 'new age' may bring. The Snake-Woman is not divested of identity, merely an empty cipher through which other cultural forces can operate, in the way Ishmael had first perceived her. Rather she has developed the ability to stage different identities, respond to different roll-calls in different contexts and therefore to work with the flexibility of identity constructs. This possibility for negotiating a more flexible and open system of interactions is particularly attractive since we know that she has not been forced to abandon her elected Indian cultural identity in order to occupy different subject positions.

Indeed, it is crucial to be aware that although Senior may choose to write of rural Jamaica, she is not interested in recycling tired, colonial pastoral idylls nor in scripting authentic nativist theories which locate sites of uncorrupted cultural identity. As Richard Patteson has pointed out, Senior 'implicitly acknowledges the interpenetration of the cosmopolitan and the insular as an essential element in the process of creolization'.[27] Nevertheless, the process of achieving a successfully creolized culture and cultural identity is not without significant obstacles, as 'The Two Grandmothers', one of Senior's best known stories, documents. Structured from a young girl's conversations with her mother, the speeches trace the formation of the girl's own cultural identity as she moves between the very different culturally determined worlds of her two grandmothers.

The opening monologue tells of the rural home of Grandma Del, her father's mother, and of the rituals of this nurturing grandmother and the role the young girl adopts in this community. She expresses a fondness for the best church dresses which grandma makes her and a contentment with her own body which is lovingly tended to by the old woman: 'I feel so beautiful in my dresses she made'.[28] However, while the emphasis on morality and spiritual belief may appear to present a clear and affirmative model of being – 'Grandma Del says my skin is beautiful like honey and all in all I am a fine brown lady and must make sure to grow as beautiful inside as I am outside'[29] – the censored genealogy and missing photographs of her grandfather still point to a part of her own identity which is being denied. In contrast, the second speech tells of her mother's mother, Grandma Elaine, who commits all the sins which Grandma Del had warned her against, and plenty more besides. For 'Towser' the doctrine of exterior beauty is supreme and whilst the young girl is clearly impressed by the glamour her maternal grandmother can offer, she is hurt by her criticism of her body: 'Mummy, what does she have against my hair? And my skin? She always seems angry about it. . . .'[30]

As the story develops, a shift in the young girl's cultural allegiances can be traced, with the denial of her rural identity and her desired identification with the world of Miami, makeup and the beauty myth: 'Can I have my hair relaxed as soon as I am twelve as you promised? Will you allow me to enter Miss Jamaica when I am old enough?'[31] Indeed, the final question which ventures a compromise to make a day-long visit to Grandma Del as long as 'We can leave there right after lunch so we will be back home in time to watch *Dallas*',[32] would seem to confirm her attachment to a new cultural hegemony beamed via satellite into the Jamaican home. However, despite her capitulation to the new value system, the problematic status of her colour remains, and the alarming question 'Mummy, am I really a nigger?',[33] which refers to an identification which has been made by her American cousin, receives no answer in the context of multi-channel glamour worship. It would appear then, that although the girl may have elected a subject position within this culture, her belonging can only be partial.

The ending of this story, like that of 'Arrival of the Snake-Woman', may appear to point to a loss of values, a lamentable denial of traditional culture, and therefore to place Senior in consensus with other Caribbean women writers and critics who have pointed to the exile of distinctly Jamaican culture, even on its own ground, as an urgent issue for cultural nationalists to address. In their introduction to *Out of the Kumbla: Caribbean Women and Literature*, Carole Boyce Davies and Elaine Savory Fido claim that:

> The greatest threat to Caribbean life at this time comes from a denial of the spiritual / intuitive / emotional strengths which have developed to sustain the cultures in the past. This denial takes the form of adherence to materialism, of attraction to the world of fast foods, video recorders, cars, multi channel television stations.[34]

For a post-colonial Jamaican culture struggling to free itself from the pervasive and persuasive iconography of English Literature, American television is the neo-colonial agent projecting 'outside' images of ideal lives and bodies onto the island's retina; as Merle Hodge points out:

> Television, which is basically American television, came to Trinidad and Tobago in 1962, the year the British flag was pulled down. The same pattern can be seen all over the Caribbean – withdrawing the most obvious trappings of colonial domination and installing a Trojan horse instead.[35]

Although Senior is often keen to portray a rural world less governed by the imperatives of a colonial culture, she is also quick to address the subtle and pervasive influence which metropolitan culture has over even the most remote communities and her stories often explore the role and position of the United States in the new configurations of cultural influence and domination.

Nevertheless, it would be too simplistic to read 'The Two Grandmothers' as a story of neocolonialism via satellite. Senior does not simply write against the cultural penetration of Jamaica by a free market economy, American television and the global campaign to colonize by credit card; rather, her stories rehearse the various ways in which these new cultural forces can operate. In 'Lily, Lily' the accumulation of capital by working class Jamaicans who had emigrated to the canal zone represents an important and disruptive intervention in the regulatory systems of naturalized hierarchies which had been imposed, entrenched and, most significantly, internalized during centuries of colonial rule. Cutting across established orders of class and 'race', the woman with capital achieves both an empowerment and a mobility of identity.

> One of these women from right here in our town, who not so long ago was walking the streets barefoot, . . . got it into her head to take off for Colón as a higgler if you please . . . a year later this same woman is back here wearing silks and satins (in broad daylight) *dripping*, just dripping with Panama gold from head to foot and this creature was actually rude to Mrs DaSilva only last week.[36]

Although 'The Two Grandmothers' may point to the problems which late capitalist cultural penetration can cause, this episode in 'Lily, Lily' points to capital as an early agent capable of mobilizing social hierarchies and identities (the two having been inextricably linked by imperial ideology).

Senior's stories do not advocate a nostalgic view of an authentic way of life or of an essentialized Jamaican identity; rather, they disclose the multiple and competing discourses in and through which a confusing proliferation of subject-positions present themselves in Caribbean cultures. Yet the stories also testify to the way in which, for both colonial and post-colonial subjects the potential horizon of identity constructions is significantly narrowed by the way in which particular constructions are channelled directly into social hierarchies. Lenora in 'Ballad' articulates the dilemma of several of Senior's protagonists, including that of 'The Two Grandmothers', who find themselves pulled between different identifications, both cultural and gendered, which are not quite 'elected' subject positions as their currencies are weighted by considerations of social status and the intersubjective necessity of identity formation.

> ... I confuse confuse because one mind in me say that I should study and pass exam so that I can go to high school and speak good and wear pretty dress and high heel shoes. ... And I confuse because another voice say that MeMa will vex. ... So maybe I should learn sewing or how to be postmistress.[37, 38]

Lenora does not reach a decision in this story, and the persistent uncertainty regarding identifications and their consequences remains an urgent question. Indeed, the tensions between constructed identities ascribed by new cultural hegemonies and lived identities which enable emotional belonging are not merely associated with childhood or adolescence, for it is the adult Ishmael in 'Arrival of the Snake-Woman' who expresses an equal sense of 'inbetweenness':

> And sometimes I am still unsure of my own self, of who I am, of where I belong, still feeling halfway between the old world where my navel-string is buried, and the new, unable to shake off the old strictures, the sentimental attachments of my earlier upbringing. ...[39]

In these stories Senior maps out a series of different but equally complex situations in which identification with and differentiation from contestatory cultural discourses and living communities cannot be comfortably resolved.

The positive aspects of a contingent and mobile identity, such as that which Miss Coolie manages to construct, which is able simultaneously to consent to and dissent from the demands of a dominant culture, needs to be acknowledged as an important means of claiming agency with a (post-) colonial context. Nevertheless, in the current climate of postmodern thought it is perhaps too easy to be persuaded by a celebratory rhetoric of plural, provisional, hybrid identities and to neglect the lived reality of certain individuals for whom subject positions are not voluntarily assumed, but assigned. To return to 'The Two Grandmothers', this fixing of positions can be observed in the protagonist's question 'Mummy, am I really a nigger?', through which the narrator's elected identity is jeopardized by the essentializing discourse of 'race' in which her new cultural 'home' continues to trade. It is significant that the black body remains a highly-charged site of conflict and denial with regard to the issue of cultural belonging, her perceived 'racial' body marking a difference which cannot be accommodated.

In 'Bright Thursdays' the overlapping discourses of belonging and the body conspire against Laura, whose mother was a servant and father a man of 'high estate'. Born between two social and cultural worlds, Laura's body bears the traces of her mixed parentage, she 'had come out with dark skin but almost straight hair'.[40] Her mother, certain that a grand destiny is inscribed in the straight line of Laura's nose, the length of her hair and the softness of her skin makes great efforts to persuade the paternal grandparents to 'adopt' her child, sending a photograph in which Laura stages a eurocentric feminine identity with her body arranged to represent the mother's fantasy in which the corporeal and cultural cannot be separated:

> The child was dressed in a frilly *white* dress trimmed with ribbons, much too long for her age. She wore long *white* nylon socks and *white* T-strap shoes. Her hair was done in perfect drop curls, with a part to the side and two front curls caught up with a large *white* bow.[41]

On the basis of this 'whitened' substitute identity, in which the body is constructed as a cipher for good behaviour and natural grace, the grandparents agree to adopt Laura and she travels to their house, across the countryside and along the social continuum. But Laura, who does not belong to the image of the photograph, becomes aware that although her body may 'pass' in the big house, both her body and her cultural origins fix her in a subordinate position, her public status as the 'adopted' child articulating the fragile and provisional nature of her belonging here.

> She didn't know her father except for a photograph of him on Miss Christie's bureau where he was almost lost in a forest of photographs of all her children and grandchildren all brown skinned with straight hair and confident smiles on their faces. When she saw these photographs she understood why Miss Christie couldn't put hers there. . . . To smile so at a camera one had to be born to certain things – a big house with heavy

mahogany furniture and many rooms, fixed mealtimes, a mother and father who were married to each other and lived together in the same house, who would chastise and praise, who would send you to school with the proper clothes so you would look like, be like everyone else, fit neatly into the space Life had created for you.[42]

In the context of her grandparents' home, Laura clearly begins to internalize the values of the dominant society, even though the mould into which such a 'Life' should be allowed to settle only applies to a small minority of the Jamaican population. Her sense of differentiation from herself becomes more serious when her father returns home on a brief visit with his glamorous American wife to whom she compares her own mother: 'she was bitterly ashamed. Knowing the mother she had come from, it was no wonder, she thought, that her father could not acknowledge her'.[43] It is particularly telling that Laura says 'the mother she had come from', a neutral expression of biological fact, rather than 'my mother', which would have signalled an identification she is willing to claim. In the ultimate gesture of disavowal, her father, to whom she had pinned secret hopes of belonging, identifies her as 'bastard'. Yet the story does not end with this gesture of rejection but with Laura's long-awaited act of self-definition: 'by the time she got to the school gates she had made herself an orphan'.[44] The ambivalence of this ending, in which agency can only function to de-identify both parents and both cultures, registers the ambivalence of a divided and plural culture which can be theorized both as a problem and as a possibility for Caribbean subjects and subjectivities seeking belonging. However, the above stories which explore the body, particularly the 'body in between', as a barrier to belonging, are again not celebrations of a wonderfully postmodern dressing up box of performative selves, but rather narratives which reveal the way in which in (post) colonial cultures identities are often still inscribed and interpreted most strongly on the body.

The most extreme and grotesque portrait of a body on which signifiers and signifieds part company is that of Clarissa, a black servant in 'Zig Zag':

Clarissa would be dressed in satin and lace and frills and beading and sequins and furs and feathers, walking up and down in the sun so hot rivulets of sweat would run down the white powder caked on her face. She looked as if she herself would just melt away encased in all her finery, melt and leave the clothing to walk on down the road by itself. . . .[45]

The list of 'ands' gives a sense of the sad excess of this performance of white female identity, whilst the idea that she may vanish inside these garments is suggestive of a more serious notion of misfitting in which subjectivity is sacrificed in the 'passing' act. While Clarissa can mimic a European feminine identity in parts, she cannot capture the whole, and thus is fragmented at the level of subjectivity as well as appearance. These depictions of the body engaged in acts of cultural deception do draw attention to the control of colonial subjects through bodies via the strategies of self-loathing, self-denial and fear of the 'other'.

    In 'Lily, Lily' the female body as a site of oppression finds multiple articulations. For the first Lily, who had fed her imagination a diet of Eurocentric romance literature and consequently felt certain that 'one day this tall, dark, handsome stranger would come riding by, come ask for Lily, come take her away . . . to live happily ever after',[46] her conquest by Mr Pym from the P&T, who had all the visible signifiers of her imagined prince, seemed 'natural'. Lily leapt into his arms for one night and the next morning 'he rode off in a mist after promising to love, honour, cherish her for the rest of their lives'.[47] It is no surprise that as a woman it is Lily who must bear the consequences, just as she must bear the child. But the birth of little Lily is not the only effect which this encounter has upon her body. Revisiting her body after this episode Lily becomes aware of the darkness of her skin,

And she no longer felt beautiful, sharp and crisp with clean edges ready to slice through life but dirty, smudged, second rate. . . . And at that moment she couldn't figure out precisely whether she was suffering like this because she was a woman or because her skin was not white like Mr Pym's.[48]

Certainly Lily's confusion points to the particular vulnerability of a black woman in a colonial patriarchal culture. This vulnerability is underlined by the experiences of the younger Lily, whose 'light' body is an interesting object of racial and sexual imbrication, and who is sexually abused by her stepfather.

Taken together, the female voices of 'Lily, Lily' offer a catalogue of wrongs against women which are further echoed by other stories in which women are treated like commodities to be selected and traded at convenience.[49] However, while I do not disagree with Evelyn O'Callaghan's observation that 'Olive Senior's stories reveal the social and historical factors that sanction male tyranny in West Indian households', it is important to recognize that this is only a partial reading of how Senior's stories demonstrate an engagement with gender politics.[50] Many stories adopt the perspective of a male character and offer a significant and searching analysis of the damaging effect that ascribed gender identities have on boys and men. Emotional confinement and repression arrest Mr Barton's possibilities for human interaction in 'The View from the Terrace'; he is isolated by a damaging version of both masculinity and coloniality which prevent him from approaching the black woman by whom he is fascinated. While this same repression had wasted the life of Eric Johns in 'The Glass Bottom Boat' by tying him to a life unlived, he is temporarily released from his stasis as a 'jobsworth' and 'husband/father' by his affair with Miss Pearson. But even this illicit relationship is increasingly characterized by loss and limitations and he is only able to break out of his fixed position through violence. The tragic irony of this story lies in the fact that his destructive gestures of release actually further condemn him to the limited world of dominant masculinity.

Even in 'The Tenantry of Birds', which tells of a wife who is manipulated by a masculinist culture, and which is probably the story most easily interpreted by orthodox feminist thought, there is a strong awareness of the complexity of subject positions which makes any exploration of gender as the priority or sole marker of identity problematic. Although the main interest of the narrative lies in the unfolding relationship between Nolene and Philip, her academic-turned-political-activist husband, there is a long digressive flashback to Nolene's childhood and her visits to her aunt and uncle in the country, which were in sharp but enjoyable contrast to her urban life. Holidays allowed her space in which to know the country; along with the duppy stories and folk songs she learnt a love for the island and its life forms, an intimacy which her husband had never understood. She also, perhaps most importantly, gained an early insight into the problems of self-definition which this act of crossing between communities evoked:

Beside her cousins who were allowed to run wild and free, . . .
she felt herself restricted, as if she were not a person in herself
but a creation, an extension of her mother who even though
she was not there was nevertheless a presence which she could
not shake off long enough to express herself, to be.[51]

In her adulthood, acts of crossing remain difficult and Nolene
knows that she cannot be like the new black woman of the moment
that her husband desires. Unlike Philip's PA Jennifer, who 'drank
and smoked and swore, was loud and argumentative and could
hold her own with the best of the men',[52] she cannot undo the
effort and training which had so successfully made a proper
woman out of the protean girl. Despite their political awareness
there is little sisterhood from these new 'enlightened' women
who are critical of 'women like her, women who still wore their
nails long and polished, who still went dressed up to the super-
market, creamed their hair and refused to wrap their heads. . . .'[53]
The absence of female solidarity is most clearly demonstrated by
Jennifer's affair with Nolene's husband and her appropriation of
her home.

Although the story draws to its conclusion with Nolene's
discovery of this fact on a return visit to her Jamaican home, it
does not end with the neat retreat to Miami which Philip had
scripted for his wife. Rather, the final gesture is a classic feminist
moment in which self-determination is claimed: 'She sat there
thinking for a long long time, getting angrier and angrier, her
very anger hardening her . . . forcing her to focus on her very
self'.[54] Importantly though, the link between her empowerment
as a woman and her mobile cultural identity is made by the
projected vision of her garden restored to its 'natural' glory which
leads her to decide that '*He* could move out'.[55] The final reference
to her childhood game to scare away wasps would seem to confirm
that although she is saved financially by a gesture of 'sisterhood'
in which her mother insisted the house remained in Nolene's
name, she is actually 'saved' by her ability to connect with a
culture capable of sustaining her emotional and cultural selves.

In many ways this story responds well to a feminist reading,
but the overlapping of cultural politics and gender politics is crucial
to its meaning. Indeed, I would suggest that this attention to the
multiple imbrications of identity which are inflected by considerations of ethnicity, sexuality and economic status as well as

gender is crucial to Senior's writing as a whole. Her stories cannot be appropriated for feminist ends in any narrow way because they do not follow the tramlines of feminist metanarratives which can tend to theorize all oppression as patriarchal oppression, universalizing the concept of both oppression and patriarchy in ways which are unhelpful in a post-colonial context. It is this resistance to 'ready-made' narratives of post-colonialism and a Caribbean canon, as well as of feminism, that is perhaps the most interesting feature of Senior's work. Not only does she dismantle comforting metanarratives of conquest and oppression which offer too simplistic models of agency and identity, but she recuperates and re-evaluates lives which have been elided by these totalizing accounts.

However, Senior does not only ask us to rethink questions of agency and identity in relation to the Caribbean subjects of her stories, she demands that, as readers, we become agents in this project. The withdrawal from closure of so many of Senior's stories can usefully be interpreted within the current intellectual climate of post-structuralist theory in which the illusory and oppressive nature of closure has been explored, a proposition of particular significance to writing in the Caribbean which has been inscribed and totalized by the closed narratives of those who conquered. However, this refusal to fix meaning from within is also a testimony to the oral tradition with which Senior is actively engaged in all her creative writing projects.

In conclusion, I want to turn to the question of agency in relation to Senior's status as a Caribbean woman writer. In his essay 'Black Art and the Burden of Representation', Kobena Mercer has suggested that writers from a minority group are 'burdened with the impossible task of speaking as "representatives", in that they are widely expected to "speak for" the marginalized communities from which they come'.[56] I believe that it is important to an understanding of Senior's works to appreciate how she both accepts and rejects this burden. It is certainly true that she does speak for her rural Jamaican community, and yet her stories do not at all play into the agendas of representation which Mercer implies above and elaborates in his discussion of the problems of 'speaking on behalf of a supposedly homogenous and monolithic community'.[57] Indeed, as I have attempted to outline, Senior's stories refute the ready-made narratives which have been generated by certain post-colonial theories and other Caribbean writers whose works have become institutionalized, as well as those of the more obvious colonial discourse in order to represent 'the voices of the formerly colonized writing out of the fullness of their lives, not just to [post-colonial readers] but to each other, and . . . in roles other than that of [the] colonized'.[58] As a consequence, in Senior's stories unstable identities can be both painful and enabling, men can be both oppressive and repressed, resistance can be unseen, and agency can take the form of collusion. The short fiction of Olive Senior offers us a culture of crossings and of complexities in which the often fragile and cusping identities of those who do not belong to society's designated categories can still be accommodated.

Notes

1. O. Senior, 'Colonial Girls School' in *Talking of Trees* (Kingston: Calabash, 1985) p. 26.
2. C. Rowell, 'An Interview with Olive Senior', *Callaloo*, 11:3 (1988) 486.
3. O. Senior, *Summer Lightning* (Harlow, Essex: Longman, 1986) p. 86.
4. Ibid., p. 99.
5. Ibid., p. 11.
6. Ibid., p. 15.
7. Ibid.
8. F. Jameson, 'Third World Literature in an Era of Multinational Capitalism', *Social Text*, 15 (1986) 65–88. For examples of Jameson's 'national allegories' see George Lamming's *In the Castle of My Skin* (1953), Geoffrey Drayton's *Christopher* (1959) and V.S. Naipaul's *A House for Mr Biswas* (1961).
9. O. Senior, *Summer Lightning*, p. 82.
10. Ibid., p. 84.
11. E. Brodber, *Perceptions of Caribbean Women; Towards a Documentation of Stereotypes* (Barbados: ISER, 1982) p. 32. in E. O'Callaghan, *Woman Version: Theoretical Approaches to West Indian Fiction by Women* (London: Macmillan, 1993).
12. O. Senior, *Summer Lighting*, p. 67.
13. Ibid., p. 70.
14. One of the stories which emerges through this tale is that of the old-time white people who 'were more like the black people than Parson Bedlow because they were out in the sun all day and burnt brown and drank rum and coffee and smoked jackass rope and cussed bad words worse than the black people. And they worked hard too, even the white women. . . . These old-time white people didn't eat much better than the slaves and didn't act much better either, but they didn't treat them badly' (*Arrival of the Snake-Woman* p. 12). This

account raises a question mark over dominant and simplistic conceptions which simply set up oppositions between colonizer and colonized and draws attention to the way in which these binarisms deny the complexity of human relationships.

15. O. Senior, *Arrival of the Snake-Woman* (Harlow, Essex: Longman, 1989) pp. 6–7.
16. Ibid., p. 10.
17. Ibid., p. 38.
18. Ibid., p. 43.
19. 'Zig Zag' in *Discerner of Hearts* might have been such a story if it had focused on Muffet rather than on Sadie.
20. O. Senior, *Summer Lightning*, p. 26.
21. Ibid., p. 29.
22. Ibid., p. 30.
23. Ibid., p. 33.
24. O. Senior, *Discerner of Hearts* (Toronto: McClelland and Stewart Inc., 1995) p. 42.
25. 'Migrations of the subject' is the subtitle of Carole Boyce Davies's book *Black Women, Writing and Identity* (London: Routledge, 1994).
26. O. Senior, *Arrival of the Snake-Woman*, p. 44.
27. R. Patteson, 'The Fiction of Olive Senior: Traditional Society and the Wider World', *Ariel*, 24 (1993) p. 18.
28. O. Senior, *Arrival of the Snake-Woman*, p. 64.
29. Ibid.
30. Ibid., p. 67.
31. Ibid., p. 71.
32. Ibid., p. 75.
33. Ibid., p. 73.
34. C. Boyce Davies and E. Savory Fido (eds), 'Introduction' in *Out of the Kumbla: Caribbean Women and Literature* (Trenton, New Jersey: Africa World Press, 1990) p. 16.
35. M. Hodge, 'Challenges of the Struggle for Sovereignty' in S. Cudjoe (ed.), *Caribbean Women Writers* (Massachusetts: Calaloux, 1990) pp. 202–8, p. 205.
36. O. Senior, *Arrival of the Snake-Woman*, p. 114.
37. O. Senior, *Summer Lightning*, p. 111.
38. The references to sewing and jam-making as suitable occupations for young women can be traced back to colonial projects which sought to socialize Jamaican women. In 1865 (significantly, the year of the Morant Bay rebellion) the Lady Musgrave Self-Help Society of Jamaica was founded with the aim to cultivate these 'feminine industries', thus shifting female economic independence into the arena of prescribed Eurocentric femininity. This society was part of a zealously pursued moral mission through which Jamaica's colonial apparatus sought to preserve and promote a sense of female duty and feminine sensibility (most commonly associated with the Victorian notion of womanhood). Efforts continued into the twentieth century with the Social Purity Association of 1917, and the Women's Social Service Club of 1918 with its attempt to 'uplift womanhood' within 'the

parameters of domesticity, morality and class-boundedness' (Reddock, 1990, p. 65). Although nominally women's organizations, these societies were in no way women-centred but were rather directed at the marginalization of women within the patriarchally organized public life of Jamaica. For a detailed account see Rhoda Reddock, 'Feminism, Nationalism and the Early Women's Movement in the English Speaking Caribbean' in S. Cudjoe (ed.) (1990) pp. 61–81.
39. O. Senior, *Arrival of the Snake-Woman*, pp. 44–5.
40. O. Senior, *Summer Lightning*, p. 39.
41. Ibid., p. 42 (emphasis mine).
42. Ibid., pp. 36–7.
43. Ibid., p. 52.
44. Ibid., p. 53.
45. O. Senior, *Discerner of Hearts*, p. 170.
46. O. Senior, *Arrival of the Snake-Woman*, p. 124.
47. Ibid., p. 125.
48. Ibid., p. 127.
49. See 'Arrival of the Snake-Woman', 'The View from the Terrace', 'The Tenantry of Birds' and 'You Think I Mad, Miss?' for examples of the commodification of women.
50. E. O'Callaghan, *Woman Version: Theoretical Approaches to West Indian Fiction by Women* (London: Macmillan, 1993) p. 5.
51. O. Senior, *Arrival of the Snake-Woman*, p. 50.
52. Ibid., p. 55.
53. Ibid., p. 56.
54. Ibid., p. 61.
55. Ibid.
56. K. Mercer's 'Black Art and the Burden of Representation' in *Welcome to the Jungle* (London: Routledge, 1994) pp. 233–58, p. 235.
57. Ibid., p. 248.
58. D. Brydon, 'New Approaches to the New Literatures in English: Are We in Danger of Incorporating Disparity?' in Hena Maes-Jelinek, Kirsten Holst Peterson and Anna Rutherford (eds), *A Shaping of Connections* (Coventry: Dangaroo, 1989) p. 89.

Bibliography

Mercer, K. *Welcome to the Jungle*. London: Routledge, 1994.
O'Callaghan, E. *Woman Version: Theoretical Approaches to West Indian Fiction by Women*. London: Macmillan, 1993.
Patteson, R. 'The Fiction of Olive Senior: Traditional Society and the Wider World', *Ariel*, 24:1 (1993) 13–33.
Pollard, V. 'Mothertongue Voices in the Writing of Olive Senior and Lorna Goodison' in S. Nasta (ed.). *Motherlands: Black Women's Writing from Africa, the Caribbean and South Asia*. London: Women's Press, 1991.
Rowell, C. 'An Interview with Olive Senior', *Callaloo*, 11, 3 (1988) 480–90.

Senior, O. *Summer Lightning*. Harlow, Essex: Longman, 1986.
—. *Arrival of the Snake-Woman*. Harlow, Essex: Longman, 1989.
—. *Discerner of Hearts*. Toronto: McClelland and Stewart, 1995.
Thieme, J. 'Mixed Worlds: Olive Senior's *Summer Lightning*', *Kunapipi*, XVI, 2 (1994) 90–5.

9

Pauline Melville's Shape-Shifting Fictions

Sarah Lawson Welsh

Cross-cultural texts of such societies as Guyana ... continually inscribe difference and transformation on landscape and on human form, literally ... in the features and voices of man, woman and child.[1]

Gareth Griffiths

The trickster. The effect of a command and the effect of transformation meet within him, and the essence of freedom can be gleaned from him as from no other human figure ... he shakes everyone off, he destroys custom, obedience ... he can talk to all creatures and things. He ... is bent purely on his own transformations.... He imitates everything badly, cannot orient himself anywhere, asks only false questions.... He is the forerunner of the fool and he will always interest people. However, his experiences have to remain incoherent. Every inner sequence, every connection would make them meaningful and would rob them of their value, i.e. their freedom.[2]

Elias Canetti

The 'shape-shifter' of the title of Melville's first collection of short stories is glossed in two epigraphs to the collection: one describes the shape-shifter as someone who is able to 'conjure up as many different figures and manifestations as the sea has waves': the other, more specifically, refers to the belief that the 'shaman or medicine-man of the Indians of Guiana, to whom nothing is impossible, can effect transformation of himself or others'. The first epigraph is attributed only to an 'Unknown poet' and the second to Walter Roth's anthropological study, *Enquiry into the Animism and Folklore of the Guiana Indians* (1909). In this way, Melville links the general and the particular, the timeless, cross-cultural archetype and a specifically Guyanese, Amerindian inflection of the concept of shape-shifting, in an introduction to her own work. More importantly, the two epigraphs encourage the composite identification of the writer, artist and magician with the shaman. However, as the narrator of 'The Truth is in the Clothes' warns, 'the gifts of the genuine shaman overlap in places with the psychological wizardry of the charlatan',[3] and true shape-shifting may be confused with the slipperiness of the 'confidence trickster'.[4] The epigraphs also challenge or blur the conceptual boundaries between the natural and the supernatural, the artist and audience, the magician's agency and the effects of magic, and are the first instance in Melville's short story collection of the deliberate juxtaposition of different points of view in order to encourage multiple readings of the same event or phenomenon, and a concomitant questioning of the assumptions, categories and oppositions upon which 'orthodox' explanations are based.

This sense of contesting explanations which act to undermine any single dominant interpretation and defer any final reading, is particularly apparent in the differing interpretations and belief systems of characters in 'The Conversion of Millicent Vernon'. In this tale Mrs Vernon's Catholicism, the Obeah practices of Mr Evans and the 'Indian Obeah man' whom Mrs Singh visits, as well as Millicent's own pantheistic belief in the Congo pump tree, are all depicted. Indeed, the overlapping bells of the Lutheran and Anglican Church which are joined by the chimes of the Catholic Church 'intermingling with them and confusing the difference',[5] not only encapsulate, in microcosm, the process of racial and cultural creolization in Guyana, but also suggest a theoretical paradigm for the reading of Melville's short stories. 'Overlapping' and 'intermingling' are central to these works, which deliberately seek to blur boundaries and 'confuse differences'. As will be demonstrated, such multiple readings are suggested in most of the stories, including 'I Do Not Take Messages from Dead People', 'The Girl with the Celestial Limb', 'The Truth is in the Clothes' and especially 'You Left the Door Open'. In this way, as O'Callaghan has noted:

Melville prevents us from taking anything for granted. With Kincaid and Brodber, she blurs the boundaries of time and space and narrative centrality [especially in stories such as 'You Left the Door Open', 'The Truth is in the Clothes' and 'Eat Labba and Drink Creek Water'.]. More importantly, she deconstructs the easy adversarial status that too often informs political rhetoric. The story 'You Left the Door Open' complicates the superficial binarism of aggressive male versus passive female victim in a chilling account of paranormal rape (by whom/of whom?). And in 'The Conversion of Millicent Vernon', racial distinctions and the hostilities they engender are subverted by reference to the 'genetic kaleidoscope' that results from racial mixing in the West Indies, so that with each generation 'a greater variety of ghosts appeared, sometimes as many as four or five mischievously occupying one body.'[6]

As the epigraphs suggest, *Shape-shifter* is a collection which deliberately crosses 'borders', moving between different age-groups, ethnicities, cultures and genders, and between different spaces, times and worlds in order to challenge received boundary demarcations and to unsettle certain assumptions. That this is Melville's main fictional agenda is strongly intimated in her own suggestion that her Guyanese background and mixed-race ancestry make her ideally suited to 'breaking down preconceptions, stirring up doubt, rattling judgements, shifting boundaries and unfixing fixities.'[7] Melville has spoken of her own shape-shifting as not only relating to her background but also to her fictional strategy of refusing to write from one particular point of view.[8] Indeed, as O'Callaghan observes, *Shape-shifter* can be read as correspondingly positing 'a concept of the writer/reader/character as a site of multiple and heterogenous "subject-positions", emphasizing not so much . . . [discrete positionalities] but "the fluid boundaries and continual commerce between them".'[9]

In an autobiographical essay Melville draws attention to the shape-shifter as trickster figure, one who deliberately deceives by changing his appearance:

There is a Yoruba folktale of a trickster god who loves to cause strife. He walks down the main street of a village wearing a hat that is red on one side and blue on the other. When he has passed, the people on one side of the street say "Did you see that god with the blue hat go by?" The people on the other side reply: "That hat was red . . ." and they fall to fighting and fisticuffs and interminable arguments while the god continues on his way, laughing.

She supplements this observation with an autobiographical note:

> I also cause confusion. I look completely English. My mother is English . . . from a London family, a tribe of Anglo-Saxons if ever there was one, blonde and blue-eyed. The photographs show St Augustine's angels in hand-me-down-clothes. My father was born in Guyana. . . . The photographs show a genetic bouquet of African, Amerindian and European features, a family gazing out from dark, watchful eyes – all except one, who turned out with the looks of a Dutchman. But then, Berbice, their birthplace, was a Dutch colony in the eighteenth century. I am the whitey in the woodpile. The trickster god now appears in another guise. He has donned the scientific mantle of genetics.[10]

Clearly then, 'the term shape-shifter applies as well to [Melville] as it does to the twelve short stories in her collection . . . Melville is just as hard to place.'[11] Born in London, brought up in Guyana, Melville has spoken of feeling connected to both Britain and the Caribbean, as the narrator of 'Eat Labba and Drink Creek Water' describes. Like 'the ambivalent Anancy figure who may be god or trickster',[12] Melville herself eludes simple definitions of racial and cultural identity by occupying an ambivalent positioning between a 'white present [and a] black past'.[13] As the protagonist of the loosely autobiographical 'Eat Labba and Drink Creek Water' is reminded, appearances can be deceptive: '"Just because you've got white skin and blue eyes you think you haven't got coloured blood in you"'.[14] In this way Melville foregrounds the need to disrupt a politics of identity based on the assumption of an easy equation between phenotype (the way genetic make-up is expressed physically) and genotype (the genetic composition of an individual), a confluence between the visible and the invisible, what she has termed the 'interior' as opposed to the exterior 'landscape' of an individual.[15] The result is a more complex and fluidly defined sense of 'all the multiple influences that go to build up an identity',[16] one which recognizes the self as inhabited by various traces of the ancestor and 'previous belongings', but which is equally importantly cross-mapped, as in the stories, by dream, fantasy and the imagination.

Although Melville claims she did not deliberately set out to show the complexity of Guyana's cultural and ethnic mix in her collection,[17] in many ways the social complexity of Guyana, its pronounced genetic hybridity, unique matrix of mythologies and histories and its particular 'geo-psyche'[18] of coastal 'exterior' versus unmapped 'interior' (another inflection of the visible and the invisible) are paradigmatic of the complexity of Melville's fictional stance, just as they are of that of her fellow Guyanese writer Wilson Harris, with whom her writing is often linked. Like Harris, Melville's foregrounding of the imagination as 'effortlessly trans-national, trans-racial, trans-gender, trans-species',[19] and her be-lief in its creative, transformative potential 'where boundaries are crossed and hybrids fertilized . . . where everything is possible . . . where things can begin to change',[20] proceeds from experience of the complex social reality of Guyana.

Like Harris, Melville acknowledges the tremendous creative potentialities of taking this hybridized society, with its complex history of overlapping ancestral presences, as in 'Eat Labba and Drink Creek Water', as the basis of an aesthetic model for a fiction which is similarly syncretic, multiple, overlapping, constantly contesting simple categories or oppositions such as time and space, life and death, the natural and the supernatural. It is a fiction in a constant process of revision – or in Harris' terms, 'infinite rehearsal', a fiction which revisits itself to consume its own bi-ases. Certainly, some of the individual stories of *Shape-shifter* work in a similar way to Harris' more intricate and extended fictions, reading and revising each other, returning to the tropes and themes of earlier fragments in a process of continual transformation. Thus, for example, a concern with clothes as mobile (and frequently deceptive) signifiers is established early on in the collection and successive stories read and reread the signifieds attached to cloth-ing. Shakespeare McNab's female impersonation in the first story, dressed in his grandmother's clothes, is thus re-read by Mrs Parrish's similar imitation of poverty in order to extort money and favours from her neighbours in 'About That Two Pounds, Mrs Parrish'; similarly, the attribution of supernatural and magical powers (as well as mythical status) to clothing as foregrounded in the King of Rags in 'The Iron and the Radio Have Gone' is taken up and expanded by a later story, 'The Truth is in the Clothes' which focuses on Maisie, a mysterious clothes designer. In this way, Melville's fiction is an example of what her fellow

Guyanese writer Grace Nichols has described as the impulse 'to keep on creating and reshaping'.[21]

Linked to this strategy is Melville's shared fascination with carnival as fictional trope – the 'riot of the imagination' as a formal dynamic:

> Pinning down my identity is not what interests me most about life. I enjoy Carnival because anybody can take on any form: an Egyptian goddess; a Mabaruma warrior; a sultan; a demon; a frog. Race, gender, class, species and divinity are all in the melting-pot, and I am a champion of mixtures and hybrids. Carnival plays with identity. It is a masquerade where disguise is the only truth.... Death comes in the guise of uniformity, mono-cultural purity, the externals of the state as opposed to the riot of the imagination.[22]

In Melville's case this fictional interest in carnival role-playing and other forms of masking, camouflage, disguise, impersonation and imposture which reveal alternative or hidden truths (as in 'The Truth is in the Clothes', 'You Left the Door Open' and 'I Do Not Take Messages from Dead People'), is also extended into her professional life; as an actress she is also a shape-shifter of sorts. The positive benefits of this trickster-like ability to role-play flexibly, to take on different disguises, is also implicit in her comments on the advantages of being 'hard to place', shape-shifting between different categories (black, white, Guyanese, British) – none of which can contain her: 'Perhaps I am the joker in the pack, able to turn up as any card.'[23] Here the 'joker figure' is not only adaptable but also potentially subversive of received categories and thus is an appropriate image for Melville's background, her acting profession and the strategies of her fiction.

Shakespeare NcNab, the protagonist of the first story in the collection, 'I Do Not Take Messages from Dead People', aspires to be the Vice-President's official biographer and so belongs to a long line of West Indian fictional characters who are aspiring writers of different kinds.[24] All fantasize about their literary prowess and accomplishments, most in sharp contrast to the rather more banal and strictly pecuniary function of their actual writing activities (McNab has a regular radio-slot telling, or rather retelling, proverbs and folktales). Similarly, he is satirized for his flights of fancy and self-inflated aspirations. Despite Shakespeare McNab's illustrious name, given to him in the hope of redeeming a child who '"don' look so bright . . . [or] pretty either"',[25] it is thus apposite that McNab merely pretends to read and study the papers from his briefcase; his talent is one of mimicry, although of a different type from Biswas' 'colonial mimicry'. Like the eponymous protagonist of Selvon's *Moses Ascending*, McNab is obsessed with accuracy in his use of words, but, despite this, he is quite spectacularly out of control with regard to his narrative; in both cases the subversive effect of the narrative (Moses' Memoirs and McNab's Anancy story with its unforeseen allegorical dimension directly relating to the Vice-President's murder of his wife) is largely unconscious and unintentional.

Here, as in all of Melville's stories, the Vice-President is characterized economically yet evocatively, his 'sullenness' holding the 'gravitational density of an imploding star'.[26] Just as the celestial imagery will be reiterated throughout *Shape-shifter*, along with a number of other recurrent motifs, so the story itself resonates with the tropes of camouflage: McNab's boss in 'camouflage jacket was a special sort of hypocrite',[27] the Vice-President is trying to cover up his corrupt and murderous activities and McNab himself will resort to cross-dressing in his grandmother's clothes in order to appear as the supernatural presence La Diablesse in a cunning ploy to regain his position and the Vice-President's favour.

The allegorical resonances of the story of Anancy outwitting Hog, which McNab tells on air, derive from more than the overlapping of Vice-President Hogg and the character Hog in the tale (later to be surreally reiterated in McNab's dream of the bulky Hogg metamorphosed into an amorphous dark mass emerging from the sea). The grimacing features of McNab after the President strikes him are directly echoed in his description of Anancy, thus linking McNab directly with this archetypal shape-shifter, trickster and impersonator of West African and Caribbean oral traditions. Whereas Anancy swaps clothes with Hog's wife in order to escape being eaten by Hog, McNab volunteers to cross-dress in his grandmother's clothes in order to first frighten and then protect the Vice-President in an attempt to regain his lost position.

This is a tactic which his grandmother strongly warns against. Death, which intrudes in one guise or another into all of the stories in *Shape-shifter*, has already been explicitly linked with eating: the Vice-President's wife is poisoned at a State banquet, Anancy is in fear of being eaten by Hog at his grand feast and

McNab's folktale programme is ironically replaced by a recipe programme. The warning thus acts as a final ominous reiteration of this link, an intimation of death as another kind of 'consumption'.

The allegorical resonances of this tale within the tale point to the possibilities of multiple or at least alternative ways of reading and of making sense of events, and more importantly, the need to be a 'discriminating' and flexible reader of all narratives, including the all-important 'social text' in order to survive. Ironically, although the President has been able to read the Anancy story allegorically, and despite apparent evidence of his susceptibility to superstition, he fails to recognize the ominous folkloric figure of La Diablesse; instead he reads Mcnab's impersonation of the supernatural Diablesse figure as his dead wife come back to haunt him. In both cases, McNab experiences a lack of control over the hermeneutic process as others interpret the narratives he spins in unsuspected and alternative ways. In this way, Melville provides an instructive gloss on Michael Dash's observation that 'In order to survive, the Caribbean sensibility must spontaneously decipher and interpret the sign systems of those who wish to dominate and control.'[28] McNab's growing awareness of this lack of control over the interpretation of the narratives he constructs and re-constructs is manifest in his growing paranoid suspicion that he has been targeted for surveillance by a group of Afro-Guyanese hitmen. This has the effect of silencing his own response to the narratives of others, for example his friend Denzil's parallel and equally subversive tale within the tale of the Vice-President and the statue of the heroic slave Cuffy. Only his grandmother's reading of events, 'Leave the country', remains consistent throughout, although it too may admit multiple interpretations, as an ominously re-inflected version of the familiar paradigm of exile in West Indian texts. The story ends with an ambivalent and unsettling sense of her awareness of the constant vulnerability of the trickster figure, especially in moments of triumph or pride, which is juxtaposed with McNab's much more limited sense of renewed security and power.

'I Do Not Take Messages from Dead People' can be viewed as merely the first in a series of stories which delight in multiple signification and which 'keep alternative readings available'.[29] This flexibility and plurality is to be found both within individual stories and within the collection as a whole. Each story refuses formal closure or containment and is open to the overlapping cross-mappings of other stories in the collection.

The second story, 'The Iron and the Radio Have Gone' is an instructive parable on the deadly sin of pride and the devastating awakening to her own racial prejudices of one Molly Summers, a white Quaker schoolteacher who visits Guyana. Like the 'Quaker Lady' in James Berry's poem 'On an Afternoon Train from Victoria to Purley, 1955',[30] Molly prides herself on the involvement of the Quaker movement in the anti-slavery struggle and energetically applies herself to present day liberal causes. However she is blind to the possible biases of following 'its one god so pale and subdued . . . that he barely existed'[31] (to be echoed in the descriptions of Christ in the Catholic Vernon household in 'The Conversion of Millicent Vernon').

Arriving in New Amsterdam, Molly sees the town in fairy-tale or picture postcard terms. Yet even in the details of her first impressions of Georgetown's night-time beauty, intimations of Anancy-like deceptive appearances are to be found: the foliage of the royal palms seems like a 'spider dancing on a stick'.[32] In the morning, a very different, defamiliarized city 'smil[es] at her with rotting teeth'[33]. Appropriately, then, for one feeling 'all at sea', the timbered veranda of her host's house gives her the sensation of the 'deck of a huge white ship . . ., [significantly] going nowhere',[34] and further images of shortage, stagnation, stasis, and ultimately death proliferate in this story.

Melville cleverly locates Molly in a longer tradition of fictional and non-fictional interlopers from Europe in the Caribbean by making her feel a disorientating unreality '[o]ne of these two countries [England and Guyana] is imaginary. . . . And I think it is this one'.[35] Molly is clearly no Antoinette Cosway,[36] as the bathetic linking of her 'unreality' with an inability to imagine the Finsbury Park shoe-shop where she recently bought her sandals makes clear. However, she suffers a similar sense of 'terrified consciousness'[37] and psychic dislocation in the Caribbean; she is similarly unable to connect her interior and exterior 'landscapes', England and the Caribbean, other than in the images of incipient madness and death with which the story ends and which provide another permutation of 'confusing the difference' in this collection.

Other intertextual traces also appear in this story. The Rasta 'King of Rags' on the streets who looks like a 'walking tree'[38] echoes McNab's disguise in the first story, just as Molly's impression of the 'English beggar' at the car window as 'enormous. His head eclipsed the sun'[39] suggests a grotesque of epic proportions parallel to that of McNab's nightmarish vision of Hogg as a black amorphous shape rising from the sea. The 'fluttering scraps of material'[40] in which the 'King of Rags' is dressed echo the Harlequin man of Conrad's *Heart of Darkness*, and his namesake in Harris' *The Tree of the Sun* (1978), with a similar suggestion of the 'wise fool', and the 'Idiot nameless' narrators of *The Eye of the Scarecrow* (1965) and *Companions of the Day and Night* (1975) – all important permutations of the trickster. As in Harris's novels this figure suggests 'that an alternative world imperfectly understood may actually be in control – the realm of the King of the Rags, a scarecrow figure with supernatural powers.'[41] He is also linked with other characters in *Shape-shifter* who seem to possess supernatural powers, including Mr Evans the Obeah man of 'The Conversion of Millicent Vernon', Maisie in 'The Truth is in the Clothes' and Dr Bartholomew in 'About That Two Pounds, Mrs Parrish'.

Although the carefully depicted social milieu of 'The Iron and the Radio Have Gone' makes it superficially closest to the final story, also set in Guyana and bridging Britain and the Caribbean, other stories in the collection are also anticipated here: Donella announces that '"Someone climbed in through the window"'[42] to steal the iron and the radio, thus prefiguring the much more troubling 'break-in' of 'You Left the Door Open'. Molly's momentary reflection on the link between the 'history of the place'[43] and some of the actions of its present inhabitants also anticipates McGregor's similarly imprisoning sense of the dynamics of black-white relations in 'McGregor's Journey'. The snapshots of damaging diasporic experiences prepare us for those of Winsome in 'A Disguised Land'. Molly's paralysed response to the 'endless . . . blue sky'[44] is to be reiterated in a different way at the opening of 'The Girl with the Celestial Limb'. Finally, Molly's sense of having been 'tricked'[45] (by the people, by appearances? by her own assumptions about herself?) will be played out in a variety of ways in 'About that Two Pounds, Mrs Parrish', 'A Disguised Land', 'The Truth is in the Clothes' and 'You Left the Door Open'.

Again, character is delineated with succinct, pithy images which act as a kind of shorthand for the reader. Molly is introduced as a 'plump white woman with a necklace of mosquito bites'[46] and, with an echo of her colonial forebears, a 'neat helmet of iron grey hair',[47] and her Guyanese host Donella is a 'stick insect' in a kimono. Melville's eye for the hypocrisies and fine lies which oil this society are much in evidence in this story. As Molly's double vision of the city suggests, it is characterized by a series of dualities, or rather duplicities, even down to the operation of its black market economy. Thus Donella's disdain for English people's lack of personal hygiene is juxtaposed with her slavish retention of the English intonation, class distinctions and social mores she acquired during her years as a diplomat's daughter in England, neatly illustrated by her retention of old issues of *Harper's Magazine* and *Tatler*. Her sloppy table-manners are in contrast to her high social pretensions; she rails about the constant shortages in Guyana despite wearing expensive clothes and employing a servant: her hypocrisy and material, emotional and spiritual meanness is tellingly revealed not only in her sparse frame but also in her habit of tearing up paper napkins to make them last. Indeed, Donella's acquaintances and 'business associates', who provide access to various black-market goods, are linked in the final pages of the story with the images of vultures greedily circling carrion; not only do they prefigure Molly's death but also, implicitly, the chronically unhealthy state of the society. Ironically, however, literal carrion is unwelcome to these characters when death intrudes into the story: '"Blast it," thought Ralph. "Don' tell me the woman has come all the way over here just to die in the back of my car"'.[48]

The lack of connection between different worlds as experienced by Molly is also explored in some of the stories set in London. In 'A Disguised Land' the roles are reversed, with a black Jamaican character, Winsome, feeling alienated in England. Like Shakespeare McNab and other characters in *Shape-shifter*, Winsome experiences ominous prophetic dreams involving death, and the dreamlike sense of disguised meaning is extended across the whole story as she struggles to 'read' the English and their signs. Nowhere is this sense of concealment and disguise stronger than in the courtroom where Winsome is tried for shoplifting, her own brand of deception. In an ingenious twist of the trope of magic which runs through the collection, Winsome's Rasta friend Levi warns her to

'watch yuhself in some of dem courts. . . . They gat certain magic writings on the walls to do harm to black people. . . . Babylon writings.'[49]

The 'writings on the walls' which are to be echoed, along with the theme of harm by supernatural means, in 'The Truth is in the Clothes', turns out to be a defamiliarized description of the Latin inscriptions on the Courtroom crests, signifying, for Levi at least, the exclusivity and ancient powers of white authority.

Winsome's initial sense, in her dream, of the kindness of the English being merely the veneer of a more treacherous reality is reiterated in those who attend her during and after her trial. Only the black cleaner, who enters the sterile 'whiteness' of Winsome's hospital cubicle in prison (later to be echoed in the harsh lights of the television studio and her prison cell), is able to disrupt the whiteness which, like its metonym, the crest in the courtroom, 'hurt her eyes'.[50] The domestic is able to present Winsome with an alternative reading of her immediate post-natal predicament, one which is grounded in a more accessible history of personal memory and which is powerfully affirmative in connecting Winsome to a black, female, Caribbean experience: '"Me mudda had me in de carner of a canefield and she was back at work a few hours later . . ."'.[51] The '"good . . . red blood"' which the cleaner contrasts with the '"pale . . . weak and sarta watery"'[52] blood of white women, echoes the picture of a pale-looking Christ in 'The Conversion of Millicent Vernon' and prepares for the culturally specific simile of the 'spreading scarlet stain [of Winsome's blood on the bedclothes] . . . like the poinciana tree in her grandmother's yard'.[53] In this way, blood and bloodlines are stressed in a passage which suggests the need for generational, gendered and cultural connection and continuity.

Significantly, in Winsome's final dream she is being buried in 'unfamiliar countryside'[54] which may be Jamaican. This cultural amnesia, specifically the erosion of native language, links Winsome's journeying to England and the subsequent severing of connections with Jamaica, with that of the Middle Passage and slavery. As in 'McGregor's Journey', a particular history resurges in the casual comments of the production assistant on the plan to return Winsome to prison: '" . . . I feel awful . . . as if I'd captured a runaway slave . . ."'.[55] In many ways, 'A Disguised Land' is indeed a modern slave narrative, one which recognizes the need to voice silenced narratives, '"You must get 'pon de television and mek dem see what these people dem a do to you"'[56] but also the problematics of doing so and the enormity of the process of negotiating power in a society where power is still overwhelmingly in white hands. Appositely then, in a direct inversion of the ending of the slave narrative, Winsome ends the story, not free but literally in captivity, constrained as much by societal structures as by the prison walls. 'A Disguised Land' acts to 'make the invisible visible' in a highly significant way, by mapping on to the more 'visible' white fictions of 'Britishness' a defamiliarizing counter-narrative of the relatively hidden fictional terrain of the black diasporic experience.

This theme of the difficulties of connection between different groups and the lack of 'connectedness' is also explored in 'McGregor's Journey',[57] which makes explicit use of myth[58] in fusing the Celtic myth of Angus the Wanderer and the ancient Greek myth of Orpheus travelling the underworld in search of Eurydice. Just as Orpheus desires to 'connect' with his lost love Eurydice, so the drunken scaffolder, McGregor yearns for genuine connection with a 'real bit of humanity',[59] quitting his job to embark on his own personal odyssey through a parallel 'underworld' of London pubs, buses and the London Underground. McGregor's epic struggle is in large part against the closing down of life's possibilities and the 'closedness' of other people to each other. Images of closure, including the ultimate closure of death, abound in the story, but are held in tension with the anarchic life-force and regenerative potential of McGregor himself. Thus, his quitting his job to go drinking is both a closure and a beginning of sorts.

McGregor's encounter with closure and death in life takes various forms: the pensioner with whom he converses in the pub, 'close[s] up in the darkness like a flower in the night'[60] and McGregor takes on another mythical mantle, that of Sisyphus 'pushing an enormous boulder uphill'[61] in an attempt to raise the spirits of a young man who can only see the closing down of prospects for his new-born son in contemporary British society. However, it is amongst the living dead of Melville's own version of the 'unreal city' on the '"travelling hearse"'[62] of the bus, that the contradictory pull between death and life is manifested most strikingly. On the one hand McGregor's quest is gently mocked; on the other, he is seen to undergo a dramatic transformation which is described in evolutionary as well as mythical terms. Thus the story provides another instance of multiple views on the same phenomena, the blurring of different kinds of discourse, here the scientific and mythological. Not only did nineteenth-century theories of evolution originally occupy a distinctly 'borderline' status in relation to orthodox religion as well as science (contesting the primacy of Creationist narratives and the categories of knowledge upon which they were based) but they also posited another highly contentious variant of 'shape-shifting' over longer periods of time: the evolution of different species over millions of years. Thus it is highly appropriate that McGregor awakes as if from a primeval sludge, his face mud-streaked. This sense of rebirth or miraculous resurrection cuts across both Christian and pagan myth and McGregor's subsequent metamorphosis into a tree invokes both the 'green man' of European pagan myth and classical metamorphoses such as Daphne, turned by the gods into a laurel tree,[63] Acteon turned into a stag and the archetypal shapeshifter of Greek mythology, Triton.

Melville has spoken of this story as dealing in part with the difficulties of black and white working class communities in Britain,[64] and with the things which divide them. This 'difficult' connection is most clearly manifested in the epiphany of McGregor's joyful dance with the black woman on the underground concourse, a moment of tentative but genuine and mutual 'connection' which is prematurely foreclosed by McGregor's sense of unease and the guard's advice that:

'Them could jus' get hold of the wrong end of the stick . . . [and] think "Here is another white man who think he own a black woman like all through history."'[65]

Here, the imprisoning modes of white-black relations determined by a history of slavery and colonialism are re-invoked in the context of a new politics of confrontation, one whose divisions are arguably just as destructive as the psychological legacies of which McGregor is here made aware. The instruction to Orpheus not to look back becomes an altogether more ambivalent one, resonant in multiple ways in relation to 'What the guard had said about history and white men',[66] the closing down of possibilities for 'dialogue' with history and new modes of relation, of human connection.

The sense of a hidden or subterranean realm as a kind of parallel or overlapping dimension which is merely hinted at in 'McGregor's Journey' becomes much more central in the slippage of time and space at the end of the occult tale 'The Truth is in the Clothes' and in the paranormal happenings and the strange synchronicity of 'You Left the Door Open'. Significantly, Maisie, the enigmatic subject of 'The Truth is in the Clothes' has a voice as 'low and sweet as an underground river'[67] and her true identity is just as hidden, gifted as she is in the art of disguise. The equation between artist and sorcerer or shaman figure, invoked in the epigraphs to *Shape-shifter*, takes its most literal form in Maisie, a dress designer travelling with a band of Sowetan musicians, who claims her clothes can shape lives.

Despite the retrospective certitude of the narrator at the opening of the story that Maisie is a 'manipulator' and that 'her powers were more akin to those of the confidence trickster'[68] than '[t]he gifts of the genuine shaman',[69] the story turns on exactly the ambiguity and refusal of certainties which the narrator wishes to deny and is as slippery as Maisie herself. As in previous tales, multiple readings of the same events or actions are suggested. Thus the accretion of occult symbolism is to be found not only in the exotic clothes Maisie designs but in the mundane example of the 'crescent'[70] shaped black eye Zephra sports. The fact that the narrator's black cat strolls in and gravitates toward Maisie may suggest it is her 'familiar', linking with her comment that 'In America they said I was a witch',[71] or alternatively it may be a playful but insignificant index to her character.

The narrator's reconstruction of Maisie in this retrospective narrative shifts from contained and particular description through a series of biblical and mythological parallels. These include Medea, maker of clothes which can heal or kill, alluded to in the latter part of the story,[72] '[a] female Ozymandias',[73] the cloth around her in her studio forming the effect of a terrain over which she soars and which shifts to give the impression of a vaster scale[74] and an iconic image of the biblical Rachel amid the alien corn, longing for home (reiterated in the musician's comment on homesickness). Yet even some of these references are to be undermined as Maisie tells the narrator that she travels widely and seems to consider no particular place home, and the name 'Medea' is revealed to be no more than a teasing slippage of the word media, itself an ambiguous term, connoting the materials in which Maisie works as an artist, the media as a means of mass communications, and traces of Maisie's role as a 'medium' of sorts, a person claiming to act as a conduit to the spirit world, as revealed in her designs.

Maisie is recurrently linked with the natural world, both as artist and as individual; in a moment of synchronicity she is glimpsed by the narrator 'sitting on a wooden bench in Africa'[75] as well as under the weeping fig in her living room, and the narrator reflects on the natural associations of her name. But as the narrator is forced to concede, Maisie is both businesswoman and artist – her magical powers may extend no further than her ability to suggest the contours of a continent in the cut of a suit (this novel mapping of Africa on to clothes echoing the Africa-shaped hearing aid worn by Avalon in 'A Quarrelsome Man'); in this reading the 'fire [which] crackled all over the cloth'[76] is no more magical than a trick of the light, an optical illusion created by careful choice of fabric. The clothes may be read in complex and multiple ways, as another variant on the self-reflexive texts within the text like the letters on the wall of the catacombs which the narrator tries to decipher, or the cryptic story title which the typewriter produces, seemingly of its own accord.

The clothing itself features a combination of the occult or mystical (the scarabs and golden bell and pomegranate on the narrator's jacket, which also links the story to the underworld mythology of 'McGregor's Journey') and the banal (the 'drumsticks' on the cloth around Maisie's head or the sun and banana tree print of Zephra's outfit, which echoes the tropical images with which Ruby is associated in 'About that Two Pounds, Mrs Parrish'). This careful overlaying of the magical and the ordinary comes close to a magic realist technique in the final part of the story where the scarabs shift from the narrator's jacket on to the walls and floor, a cat is seen to levitate, and a hole in the wall provides the means of entry into another imaginative realm or dimension, which is in part a kind of regression into the narrator's unconscious.

The mythical and cross-cultural permutations of journeying which are respectively explored in 'McGregor's Journey' and 'Eat Labba and Drink Creek Water' are joined in this story by a different sense of journeying: into the past, into the catacombs and passages of another kind of 'hidden realm', an 'interior landscape' of the psyche. As in Harris's fiction, Melville is concerned in this story with 'the penetration of masks to unravel deeply buried and unconscious residues of individual and historical experience; the need to trace and elucidate real motivations behind paradoxical or deceptive appearances'.[77] The latter part of the story is characterized by the same kind of metaphoric condensation, metonymic displacement and slippage of the signifier which

characterizes dream sequences and can be read as another permutation of Melville's concern to make the 'invisible' 'visible'.[78]
That the usual boundaries of time and space have been collapsed
is suggested by the narrator's comment:

> ... I had lived in my ground floor London flat for five years
> without ever realizing that Jamaica was just on the other side
> of my back wall ... Now I would be able to return whenever
> I wanted, by going through the hole in the wall.[79]

However, an alternative reading is also suggested, that Jamaica
is simultaneously to be found in London, as the opening of 'A
Quarrelsome Man' and the diasporic experiences of characters
such as Tuxedo and Winsome suggest in different ways elsewhere
in the collection.

Similarly, interior space is dislocated as the narrator passes
through a series of spaces all linked in some way with the
preceding story: an empty house in which the narrator once lived
reminds us of Maisie's London studio; the 'evangelical church
hall' which, as in 'The Conversion of Millicent Vernon' 'confuses
the difference' by amalgamating different denominational elements,
is the location in which an 'overlapping' sermon is heard, echoing the motifs on the robe Maisie made for the narrator and the
Medea-like potential of her clothes to heal and kill. In a Jamaican locale, familiar to the narrator, the Anglican vicar's 'white
surplice'[80] of the last scene has metamorphosed into a 'dazzling
white robe [which] reminded me of the garb worn for the
pocomania ritual'[81] and Mr Elliott's servant Dolores is teasingly
also connected with clothes and the Medea figure; finally Mr
Elliott's bedroom opens on to a room which the narrator recognizes as where she should be. Only here is the blocked writing
of the story about Maisie released, as the story (which may be
the story we have just read) begins to write itself. Melville has
spoken of the ending of this story as exploring the need to go
back to one's origins before beginning to write[82] and thus it is
significant that this final room suggests childhood memories, as
well as a certain circularity in its echoes of the empty old house
at the beginning of this sequence. As 'Eat Labba and Drink Creek
Water' will make even clearer, there is a sense here of a 'journey
into the past and hinterland which is at the same time a movement of possession into present and future',[83] and a cleverly oblique

commentary on the genesis of art and its self-reflexivity.

Despite its more serious tone and violent subject-matter, 'You Left the Door Open' is in many ways the central story of *Shape-shifter*, encapsulating in microcosm all of its concerns and motifs. These include: ambiguity, boundary crossing, shape-shifting, impersonation and disguise, the role of art and the imagination, the use and abuse of power, fear, magic, dreams, madness, interior landscapes and the psyche. In addition, the Anancy-like use of story-telling and the 'cunning obsequiousness of the slave'[84] as survival mechanisms are recurrent concerns as is the 'confusing [of] the difference' between the human and the animal, the living and the dead, science and the supernatural, reality and unreality.

'You Left the Door Open' is also the most self-reflexive story in the collection. Not only does the narrator remind us that the 'lens . . . determines what is seen',[85] but she also presents examples of different ways of 'reading' the break-in and attack on the female protagonist by an unknown man, and the status accorded to their respective discourses, from psychology to demonology to forensics. That certain readings are deemed more valid than others is beautifully encapsulated in the policewoman's empirical bias, her refusal to record the narrator's description of her assailant as appearing to have the '"soul of a wolf"'.[86] However, the narrative voice warns against discounting less orthodox explanations, by reminding us that 'Some events defy scrutiny',[87] and this might be taken to apply to much of the collection. Indeed, as in most of the stories, 'impenetrable ambiguity'[88] remains to the end.

Unlike the deliberate aura of mystique surrounding Maisie in 'The Truth is in the Clothes', the narrator of this story candidly declares her position as shape-shifter in demystifying terms: 'I am a cabaret artist. I specialize in impersonations'.[89] However, her cross-dressing creation of the fictional Charlie, a minor criminal, quickly takes on ominous tones, as, Jekyll-like, she feels controlled by his 'vicious and predatory' impulses and desire to 'hurt people'.[90] Indeed, as Morris has suggested, 'Charlie' is ambiguously constructed as the narrator's Jungian shadow, as well as overlapping with a present-day criminally insane man charged with a series of attacks on women, and, in a chilling instance of synchronicity, with one Charlie Peace, a nineteenth-century murderer and cabaret artist who evaded arrest by taking on different disguises. Accordingly, the assailant's explanation of his 'entry' which forms the story title, resounds in ways beyond the most immediate orthodox interpretation. An interesting subtext of this sense of doors opening into other dimensions is provided by the narrator's picture of the leopard painted in Haiti. Haitian paintings such as this are regarded as 'multi-dimensional', with the artist acting as a medium, and his painting as a bridge between the human and spirit worlds. Brathwaite's comment on the late Guyanese painter Aubrey Williams makes this clear:

> Williams is the medium. His paintbrush is the door, the porte cabesse or central pole, down which the gods often descend into the tonelle during vodun worship.[91]

Yet the role of the painting is ambiguous. The narrator considers it to have talismanic powers and thus is loath to loan the painting to a friend, but whether the subsequent attack is or is not linked to the absence of its protective influence is unclear.

The recurrent references to the narrator as wild and animal-like[92] suggest that she is forced to become the leopard itself, her own protector. Significantly, in a dream after the attack, the leopard recurs in a domestic setting 'half-painting and half-real'.[93] The narrator's feeling that 'when he was face to face with the mirror, something terrible would happen'[94] echoes the half-glimpsed portents of the narrator's earlier – equally ambiguous – encounter of self with the 'self' she has created in the bathroom mirror, also half artistic creation and half real. It also captures the mixture of terror and horrid fascination with which she subsequently attempts to re-enter the events of the night of her attack to scrutinize its 'impenetrable ambiguity' and to make sense of the paradoxical lack of 'traces' left by such a violently physical encounter, as well as her growing intimation that what she is uncovering may be part of her own psyche, a bizarre variant on 'the enemy within' rather than an external 'foe'. As a character in 'The Girl with the Celestial Limb' says '"there is a reality which we uncover by our observations"'[95] but '"[Einstein] didn't ... consider the possibility of multiple universes"'.[96] The latter possibility is exactly what the narrator of 'You Left the Door Open' must confront: 'Had the spirit of a nineteenth-century murderer and cabaret artist entered a contemporary small-time burglar? Did we all overlap?'[97] However, as in 'The Truth is in the Clothes', the supernatural is

stubbornly accompanied by the natural, the banal and the pro-
saic. Thus a further, more ordinary kind of 'overlapping' is constituted by the shape-shifting 'slippage' of roles and agency in
the final section of the story. The policeman who visits the house
of the narrator-as-crime-victim is also an ex-repertory actor and
foregrounds the narrator's similar occupation as a 'performer' (in
itself an ambiguous term). This reading blunts the potential
synchronicity of the story's ending as the narrator encounters
the man accused of a subsequent attack in the area, wearing the
same type of clothes favoured by both Charlie Peace and herself
in her own impersonation of a petty criminal (also named Charlie).
Perhaps, then, she is just a consummate 'performer' and able to
gauge these things well. Similarly, the accused's claim that someone
is attempting to 'get into him and tell him what to do'[98] signifies
doubly as the sign of his mental illness or supernatural manipulation by the spirit of Charlie Peace. As so often in Melville's
stories, an 'impenetrable ambiguity' remains.

In sharp contrast to the impressions of other characters in *Shape-
shifter*, the narrator of the final story 'Eat Labba and Drink Creek
Water' reflects of Guyana that 'Everything is more visible there'.[99]
Yet this reading of contemporary Guyanese society, personified
in the pragmatic and politically aware Evelyn, and borne out by
the mad aunts' outspokenness, is accompanied by a contesting
reading, provided by one of the aunts, that: '"Everything's gone
middly-muddly over here"',[100] thereby affirming the concept of
multi-focality, different versions of the same reality.

'Eat Labba and Drink Creek Water' is fragmentary in form,
constructed, like Brodber's fiction, from a series of disconnected
voices and making use of a range of oral resources including
song, folklore, superstition and the words of children's games.
Likewise it eschews strict narrative temporality for a more fluid,
'spatial' mapping of experience and events, and a more holistic
sense of time. As in Harris' novels, this involves slippage between
different tenses and the collapsing of the boundaries between
the living and the dead, a recurrent theme in *Shape-shifter*. Thus
the narrator's (memory of?) playing in the lake constitutes a
Harrisonian 'catalyst of experience within the density of place
[which causes her to] sense presences . . . the sense of unfathom-
able age and youth',[101] in a passage which invokes an overlapping, multi-dimensional sense of time: an Amerindian woman
(living? dead?) in a canoe, the spirit of the 'pale boy', Wat, travelling

centuries before with an expedition in search of the riches of El Dorado, is rumoured to be 'trapped'[102] under the waters nearby.

As in Margaret Atwood's *Surfacing*, the retreat into a geographical interior allows the narrator to map her own 'interior landscape', to reconstruct a personal history which not only involves encounter with the most immediate 'natives of her person' (the aunts), but also admits the surfacing of a series of other traces and ancestral presences.[103] In this context, Brathwaite's following comment is pertinent:

> In the Caribbean, whether it be African or Amerindian, the recognition of an ancestral relationship with the folk or aboriginal culture involves the artist and participant in a journey into the past and hinterland which is at the same time a movement of possession into present and future. Through this movement of possession we become ourselves, truly our own creators, discovering word for object, image for the Word.[104]

However, an alternative, less positive sense of 'doubling back' and self-defeating circularity is also intimated in the Anancy-like boat called by the Arawaks the '"eight-legged sea-spider" . . . seem[ing] to travel far on the same spot',[105] the New Amsterdam 'telegraph poles whose wires carry singing messages from nowhere to nowhere'[106] and the mad aunt, crippled by her obsessive return to divisive racial distinctions, the fearful blackness in the family which like 'molasses will always stick to you'.[107]

In this way, Guyana is constructed as vast and self-sufficient but also as isolated and plagued by shortage and poor communications. Appropriately, Melville has similarly spoken of Guyana as being in a kind of 'limbo': part of South America as well as the Caribbean, belonging fully in neither category.[108]

The fragmented form of 'Eat Labba and Drink Creek Water' is also paradigmatic of the larger fragmentations of Caribbean history. Central to this are the sequence of 'journeys', arrivals and departures and the exploration of the trope of the journey in its various permutations in the story: imaginative and dream journeying, the journeys of the dead (the body of the Amerindian 'falling through the mists'[109] as if through time, 'Wat's body, loosened from its grave . . . [on] a quest of its own'[110] through a labyrinth of waterways) as well as literal migrations, quests and odysseys and a series of voyages into the archives of personal memory and a collective past. Lamming's sense of a 'journey to an expectation' is glossed in a variety of ways in this story, from the cross-cultural expectations of the conquistador in Guyana searching for the mythical El Dorado and the modern day tourist's vague sense of Caribbean geography and culture which begs comparison with the starting point of Kincaid's *A Small Place*, to the equally idealized expectations of the West Indian journeying to London, reciting, as, if by rote, a litany of those factors which constitute the 'pull of the metropolis'. There is also the wonderfully parodic account of the 'golden city' which is London. Melville appropriates the language of European travellers' accounts, with their fanciful descriptions of the grotesque, outlandish inhabitants of the New World, and the language of the conquistadors in search of the gold of El Dorado, and turns it toward another city mythically 'paved with gold': London.

Like a number of texts by Caribbean writers based in Britain,[111] 'Eat Labba and Drink Creek Water' is concerned with the problems of return to the Caribbean and specifically with the overlapping versions of Guyana which are encountered in myth and dream, and its different expectations and realities. Lamming's 'journey to an expectation' is inverted in the opening pages of the story as the narrator and her Jamaican friend discuss their mutual need to 'go back'. However, the story goes on to deconstruct this easy duality by acknowledging the complex trajectories of desire which accompany such journeys and which problematize any concept of 'home', 'return' or 'arrival': 'whichever side of the Atlantic we are on, the dream is always on the other side.'[112]

Arguably, O'Callaghan's observation that *Shape-shifter* is characterized by a range of subject-positions with '"fluid boundaries and continual commerce between them"'[113] finds its apotheosis here, as boundaries are continually crossed and blurred. Demerara is described as 'built on stilts, belonging neither to land nor to sea but to land reclaimed from the sea';[114] likewise, the father's birth certificate pronounces him '"Coloured. Native. Creole"'[115] yet his mixed racial origins 'over-spill' the categories which seek to contain and define him, thereby destabilizing the boundaries of such classifications; they are then 'rubbished' by the colonial authorities and replaced with a birth certificate in a deceptive move to conceal his 'difference' in England. Finally the narrator, like Melville, presents a confusion of categories, as an '"ice-cream face"'[116] looking white but with mixed race origins, her complex dual identities in Britain and the Caribbean giving her the sense of travelling on a 'frail spider's thread . . . attached to Big Ben at one end and St George's Cathedral, Demerara, at the other'.[117] In this, the most impressionistic and autobiographical of Melville's stories, the narrator weaves an Anancy-like fictional web which bridges time and space, past and present, the real and the mythical, the natural and supernatural, London and the Caribbean, 'communicat[ing] much by indirection, by symbolic hints . . . traffic[king] in intuition . . . travel[ling] dream and myth'[118] in true shape-shifting style.

Notes

1. G. Griffiths, 'Wilson Harris and Caribbean Criticism' in H. Maes-Jelinek (ed.), *Wilson Harris – The Uncompromising Imagination* (Coventry: Dangaroo Press, 1991) p. 67.
2. E. Canetti, *The Human Province*, translated from the German by Joachim Neugroschel (London: Pan Books, 1986) pp. 174–5. I am indebted to Roy Woolley for drawing this passage to my attention.
3. P. Melville, *Shape-shifter* (London: The Women's Press, 1990) p. 99.
4. Ibid.
5. Ibid., p. 27.
6. E. O'Callaghan, *Woman Version – Theoretical Approaches to West Indian Fiction by Women* (London and Basingstoke: Macmillan, 1993) p. 108.
7. M. Busby (ed.), *Daughters of Africa* (London: Jonathan Cape, 1992) p. 740.
8. P. Melville, recorded conversation with Caryl Phillips, ICA Guardian Conversations, 1990.
9. E. O'Callaghan, *Woman Version – Theoretical Approaches to West Indian Fiction by Women* (London and Basingstoke: Macmillan, 1993) p. 108.
10. M. Busby (ed.), *Daughters of Africa* (London: Jonathan Cape, 1992) pp. 739–40.
11. L. Chunn, 'The Shape of Good Things to Come', *The Guardian* (14 February 1990) 42.
12. M. Morris, 'Cross-Cultural Impersonations: Pauline Melville's *Shape-shifter*', *Ariel*, 24:1 (January 1993) p. 79.
13. M. Busby (ed.), *Daughters of Africa* (London: Jonathan Cape, 1992) p. 740.
14. P. Melville, *Shape-shifter*, p. 162.
15. M. Busby (ed.), *Daughters of Africa* (London: Jonathan Cape, 1992) p. 740.
16. Ibid.
17. ICA video.
18. K. Brathwaite, 'History, the Writer and X-Self', source unknown.

19. M. Busby (ed.), *Daughters of Africa* (London: Jonathan Cape, 1992) p. 743.
20. Ibid.
21. G. Nichols, 'The Battle with Language', Selwyn Cudjoe, ed., *Caribbean Women Writers* (Wellesley, Massachussetts, Calaloux Publications: 1990) p. 288.
22. M. Busby (ed.), *Daughters of Africa* (London: Jonathan Cape, 1992) pp. 742–3.
23. Ibid., p. 741.
24. Mr Biswas in Naipaul's *A House for Mr Biswas* (1961) is a one-time journalist who aspires to write novels; Moses Aloetta in Selvon's *Moses Ascending* (1975) has ambitious plans for the 'magnus opus' of his memoirs and B. Wordsworth in Naipaul's *Miguel Street* is an aspiring poet, distilling verse at the rate of one line a month. However, there is a more serious undertow to the satirical treatment of writing in these texts: that of the need for the colonial subject to write the self, to inscribe himself in a 'great tradition' or make his counter-discursive mark thereby dismantling the European belief in the lack of West Indian writing or the (post)colonial subject's 'incapacity' to write; this is counterbalanced with the sense of pathos derived from B. Wordsworth and Biswas' acts of colonial mimicry and by a simultaneously wry reflection on the obstacles traditionally facing the West Indian writer: dearth of publishing facilities and also potentially of audience.
25. P. Melville, *Shape-shifter*, p. 3.
26. Ibid., pp. 3–4.
27. Ibid., p. 3.
28. Michael Dash, 'In Search of the Lost Body: Redefining the Subject in Caribbean Literature', in Stephen Slemon & Helen Tiffin (eds), *After Europe* (Coventry: Dangaroo Press, 1989) p. 26. Dash locates 'those who wish to dominate and control' within the larger project of what he calls: 'Prospero's signifying grasp' (p. 18): the whole ideological apparatus of control, exacted through language and education and involving the privileging of European texts, European signifying practices and European epistemologies, which accompanied the colonization process. Dash argues that the historical construction of the colonial subject as already signified within the colonizer's discourse and subsequently denied agency in 'confer[rring] meaning on his/her world' (p. 17) makes 'the task of consciousness . . . or "subjectification"' imperative. To be able to interpret accurately and understand the basis of such oppressive 'systems of knowledge and signification [which were and are] enforced in order to produce docility, constraint and helplessness' (p. 17) in the colonial subject is a crucial step in this process. In Melville's story the desire to control or delimit meaning which is part of a wider battle over signification is an ironic reminder of the legacies of the terrain which Dash explores.
29. M. Morris, 'Cross-Cultural Impersonations: Pauline Melville's *Shape-shifter*', *Ariel*, 24:1 (January 1993) p. 83.

30. J. Berry, 'On an Afternoon Train from Purley to Victoria, 1955', *Chain of Days* (Oxford: Oxford University Press, 1985) p. 25.
31. P. Melville, *Shape-shifter*, p. 16.
32. Ibid., p. 17.
33. Ibid., p. 18.
34. Ibid.
35. Ibid.
36. The Creole heiress from Jean Rhys's *Wide Sargasso Sea* (London, André Deutsch: 1966).
37. K. Ramchand, *The West Indian Novel and its Background* (London: Faber & Faber, 1970) pp. 223–6.
38. P. Melville, *Shape-shifter*, p. 18.
39. Ibid., p. 25.
40. Ibid., p. 19.
41. M. Morris, 'Cross-Cultural Impersonations: Pauline Melville's *Shape-shifter*', *Ariel*, 24:1 (January 1993) p. 84.
42. P. Melville, *Shape-shifter*, p. 17.
43. Ibid., p. 21.
44. Ibid., p. 24.
45. Ibid., p. 26.
46. Ibid., p. 15.
47. Ibid., p. 16.
48. Ibid., p. 26.
49. Ibid., pp. 44–5.
50. Ibid., p. 47.
51. Ibid., p. 48.
52. Ibid., p. 48.
53. Ibid., p. 48.
54. Ibid., p. 53.
55. Ibid., p. 52.
56. Ibid., p. 50.
57. For an extended analysis of 'McGregor's Journey' see M. Condé 'McGregor as Orpheus: Pauline Melville's "McGregor's Journey"', *Journal of the Short Story in English*, 26 (Spring 96), pp. 63–74.
58. Melville's appropriation, as a Caribbean writer, of European mythologies in this and other stories in *Shape-shifter* is significant. Myth, culture and language are seen to be – like the stories themselves – in a state of flux and negotiation. Not only does Melville re-inflect and revitalize Old World mythologies by exploring them in some startlingly new, post-colonial contexts, but she also manages to impart something of the privileged status of classical mythology to her own stories set in the Caribbean and multicultural Britain. These too, she suggests, are potent, resonant narratives, waiting to be told – and waiting to be heard. (I am indebted to David Keogh for the basis of some of these points.) See also Mary Condé's article, 'McGregor as Orpheus: Pauline Melville's "McGregor's Journey"' in *Journal of the Short Story in English*, 26 (Spring 1996).
59. P. Melville, *Shape-shifter*, p. 97.
60. Ibid., p. 91.

61. Ibid., p. 91.
62. Ibid., p. 95.
63. This echo is also appropriate to Melville's shape-shifting theme, since Daphne is wooed by one Leucippus who disguises his sex by dressing as a huntress only to be discovered by his rival, Apollo and killed.
64. ICA video.
65. P. Melville, *Shape-shifter*, p. 97.
66. Ibid., p. 98.
67. Ibid., p. 100.
68. Ibid., p. 99.
69. Ibid.
70. Ibid., p. 100.
71. Ibid., p. 104.
72. Maisie is most clearly linked to Medea in that the latter made a poisoned robe with which she killed her husband; however, Medea was also a musician (thus providing another link with Melville's story), skilled in the art of herbal remedies, able to regenerate as well as destroy and a trickster of sorts, deceiving her husband's family by making the pieces of an old ram appear as a young lamb.
73. P. Melville, *Shape-shifter*, p. 106.
74. Ibid.
75. Ibid., p. 102.
76. Ibid., p. 103.
77. Hena Maes-Jelinek, 'Carnival and Creativity in Wilson Harris' Fiction' in Michael Gilkes (ed.), *The Literate Imagination: Essays on the Novels of Wilson Harris* (Basingstoke: Macmillan, 1989) p. 49.
78. M. Busby (ed.), *Daughters of Africa* (London: Jonathan Cape, 1992) p. 741.
79. P. Melville, *Shape-shifter*, p. 111.
80. Ibid., p. 110.
81. Ibid., p. 111.
82. ICA video
83. K. Brathwaite, 'Timehri', *Savacou*, 2 (September 1970) p. 43.
84. P. Melville, *Shape-shifter*, p. 125.
85. Ibid., p. 113.
86. Ibid., p. 114.
87. Ibid., p. 113.
88. Ibid., p. 113.
89. Ibid., p. 114.
90. Ibid., p. 115.
91. K. Brathwaite, 'Timehri', *Savacou*, 2 (September 1970) p. 44.
92. P. Melville, *Shape-shifter* see p. 118.
93. Ibid., p. 132.
94. Ibid.
95. Ibid., p. 144.
96. Ibid.
97. Ibid., p. 133.
98. Ibid., p. 134.

99. Ibid., p. 149.
100. Ibid., p. 162.
101. W. Harris, 'A Talk on the Subjective Imagination' in H. Maes-Jelinek (ed.), *Explorations* (Mundelstrup, Denmark: Dangaroo Press, 1981) p. 61.
102. P. Melville, *Shape-shifter*, p. 149.
103. In Erna Brodber's *Jane and Louisa Will Soon Come Home* (1980), this 'interior' is not geographical but a retreat into the hinterland which is madness, also a recurrent theme in Melville's collection; here again a similar syncretic emphasis on the need to acknowledge *all* the ancestors is to be found.
104. K. Brathwaite, 'Timehri', *Savacou*, 2 (September 1970) p. 44.
105. P. Melville, *Shape-shifter*, p. 158.
106. Ibid., p. 153.
107. Ibid., p 157.
108. ICA video
109. P. Melville, *Shape-shifter*, p. 150.
110. Ibid., p. 160.
111. For example: Caryl Phillips' *The Final Passage* (1985), Amryl Johnson's *Sequins for a Ragged Hem* (1987), Linton Kwesi Johnson's 'Reggae fi dada' in *tings an times* (1992).
112. P. Melville, *Shape-shifter*, p. 149.
113. Diana Fuss cited in E. O'Callaghan, *Woman Version – Theoretical Approaches to West Indian Fiction by Women* (London and Basingstoke: Macmillan, 1993) p. 108.
114. P. Melville, *Shape-shifter*, p. 152.
115. Ibid., p. 153.
116. Ibid., p. 156.
117. Ibid., p. 149.
118. M. Morris, 'Cross-Cultural Impersonations: Pauline Melville's *Shape-shifter*', *Ariel*, 24:1 (January 1993) p. 88.

Bibliography

Brathwaite, E.K. 'Timehri', *Savacou*, 2 (September 1970) 35–44.
——. 'History, the Writer and X-Self', source unknown.
Busby, M. (ed.). *Daughters of Africa*. London: Jonathan Cape, 1992, pp. 739–43.
Canetti, E. *The Human Province* (translated from the German by Joachim Neugroschel). London: Pan Books, 1986.
Chunn, L. 'The Shape of Good Things to Come', *The Guardian* (14 February 1990) 42.
Dash, M. 'In Search of the Lost Body: Redefining the Subject in Caribbean Literature' in Stephen Slemon and Helen Tiffin (eds). *After Europe*. Coventry: Dangaroo Press, 1989.
Gilkes, M. (ed.). *The Literate Imagination: Essays on the Novels of Wilson Harris*. London and Basingstoke: Macmillan, 1989.

Harris, W. *Explorations*. Mundelstrup, Denmark: Dangaroo, 1981.

Lamming, G. *The Pleasures of Exile*. London: Michael Joseph, 1960.

Maes-Jelinek, H. (ed.). *Wilson Harris – The Uncompromising Imagination*. Coventry: Dangaroo Press, 1991.

Melville, P. *Shape-shifter*. London: The Women's Press, 1990.

——. Recorded Conversation with Caryl Phillips, ICA Guardian Conversations, 1990.

Morris, M. 'Cross-Cultural Impersonations: Pauline Melville's *Shape-shifter*', *Ariel*, 24:1 (January 1993) pp. 79–89.

O'Callaghan, E. *Woman Version – Theoretical Approaches to West Indian Fiction by Women*. London and Basingstoke: Macmillan, 1993, pp. 107–8.

Savory, E. 'The Truth is in the Clothes', *Review of Shape-shifter*, *CRNLE Reviews Journal*, No. 1 (1994) pp. 123–31.

10

Jamaica Kincaid's Writing and the Maternal-Colonial Matrix

Laura Niesen de Abruna

Acknowledged as one of the leading women writers from the Caribbean, Jamaica Kincaid was born in 1949 in St John's, Antigua. At the age of 19 she left the island for the United States, where she took various jobs before establishing herself as a writer. Kincaid's father was a carpenter and cabinet-maker. Her grandmother was a Carib Indian, and her mother, Annie, is from Dominica. In 1966 Kincaid went to the United States to pursue her education. She attended college for one year, but became alienated before the second year started and dropped out. Soon afterwards she began to submit freelance articles to magazines, two of which were published in *Ms.*. With the help of her friend George Trow, she became a contributor to the *New Yorker*. From 1976 to the present, she has been a staff writer for the *New Yorker*, contributing some 80 pieces, a few as letters with her name attached, some unsigned, to the 'Talk of the Town' section, and over 14 short stories. Her first volume of short stories, *At the Bottom of the River*, published in 1978, presented modernist dream visions of life in Antigua. Her best work to date is the coming-of-age novel, *Annie John*, which appeared in 1983. Her collection of short essays on Antigua, *A Small Place*, was published in 1988. Her novel *Lucy* appeared in 1990. Her most recent novel is entitled *The Autobiography of My Mother* (1996) and picks up the theme of the maternal matrix, as Kincaid presents her mother's life in the first person. Kincaid now lives in Vermont with her husband Allen, a music professor at Bennington College, and their two children, Annie and Harold Shawn.

Kincaid is notable for her presentation of women's experience. Jean Rhys was the first or at least the first published among Caribbean women writers to present the mother–daughter matrix as part of the full range of women's experiences in the Caribbean. Like Rhys, Kincaid employs a wide range of modernist and postmodern strategies, such as dreams and associative thinking, as parts of the narrator's strategies of resistance to the dominant culture. In *Lucy*, and in the *New Yorker* stories, in *Annie John*, *A Small Place*, and *The Autobiography of My Mother*, Kincaid puts little distance between herself and the narrator who recounts a portion of her life and analyses its trajectory. The one exception to this is *At the Bottom of the River*, which treats the mother–daughter matrix but always through the literary mediation of dream associations and their language. Kincaid's greatest contribution to the full presentation of female life is her exploration of the mother–daughter bond, and specifically, the effects of the loss of the maternal matrix on the relationship between the mother and daughter. In *Annie John*, as well as in *Lucy* and *The Autobiography of My Mother*, the alienation from the mother becomes a metaphor for the young woman's alienation from an island culture that has been completely dominated by the imperialist power of England. In *Lucy*, this point is made through the narrator's very name. She feels that her mother's teasing explanation of the name 'Lucy' as a diminutive of 'Lucifer' is accurate because it represents her sense of herself as fallen away from a relationship with a kind of god, and at several points in the novel she refers to her vision of her mother as 'godlike.' In most of Kincaid's work, her narrators perceive and present their early, preoedipal relationship with their mothers as a type of Eden from which they have irretrievably fallen away.

Recent critics have found that an emphasis on the personal area of experience, like the mother–daughter relationships in Kincaid's *Lucy* and *The Autobiography of My Mother*, is a characteristic of women's writing in general and of Caribbean women's writing in particular. In their anthology entitled *Her True-True Name*, the Jamaican writers Betty Wilson and Pamela Mordecai have testified to a flowering in the 1980s of women's writing dealing with such concerns as surviving sexism, negotiating mother–daughter relationships, and an interest in relational interaction, or 'bonding'. Most of this literature is concerned with bringing personal and emotional issues into the public and literary arenas. In her anthology of black women writers, *Watchers & Seekers: Creative Writing by Black Women*, Rhonda Cobham argues for the centrality of either bonding or the absence of bonding in the texts of Caribbean women writers, especially in their focus on the emotional interdependence of mothers and daughters, granddaughters and grandmothers, friends, and sisters:

> Their perspectives may be critical, nostalgic or celebratory, sentimental or distanced. But repeatedly there emerges a sense of sisterly solidarity with mother figures, whose strengths and frailties assume new significance for daughters now faced with the challenge of raising children and/or achieving artistic recognition in an environment hostile to the idea of female self-fulfillment.[1]

Kincaid focuses intensely in all of her work on the relationship between her narrator and her mother. And there is always a correlation between the political difficulties afflicting the island-'mother' country relationship and the problems affecting the mother–daughter family relationships in these texts. The characters' separation from the mother, or the 'mother' country, evokes extreme anxiety that appears as cultural and psychic alienation. In all of Kincaid's work, it is the absence of the once-affirming mother or an affirming 'mother' country, that causes dislocation and alienation. In both *Annie John* and *Lucy*, the narrators Annie and Lucy experience great tensions in their experiences with their mothers because of the early intensity of the bond and its later complete severance. For Annie, the severance is initiated by her mother and occurs before she leaves the island. For Lucy, the separation seems to be initiated by her and is demonstrated in her habit of not opening the 19 or so letters that arrive from her mother. In both novels, the importance of female bonding is central, and is centred on the narrator's relationship with her mother. In both texts the character's personal alienation is explored first directly and then as a metaphor for the alienation of the daughter-island from the mother-country. The metaphorical exploration offers a criticism of the neocolonial situation that inhibits the lives of both Annie and Lucy. Both women are victims of their environments and both are in states of extreme anger because of this situation. At the end of *Annie John*, Annie can find her own identity; she is able to do this through her identification with her mother and her grandmother, Ma Chess, who fills the maternal role when

Annie's mother can no longer cope with Annie's psychological breakdown and physical illness.

In *Lucy*, the narrator is much older, 19 rather than 15, and her relationship with her mother is much less clear to her than it is to Annie. Because Lucy is in the United States working as an au pair, she has no group of female relatives who could form a support group for her. In fact, she seems to long for total anonymity because those who know her harshly evaluated and judged each of her actions. She has a tremendous amount of anger about her relationship with her mother. Again, Lucy feels that the closeness she experienced with her mother was a kind of trap set by their biological connection. As her mother says to her, '"You can run away, but you cannot escape the fact that I am your mother, my blood runs in you, I carried you for nine months inside me."'[2] Yet Lucy would die of longing for her mother if she read even one letter.

The most dramatic example of Lucy's anger is her response to her father's death. She thinks of saying to her mother's friend, Maude:

'I am not like my mother. She and I are not alike. She should not have married my father. She should not have had children. She should not have thrown away her intelligence. She should not have paid so little attention to mine. She should have ignored someone like you. I am not like her at all.'[3]

She seems to have very few feelings of regret about her father, whom she describes as having behaved very badly, in a way that Antiguan women would have expected. It is with her mother that the conflict continues. Her letter is extremely cold:

It matched my heart. It amazed even me, but I sent it all the same. In the letter I asked my mother how she could have married a man who would die and leave her in debt even for his own burial. I pointed out the ways she had betrayed herself. I said I believed she had betrayed me also, and that I knew it to be true even if I couldn't find a concrete example right then. I said that she had acted like a saint, but that since I was living in this real world I had really wanted just a mother. I reminded her that my whole upbringing had been devoted to preventing me from becoming a slut; I then gave a brief description of my personal life, offering each detail as evidence that my upbringing had been a failure and that, in fact, life as a slut was quite enjoyable, thank you very much. I would not come home now, I said. I would not come home ever.[4]

Lucy is, of course, in the process of working out her relationship with her mother from the distance of the United States. She sees in Mariah a number of different people, but she often sees Mariah as a sort of substitute for her mother. With Mariah she has the closeness of conversation and intimacy that she could not have experienced with her 'saint-like' mother. It is Mariah who points out to Lucy that she is filled with anger and later suggests, even as her own marriage is falling apart, that Lucy must forgive her mother in order to thaw her cold heart: '"Why don't you forgive your mother for whatever it is you feel she has done? Why don't you just go home and tell her you forgive her?"'[5] These words allow Lucy to recognize the real source of her anger in the treatment she had received from her mother, which Lucy perceives as a series of betrayals.

The first betrayal is the betrayal of the first child in a family into which other children are born. But the other children were all male children, each of whom would be considered by her parents as potential candidates for the university in England or to study as a doctor or a lawyer. Lucy feels this discrimination stingingly. She seems not to respect her father, an old man who had fathered thirty children and left their mothers. But she could not accept the betrayal by her mother:

I did not mind my father saying these things about his sons, his own kind, and leaving me out. My father did not know me at all; I did not expect him to imagine a life for me filled with excitement and triumph. But my mother knew me well, as well as she knew herself: I, at the time, even thought of us as identical; and whenever I saw her eyes fill up with tears at the thought of how proud she would be at some deed her sons had accomplished, I felt a sword go through my heart, for there was no accompanying scenario in which she saw me, her only identical offspring, in a remotely similar situation. To myself I then began to call her Mrs. Judas, and I began to plan a separation from her that even then I suspected would never be complete.[6]

Lucy's anger is different from Annie's. Annie's anger comes from her mother's indifference to her once she attains puberty. Lucy's anger comes from her mother's lack of faith in her abilities and talents. Although Mariah points out to Lucy that part of her mother's attitude comes from cultural conditioning, that is something that Lucy is unwilling to accept. For, at this point, and indeed even at the end of the novel, the mother remains a figure who is not an individual, partly conditioned by history, culture, and class. Instead, the mother remains the 'god', as she is referred to so often, or the 'monster', as in the stories collected in the anthology, *At the Bottom of the River*. This is one of the major problems with the novel, since the narrator never moves away from a childlike view of her mother as both superhuman and subhuman. In fact, her response is melodramatic and fixated at the preoedipal level: ' . . . for ten of my twenty years, half of my life, I had been mourning the end of a love affair, perhaps the only true love in my whole life I would ever know'.[7] Unfortunately, this statement is made by a 20-year-old narrator who has also claimed that she is breaking the bond she felt with her mother. The intensity of that bond is remarkable, although its sources are not revealed in the text.

According to Lucy, she has never had any love for the men she saw around her either in Antigua or in the United States. The couple with whom she lives, Mariah and Lewis, are moving toward the end of their marriage. Lewis is having an affair with Mariah's best friend, Dinah, and neither Dinah nor Lewis has any feelings of concern for Mariah or her four children. For Lucy, Lewis's behaviour in rejecting his wife Mariah for Dinah comes as no surprise, but as behaviour expected from men:

> A woman like Dinah was not unfamiliar to me, nor was a man like Lewis. Where I came from, it was well known that some women and all men in general could not be trusted in certain areas. My father had perhaps thirty children; he did not know for sure. He would try to make a count but then he would give up after a while. One woman he had children with tried to kill me when I was in my mother's stomach. She had earlier failed to kill my mother. My father had lived with another woman for years and was the father of her three children; she tried to kill my mother and me many times. My mother saw an obeah woman every Friday to prevent these attempts from being successful.[8]

In a situation in which the parental focus is so asymmetrical, the bond between the mother and the daughter will attain great importance.

In both *Annie John* and *Lucy* the process of leaving the mother is complicated by the similar process of leaving an island dominated by British cultural imperialism. Lucy's anger about this is best seen in her reaction to reading a poem about daffodils, probably Wordsworth's. As a ten-year-old on a tropical island, Lucy was forced to memorize and recite a poem about daffodils approved by the Queen Victoria Girls' School. The flowers, which do not grow in the Caribbean, are symbolic of the many ways British culture had been forced on the young women in Antigua. After reciting the poem, Lucy tried to repress all of its lines. She is herself surprised when Mariah's mention of daffodils unleashes strong emotions: 'I had forgotten all of this until Mariah mentioned daffodils, and now I told it to her with such an amount of anger I surprised both of us'.[9] Later, when Mariah again presses the issue of these flowers, Lucy finds that she wants to kill them: 'There was such joy in her voice as she said this, such a music, how could I explain to her the feeling I had about daffodils – that it wasn't exactly daffodils, but that they would do as well as anything else?'[10] Finally, Lucy is able to push this anger into full consciousness as she explains to Mariah, '"Mariah, do you realize that at ten years of age I had to learn by heart a long poem about some flowers I would not see in real life until I was nineteen?"'[11]

In a 'Talk of the Town' article for the *New Yorker* which appeared in 1977, Kincaid, who rejected her British name Richardson, recalled that most of the African-Caribbean people of Antigua worked as carpenters, masons, servants in private homes, seamstresses, fishermen, or dockworkers. She added that, 'A few grew crops and a very small number worked in offices and banks'.[12] When Kincaid was seven, she was herself apprenticed to a seamstress for two afternoons a week. People who worked in offices and banks were white, and the wealthiest ran a country club called the Mill Reef Club. The whites owned the banks and the offices and reserved most of the island's pleasant beaches for themselves. All of these historical and political contexts are important to Kincaid's fiction. Despite her affection for her surrogate family in the United States, Lucy is still the 'Visitor', and she questions the basis of the family's comfortable life. For example, Lucy comments ironically on the connection between the endangered species for which Mariah evinces such concern and her family wealth. And Lucy is offended when Mariah boasts that she has some 'Indian' blood in her: 'How do you get to be the sort of victor who can claim to be the vanquished also?'[13]

Much of Kincaid's distrust of the postcolonial environment went unnoticed by the reviewers of *Annie John* and *Lucy*. Like *Annie John*, *Lucy* was received in many academic circles as a book about mothers and daughters, a popular topic in feminist literary criticism, especially since the late seventies, when Nancy Chodorow and Carol Gilligan published their influential studies. In both of Kincaid's novels, female bonding is the primary subject and receives the most narrative attention, whereas within *Annie John*, for example, there are only two direct statements of resentment made about the political situation. One is a comment the narrator makes while observing a classmate, Ruth, who is the child of British missionaries:

> Perhaps she wanted to be in England, where no one would remind her constantly of the terrible things her ancestors had done; perhaps she had felt even worse when her father was a missionary in Africa. I could see how Ruth felt from looking at her face. Her ancestors had been the masters, while ours had been the slaves. She had a lot to be ashamed of. . . . I am quite sure that if the tables had been turned we would have acted quite differently.[14]

Earlier in the novel, while Annie and her friend 'The Red Girl' watch a cruise ship with wealthy passengers go by, she fantasizes that they wreck the ship: 'How we laughed as their cries of joy turned to cries of sorrow'.[15]

A Small Place, published in 1988, makes explicit Kincaid's resentment of the British upper class and forces us to look at *Annie John* and *Lucy* from a different angle. In *A Small Place* Kincaid recites an elegy for an Antigua that no longer exists. The British have ruined much of the island:

> And so everywhere they went they turned it into England; and everybody they met they turned English. But no place could ever really be England, and nobody who did not look exactly like them would ever be English, so you can imagine the

destruction of people and land that came from that. The English hate each other and they hate England, and the reason is they have no place else to go and nobody else to feel better than.[16]

At the age of seven, Kincaid remembers waiting for hours in the hot sun to see a 'putty-faced princess' from England disappear behind the walls of the governor's house. Later she found that the princess was sent to Antigua to recover from an affair with a married man! In schools and libraries the British found opportunities to distort and erase Antiguan history and to glorify British history in its place. One of the crimes of the colonial era was the violation of the colonized peoples' languages: 'For isn't it odd that the only language I have in which to speak of this crime is the language of the criminal who committed the crime?'[17]

The thematic connection between *Annie John* and *A Small Place* is made clear in an interview with Selwyn Cudjoe in *Callaloo*. In this interview Kincaid discusses her ideas in *A Small Place*, particularly her dislike of colonialism, which she had developed by the age of nine:

> When I was nine, I refused to stand up at the refrain of 'God Save Our King.' I hated 'Rule Britannia'; and I used to say that we weren't Britons, we were slaves. I never had any idea why. I just thought that there was no sense to it – 'Rule Britannia, Britannia rule the waves, Britons never shall be slaves.' I thought that we weren't Britons and that we were slaves.[18]

Elsewhere in the interview Kincaid indicates the instinctive rebellion she felt against England, despite the omnipresent validation of British culture: 'Everything seemed divine and good only if it was English'.[19] Although Kincaid eschews an overtly political allegiance, there is a close connection between Kincaid's anticolonialist essays in *A Small Place* and the feelings ascribed to the young narrators of *Annie John* and *Lucy*.

In her review of Jamaica Kincaid's *Lucy*, Nicolette Jones suggests that the 19-year-old narrator is both innocent and wise. In that novel, Lucy is able to see through Mariah's good intentions, but she is also warm enough to care for Mariah and her children; 'It is a significant achievement that Kincaid allows Lucy to expose faults in her friend without undermining her grounds for affection'.[20] In the novel Lucy is both warm and remote; even in the midst of a love affair, she maintains a detachment from her lover. Jones refers to this as 'the emotional deficiency that will always make her an outsider'.[21]

It is precisely this warmth that is lacking in Kincaid's latest novel, *The Autobiography of My Mother* (1996). In the *New York Times Book Review*, Cathleen Schine claims that this is a 'shocking' book in which the narrator is 'intoxicated with self-hatred', producing a 'truly ugly meditation on life'.[22] The novel starts with the claim 'My mother died at the moment I was born, and so for my whole life there was nothing standing between myself and eternity; at my back was always a bleak, black wind'.[23] Although *The Autobiography of My Mother* is based on the real facts of Kincaid's mother's life, this claim of maternal death is purely fictional, although it is used to explain a psychic crippling. As John Skow says in his review for *Time*, Kincaid's primal theme, repeated well past the point of obsession, has been her abiding resentment of her mother, connected with, but not overriding, her resentment of a cultural imperialism.

Notes

1. R. Cobham and M. Collins (eds), *Watchers & Seekers: Creative Writing by Black Women* (New York: Bedrick, 1988) p. 6.
2. J. Kincaid, *Lucy* (New York: Farrar Straus Giroux, 1990) p. 90.
3. Ibid., p. 123.
4. Ibid., pp. 127–8.
5. Ibid., p. 129.
6. Ibid., pp. 130–1.
7. Ibid., p. 132.
8. Ibid., p. 80.
9. Ibid., pp. 18–19.
10. Ibid., p. 29.
11. Ibid., p. 30.
12. J. Kincaid, 'The Talk of the Town', *New Yorker* (17 October 1977) p. 37.
13. J. Kincaid, *Lucy*, p. 41.
14. J. Kincaid, *Annie John* (New York: New American Library, 1983) p. 76.
15. Ibid., p. 71.
16. J. Kincaid, *A Small Place* (New York: Farrar Straus Giroux, 1988) p. 24.
17. Ibid., p. 31.
18. S. R. Cudjoe, 'Interview with Jamaica Kincaid', *Callaloo*, 12 (1989) p. 397.

19. Ibid., p. 398
20. N. Jones, 'An Innocent Abroad', Review of *Lucy* by Jamaica Kincaid, *The Sunday Times* (23 June 1991) p. 5.
21. Ibid.
22. C. Schine, 'A World as Cruel as Job's', Review of *The Autobiography of My Mother* by Jamaica Kincaid, *The New York Times Book Review* (4 February 1996) p. 5.
23. J. Kincaid, *The Autobiography of My Mother* (New York: Farrar Straus Giroux, 1996) p. 3.

Bibliography

Ashcroft, B., G. Griffiths and H. Tiffin. *The Empire Writes Back: Theory and Practice in Post-Colonial Literatures*. London and New York: Routledge, 1989.

Boyce Davies, C. and E. Fido (eds). *Out of the Kumbla: Caribbean Women and Literature*. Trenton, New Jersey: Africa World Press, 1990.

Cobham R. and M. Collins (eds). *Watchers & Seekers: Creative Writing by Black Women*. New York: Bedrick, 1988.

Cudjoe, S.R. 'Interview with Jamaica Kincaid', *Callaloo*, 12 (1989) pp. 396–411.

Cumber-Dance, D. (ed.). *Fifty Caribbean Writers*. New York: Greenwood, 1986.

Davis, T. 'Girl-Child in a Foreign Land', Review of *Lucy* by Jamaica Kincaid, *New York Times Book Review* (28 October 1990) p. 11.

Ferguson, M. *Jamaica Kincaid: Where the Land Meets the Body*. Charlottesville, VA: UP of Virginia, 1994.

Freeman, S. Review of *At the Bottom of the River* by Jamaica Kincaid *MS.*, (12 January 1984) pp. 15–16.

Gates Jr. H.L. (ed.). *Reading Black, Reading Feminist: A Critical Anthology*. New York: Meridian, 1990.

James, L. Review of *Lucy* by Jamaica Kincaid in *Wasafiri*, 15 (1992) p. 37.

Jones, N. 'An Innocent Abroad', Review of *Lucy* by Jamaica Kincaid, *Sunday Times*, (23 June 1991) p. 5.

Kenney, S. 'Paradise with Snake', Review of *Annie John* by Jamaica Kincaid, *New York Times Book Review* (7 April 1985) p. 6.

Kincaid, J. 'The Talk of the Town', *New Yorker*, (17 October 1977) p. 37.

———. *At the Bottom of the River*. New York: Vintage, 1978.

———. *Annie John*. New York: New American Library, 1983.

———. *A Small Place*. New York: Farrar Straus Giroux, 1988.

———. *Lucy*. New York: Farrar Straus Giroux, 1990.

———. *The Autobiography of My Mother*. New York: Farrar Straus Giroux, 1996.

Maguire, G. Review of *At the Bottom of the River* by Jamaica Kincaid, *Horn Book*, 60 (1984) p. 91.

Milton, E. Review of *At the Bottom of the River* by Jamaica Kincaid, *New York Times Book Review* (15 January 1984) p. 22.

Mordecai, P. and B. Wilson (eds). *Her True-True Name: An Anthology of Women's Writing from the Caribbean* London: Heinemann, 1989.

Niesen de Abruna, L. 'Family Connections: Mother and Mother Country in the Fiction of Jean Rhys and Jamaica Kincaid' in S. Nasta (ed.) *Motherlands: Black Women's Writing from Africa, the Caribbean and South Asia.* New Brunswick, NJ: Rutgers UP, 1991 pp. 257–89.

O'Callaghan, E. 'Feminist Consciousness: European/American Theory, Jamaican Stories', *Journal of Caribbean Studies*, 6:2 (1988) pp. 143–62.

Schine, C. 'A World as Cruel as Job's', Review of *The Autobiography of My Mother* by Jamaica Kincaid, *New York Times Book Review* (4 February 1996) p. 5.

Skow, J. 'Sharper than a Serpent's Pen', Review of *The Autobiography of My Mother* by Jamaica Kincaid, *Time* (5 February 1996).

Spivak, G.C. *In Other Worlds: Essays in Cultural Politics.* New York: Routledge, 1987.

Tyler, A. 'Mothers and Mysteries', *New Republic*, 189 (1983) pp. 32–3.

Wiche, J. Review of *At the Bottom of the River* by Jamaica Kincaid, *Library Journal*, 108 (1983) p. 2262.

11

The Fiction of Zee Edgell

Adele S. Newson

In his 'Belize: An Introduction' written for *Latin American Research Review*, Bruce Ergood deprecates Belize's relative absence in scholarship about Central America. He echoes Wilfred Elrington's characterization of the new nation in Central America as 'the omitted land', and concludes that 'real differences exist between the viewpoints of Belizean and U.S. analysts'.[1] His review, then, is a call for inclusion as well as for a sympathetic treatment of Belize in the histories of Central America. This call, he suggests, should be directed to a person who has experienced the system from within and is able to speak with conviction.[2]

Belizean writer Zee Edgell ably answers Ergood's call with two novels published to critical and popular acclaim; *Beka Lamb* (1982) and *In Times Like These* (1991) chart, in miniature, the development of Belize over a 30-year period.

Of Creole descent, Zelma (Zee) Inez Tucker Edgell grew up in British Honduras during the early 1950s, the daughter of Clive and Veronica Tucker. Her desire to write was nurtured by Sister Andretta Reyes, principal of Holy Redeemer Upper School, who praised an essay on Edgell's writing ambitions. Edgell says that

> I discovered that by writing I could overcome some of the obstacles that faced me as a woman, a Belizean, and later on as someone who was living away from Belize. It helps me to be. If I don't write – I feel unconnected.[3]

In the early 1960s she worked as a reporter on the *Daily Gleaner* in Kingston, Jamaica, and later went to London to study journalism. From 1966 to 1968 she edited a small newspaper in Belize and taught at St Catherine Academy. She began writing after her marriage to Alvin Edgell, a US citizen, with whom she has two children, Holly and Randy. She has travelled widely with her husband and children, living in Nigeria, Britain, Afghanistan, Bangladesh, and the United States. After returning to Belize to serve as Director of the Women's Bureau, she is currently an assistant professor at Kent State University, Ohio.

In an interview with Gay Wilentz, Edgell explains,

> I wanted to record my point of view – from this writer's perspective – what I thought I had seen. Not necessarily what was, but what I thought I had seen. It was there. We don't have a history written by the Belizeans yet, so that I wasn't in any position to write a history, but I felt that history was sufficient to write a novel.[4]

Set between 1951 and 1981, the two novels cover years in which the former British colony experienced sweeping social and political change. In 1954 the Belizean constitution was adopted and in 1964 Belize achieved home rule. Belize was granted full independence on September 21, 1981. One critic believes that *Beka Lamb* might be viewed as a 'literary declaration of independence . . . a direct response to the often asked and heavily loaded question: Can anything good come out of the multi-racial society of the Caribbean Basin?'[5] The same reviewer sees the 'political undercurrent . . . [as] peripheral to the plot of the novel', citing instead Edgell's affirmation of the 'Creole ideal'.[6] Indeed, as storyteller Edgell does more than merely respond to the questions: *Do you remember when the People's United Party was formed? Do you remember those urgent impulses toward decolonization?* Rather, in both novels, the socio-political and the personal are inextricably but unobtrusively tied together: people recall great sweeping social events in terms of their private enterprises.

Edgell produces both history and literature, in the time-honoured tradition of story tellers as described by Trinh T. Minh-ha. Each novel, based on the act of remembering, allows characters to gain insight into their own lives and into a society rich with diverse populations. Renée Hausmann Shea asserts that:

> Edgell's gift is creating and exploring characters who struggle with issues that matter to them and ultimately to us. In depicting these struggles, she blurs the lines between private and public, suggesting, perhaps, that there is no line when sex and race are at issue.[7]

Roger Bromley echoes these sentiments in saying of *Beka Lamb*:

> ... [T]he meanings of the private and the socio-political are never really separable. At every point in the novel, yet not polemically or obtrusively, the personal and the historical intersect as the dominant themes of gender and politics assume the form of a cultural mediation of the making of Belize.[8]

The novel tells the story of how a nation came to its sovereignty. Bromley adds that the political and fictional process are not unrelated: the development of an adolescent girl is likened to the development of a country. Each requires nurturing and an awareness that things break down. Bromley believes that

> the making of the text is a part of the social construction itself. The writing is not ornamental, a cultural 'extra', but an integral feature of socio-political fabric. Society, in other words, is not a set of fixed forms which fiction sets out to discover and then illustrate, but is a making, a never finally settled activity.[9]

Beka Lamb is firmly within the tradition of the black female *bildungsroman*, in which one commonly finds a confrontation between the protagonist and a mother figure (leading either to tragic fragmentation or to greater bonding), a communal spirit embracing several protagonists and offering a variety of 'ways of being in the world', and an act of remembering and of looking back to reassess the maturation process from the vantage point of maturity, suggesting both a political act and an act of education for a specific and larger audience. The end of the novel suggests the start of yet another phase of a continuing journey.

In Times Like These examines the self in the context of the society it inhabits. The protagonist begins her journey with the knowledge that she is a 'displaced' person, existing outside a value system and milieu once familiar to her. Her impulse to romanticize her former existence and her often painful attempts to retrieve it drive the narrative.

Edgell's writing is a mixture of fiction, autobiography, and self-discovery narrative. Her authority derives from the oral tradition of people of African descent. Alternate cosmologies, as Trinh T. Minh-ha suggests in *Woman, Native, Other*, reveal themselves in spite of the tensions for women of colour writing today. These tensions originate in multifaceted forces of power and dominance. The male tradition of writing invites women writers to adopt the power position of 'author', asserting claims to truth and knowledge with arrogant confidence. In this process women of colour are inevitably invited into a conversation of 'us' about 'them' in which 'they' are silenced because the act of defining the lives of 'others' automatically and ironically marginalizes the very people who are the object of scholars' analyses.[10] As Minh-ha explains:

> If we rely on history to tell us what happened at a specific time and place, we can rely on the story to tell us not only what might have happened, but also what is happening at an unspecified time and place. No wonder in old tales storytellers are very often women, witches, and prophets. The African griot and griotte are well known for being poet, storyteller, historian, musician, and magician – all at once.[11]

In the end, Edgell calls on the people themselves to tell their stories; she is, she says, only a medium, saying of *Beka Lamb*, 'I only wrote it'.[12] Edgell dedicates *In Times Like These* 'to Belizeans everywhere'.

Hers is an ambitious project which gives voice to all the diverse peoples of Belize:

> The town didn't demand too much of its citizens, except that in good fortune they be not boastful, not proud, and above all, not critical in any unsympathetic way of the town and country. Then in bad times, whether individuals forsook the common reality, murdered or went bankrupt, Belizeans generally rallied around to assist in whatever ways they could. The townspeople rewarded those citizens perceived as truly loyal, with a devoted tolerance that lasted for generations. . . . In times of danger, it was a tradition for all races to present a united front.[13]

Belizeans, then, see themselves as communal beings. As diverse as the community is, it is nonetheless strengthened in times of adversity. The personal is indeed the political. Edgell's novels constitute a feminist-historical project while adhering to conventions of the black female *bildungsroman* to convey how 'women and a nation struggle toward independence'.[14]

Beka Lamb is the first novel written by a Belizean to reach an international audience.[15] Belize's main racial groups are those of African descent, those of mixed African and European (mulatto and Creole) descent, those of mixed native Indian and Hispanic (mestizo or pania) descent, the Caribs or Garinagu people, and the indigenous Mayas. Edgell chooses as heroine the 14-year-old middle-class Creole girl, Beka Lamb, who grows into maturity during the course of the novel. The story begins on a November day, the day Beka wins the essay contest at St Cecilia's Academy and recalls the events of seven months earlier. These events, including the death of her maternal great-grandmother and the untimely death of her friend Toycie, catapult Beka into womanhood, and as Beka advances toward womanhood, so too does Belize itself race toward political maturity. The problem for Beka as well as for the country is one of 'How to be in the world' given the external and internal threats to their sovereignty. A grim reality is expressed in the Creole saying, 'Anything whe come da Belize sooner or later bruck down',[16] and this warning looms over the lives of the two girls Beka and Toycie.

At the start of the novel, Beka is at the starting point of her journey to adulthood. She wins an essay contest and has, as her mother remarks, made the transformation from a '"flat-rate Belize creole" into a person with "high mind"'.[17] The personal and political merge when the reader discovers that 'befo' time' (traditionally) prizes were awarded to bakras (local whites), panias, or expatriates. The importance of ethnicity in this novel cannot be overstated; racial and ethnic tensions still rage in present-day Belize. Harriot Topsy argues that 'a war is going on between several ethnic groups, and the majority Creoles (who claim 40 to 45 per cent of the population) are leaving the country as a result'.[18]

At fourteen, Beka is immersed in her society. Ever curious, she turns to her paternal grandmother Ivy for information about 'befo' time'. Gran Ivy's responses situate her as the ancestral figure and as the traditional storyteller, the link to the people's past. Lilla, Beka's mother, is a model of 'unconnected present' who believes that Ivy's stories will 'make Beka thin-skinned and afraid to try'.[19] Beka's domestic education is the product of two conflicting practices, two entirely different ways of being in the world. This fact, coupled with the death of her best friend, Toycie, the devaluation of the Belize currency, the activity of the People's Independent

Party, and the presence of British soldiers, familiarizes the young Beka with issues and events that seem well beyond her years. This milieu has much to do with her troubling habit of lying. Lorna Down suggests that '[f]antasy provides a bridge between what is real and what is hoped for and what is expected of her'.[20] This practice, the reader understands, must be controlled as Beka races towards womanhood. Yet it is more than an element of ordinary childhood behaviour: it is, in part, connected with her status as a colonial child. Significantly, 'What Beka recognized in herself as "change" began, as far as she could remember, the day she decided to stop lying.'[21] Coming to womanhood involves the choice of whether to be a good colonial citizen or to be independent.

Beka's dream of being left on the wrong side of town is central to an understanding of this choice. In the dream, Beka goes to 'that side' of town where the sailors work, and where the government house and the library of Bliss Institute are located. Desperate to reach Northside before the bridge swings to the middle of the creek, Beka runs furiously, but:

> It was too late. The bridge, shuddering beneath her feet, began turning slowly away from the shore. Back and forth along the narrow aisle she ran, stopping again and again to shout and beat on the high iron wall separating the main traffic line from the pedestrian aisle. . . .
>
> Laughing uproariously, the crowd pressed against the barriers, pointing elongated fingers to where she now stood exhausted, clinging to the railing. She felt shrunken except for her head which had grown to the size of a large calabash. . . . Sailors standing on the decks of their boats stretched muscled brown arms upwards, calling,
>
> "Jump, nigger gial, jump! We'll ketch you!"[22]

This dream is the central metaphor of the novel, and may be compared with an incident from *I Know Why the Caged Bird Sings* in which Maya Angelou records her 'lifelong paranoia . . . born in those cold, molasses-slow minutes' during which her parental grandmother is accosted by a group of 'powhitetrash' girls in front of her own store. Beka is not a good swimmer and the creek represents the primary threat to her existence. 'Nigger Gial' is not only the name the sailor bestows on her, it is also, curiously, the name of 'the Blanco's skiff' moored off the caye the Lambs visit during the summer vacation.[23] It is a familiar, appropriated name used neutrally in Belize, used here as a vehicle for race.

As Toni Morrison does in her prologue to *The Bluest Eye*, Edgell uses memory in order to explain. In keeping wake for Toycie, Beka is attempting to cope with her own development, which is also the story of Toycie's destruction. The wake is a means of remembering and paying respect, but it is also '"a help to the living"'.[24] Beka's keeping wake in the form of a conscious remembering of Toycie is the key to her salvation. Indeed, the novel was originally titled *A Wake for Toycie*, 'but the publisher didn't like that title'.[25]

Mothers, biological and surrogate, are central to the story of Beka's development. When the bonds of colonization break down, the colonial mother must be replaced with a new indigenous one: the Caribbean mother. (Miss Ivy, we learn early in the novel, is one of the first members of the two-year-old People's Independence Party.) Lorna Down observes:

> The personal stories of the girls Beka and Toycie are used as a way of examining the colonial society. The relationship between Toycie and Emilio in particular suggests the exploitative colonial one.[26]

Beka's successful entry into adulthood is a function of the mothers who nurture her. Toycie's death is at least partly attributable to the absence of her biological mother who has been abroad for 15 of Toycie's 17 years, leaving her with her aunt Elia. Toycie tells Beka,

> '[Y]ou're still luckier than me. You have Miss Lilla, your Daddy and Miss Ivy. . . . My own mother scarcely writes to me anymore. I'd feel better if she were dead. She went to America when I was two and has never come back. She's married to a man in Brooklyn who doesn't even know she has me back here.'[27]

Beka Lamb is mothered by Lilla Lamb (her biological mother), Granny Ivy (her paternal grandmother), and Granny Straker (her maternal great-grandmother). Each 'mother' exerts personal and political influences which help to shape the young girl's way of being in the world, in so far as they each provide models of choices.

Lilla Lamb is genteel. A model colonial subject, she cultivates rose bushes rather than bougainvillea, crotons, and hibiscus. The latter grow easily in the yard, 'but Lilla kept those trimmed back, and continued to struggle year after year in her attempt to cultivate roses like those she saw in magazines which arrived in the colony three months late from England'.[28] She values education as a means to help Beka "to reach a clearing"'.[29] But interestingly, to break Beka of the destructive habit of lying, Lilla recommends the keeping of a journal, instructing Beka to write down her lies, an original and creative suggestion.

Granny Ivy, on the other hand, is a nationalist who believes in self-rule. Through her stories, Granny 'always trie[s] to explain the present to Beka with stories about the past'.[30] Desiring the goodwill of her neighbours, Lilla believes it is best to cut down Beka's bougainvillea bush, which is annoying her neighbour, but Granny Ivy disagrees with the idea because the bush is 'the first thing [Beka] planted that took root'.[31] She adds that peace and happiness

'... only visit in spells, Lilla, best to accept it. I have lived these sixty odd years, and I haven't yet met anyone at peace or happy.... If we cried every time somebody's life fall apart, this country would be called the one true valley of tears.'[32]

Essentially, both Lilla and Gran Ivy are compelled to urge Beka into adulthood. Though their methods and ideas vary, their goal is the same. Both Beka's father Bill Lamb and his mother Ivy are nationalists in that they believe in the promise of the country and its people. They differ politically in that Bill favours federation while Granny Ivy favours independence first.

Great Grandmother Straker, ill at the start of the story, functions as the surrogate presence removed from the family. She serves, at the same time, as family historian and chronicler of the country's economic history. She dies in her sleep, over the age of 80, while the family is at the Caye on vacation. Known as Old Mother Straker, she is lauded as 'one of the last. Not too many left now of the old people that remember things from the time before. The young ones aren't interested'.[33] Beka, however, is one who questions and craves information about the past. This interest is yet another signal that she will cross the bridge to womanhood with her sense of self and community intact. Toycie, her counterpart, has neither Beka's host of maternal surrogates nor a grounding in history to support her crossing.

Beka and Toycie have a solid friendship. Though 14 and 17 respectively, their friendship thrives because 'Toycie remember[s] what it [is] like to be fourteen, and Beka ha[s] the ability to pretend seventeen.'[34] This is where the similarity ends, however. Beka's father is a businessman of moderate means and she lives with her extended family. Both Toycie's parents are absent and she is raised by her aunt, who is a domestic. Toycie is artistic and a dreamer of the fanciful and Beka is given to a pragmatic politics. Toycie's passivity in relation to Emilio is the cause of her breakdown.

Two central problems dominate the novel: Beka's failure at school and Toycie's involvement with Emilio Sanchez Villanueva, a young pania and therefore from a racial group who, as Beka reminds Toycie, '"scarcely ever marry creole like we"'.[35] Both problems are firmly situated in the socio-political and socio-economic realities of the country. Bill Lamb is angry that what he pays in school fees, '"could feed a poor family for six months"'.[36] Granny Ivy says of Toycie's relationship with Emilio, 'Toycie was trying to raise her colour, and would wind up with a baby instead of a diploma, if she wasn't careful'.[37] During the summer holiday, Toycie accompanies Beka's family to St George's Caye where she secretly meets with Emilio at the expense of the relationship she has with Beka. The essence of the multi-ethnic conflict in Belize is engendered in the personal relationship between Toycie (the Creole girl) and Emilio (the pania boy). As a lover she is a satisfactory experiment, a means of affirming his rite of passage to adulthood. Given the social, class and ethnic structure of Belize, she could never be satisfactory as wife. Ethnicity and social class are powerful agents working against the two young lovers.

In the period of two months, things break down for both girls at an alarming pace, but for Beka, the adversities are turned to use and she is supported by her family. In an effort to stay Beka's fanciful inclinations, Lilla Lamb presents her with exercise book and pen, advising:

'[E]verytime you feel like telling a lie, I want you to write it down in there and pretend you are writing a story. That way, you can tell the truth and save the lie for this notebook. And when we tell you stories about before time, you can write them down in there, too, for your children to read.'[38]

In providing Beka with the notebook and in accepting the tradition of the wake, Lilla is providing a model for Beka by which she can overcome adversities.

The funeral and wake for Granny Straker serves as the cata- lyst for the changes affecting the two girls, both good and bad. Beka's father decides to allow her to go back to school and Toycie is pregnant. Toycie is killed during the heavy storm, having wandered off during the preparation for the hurricane. But Beka does not 'break down'. The collaboration for folksongs (to be sung in honour of Mother Provincial's visit) between herself, Sister Gabriela, and Granny Ivy, after the death of Toycie, establishes this fact. Lilla undertakes to plant poinciana. Beka wins first place in the essay contest honouring the seventy-fifth anniversary of the Sisters of Charity in the colony of Belize, and the beginning of the march for independence is heralded: 'Belize people are only just beginning! Soon we'll all be able to vote instead of only the big property owners, then we may get self-government and after that, who knows?'[39] At the end of the novel, Beka's personal triumph is coupled with that of her country.

In Times Like These is Edgell's second novel and a companion piece to *Beka Lamb*. According to Edgell, 'People don't realize that although this novel is set in a certain year, many of the events, flashbacks, deal with *Beka Lamb*.'[40] The novel is a mixture of adventure, romance, and drama. Edgell herself calls the novel 'a simple story about a young woman with twins who returns to her home to introduce them to her father'. Pavana Leslie, the central character, returns to Belize after some 15 years to recon- nect with lost values. A former member of the international set, Pavana works as an administrative assistant to Julian Carlisle, an official working for the United World, a development organiza- tion. Stationed in East Africa, Pavana understands herself to be wandering 'down an interminable side road' entering the realm of caricature and burlesque.[41] Like Beka Lamb, who abhors the name *phoney*, which 'pepper[s] her insides good and hot',[42] Pavana 'value[s] her individuality and ha[s] an absolute distaste for the poseur'.[43] Her decision to return to Belize is influenced by a sense of 'uprootedness' coupled with a resurgence of patriotism, as Belize is in the throes of sweeping social and political change.

Set principally in Belize in March 1981 – a year 'Belizeans were unlikely to forget in a hurry'[44] – the novel examines the country's bid for independence from both British and Guatemalan claims, the preoccupation of the emigrée attempting to readjust to Belizean society and the plight of the single mother. The economy is in a shambles and a secret new crop becomes the country's biggest export item. More importantly, 'the heads of agreement' are a subject of immediate concern for Belizeans, so named for the headings of the agenda for Guatemala, Great Britain and Belize, in the discussion of Guatemala's claim of part of Belize by rights inherited from Spain. The popular belief is that Belize may well become a colony again. Indeed, as a condition of independence, Great Britain mandates that Guatemala, Belize, and Britain try once more to find a compromise. Renée Hausmann Shea calls the novel a *bildungsroman*, but this time it is a 30-something character who is 'trying to become the person she wanted to be'.[45] Similarly, the country itself is coming into autonomy, into the self that it believes it can be. That self rejects colonialism and victimization in all their myriad forms. Pavana's resolve to accept the position in the Ministry of Community Development is inspired by her feeling 'helpless in the face of the bafflement, anger and sadness with which most citizens viewed not only the proposed agenda but a vast array of other difficulties facing the country'.[46]

When Pavana, a Creole Belizean, leaves Belize to enrol in journalism classes in London she is full of hope and naïvety, social and political. In London, she encounters a Belizean, Alex Abrams, a student reading law at university. Alex possesses an overabundance of political aspirations, charm, and rhetorical skills. He is looked upon by the West Indian student population as a demigod. Sensing Pavana's displacement and discomfort in London, he befriends her, and ultimately the two become lovers. At the start of the novel, Pavana is 21 and pregnant. She is considering abortion as a means of avoiding the cultural pattern of her countrywomen. Alex, the father, is intent upon marrying a German woman he believes to be better able to advance his political aspirations once he returns to Belize. He provides Pavana with money for an abortion, which she decides against at the eleventh hour. Thereby, she offers yet another way of being in the world for women in her position. She has twins, Lisa and Eric, and does not inform Alex of their existence until her return to Belize.

The present begins after Pavana accepts the position of Director of the Women's Unit with the Ministry of Community Development in Belize, some years after her experiences in London and East Africa. The position requires her to work for the development of Belizean women. In this way Edgell explores the intricacies of working for the development of women within a framework of a pluralistic country (Mayan, Creole, Mestizo, Garinagu, East Indian, Chinese, and others). Yet Pavana's appointment is fraught with controversy. She is not a political affiliate and the ruling party wants a party member to direct the unit. As one male official explains, '"It's just another government unit"'.[47]

If the novel is intended as a realistic representation of Belizean society, then it suggests that despite the declaration of the era's being that of the Decade of Women, Belizean women, regardless of social class and heritage, are among the most oppressed women in the world, living still in the 'befo' time'. In a radio interview Pavana conducts in the interest of public education programming, a woman who attended one of Pavana's workshop shares her life with the listener:

'My husband and I have ten children, and we are grateful for them. . . . Sometimes I give them a little trouble you know. My mouth is a little fast. So my husband has to punish me sometimes, but I deserve it. He punishes me because he loves me. He's not like some who beat their wives for little or nothing, especially when they are drunk.'[48]

In spite of the time and effort invested in the total independence effort, '"the lives of women have improved very little"'.[49]

The novel is rich in its depiction of what is commonly termed 'women's problems' – that of paternal abandonment and the task of rearing children without aid from the fathers. Abandonment, bundled within the phrase 'taking slaveman's revenge', is the personal practice that engenders the political powerlessness of Belizean women, even from the educated classes.

In the midst of the action is the failed love affair between Pavana and Alex. Their relationship is a study of personal victimization. During the winter of 1967, Pavana arrives in London where she meets Alex. He is involved with a German student, Helga Konig, whom he eventually marries. When she goes to Germany for six months, Alex courts Pavana as Pygmalion courted Galatea. Yet the more she accomplishes, the less affinity he has with her. When she is no longer able to sustain the role of ingenue, he distances himself from her. He appears to be 'always at his best with her only when she seem[s] vulnerable or helpless . . . this was the nature of their relationship, always had been'.[50] A star among the Caribbean student population abroad, Alex convinces her

> [T]hat they [are] a new breed in the Caribbean; that they would attempt to create an economically viable, progressive, creative and just society, a society that would offer the possibility of participation for everyone. . . .[51]

Once Alex marries Helga and returns to Belize, his idealism wanes and he becomes desperate to hold on to office. After Alex's rejection, Pavana 'eschew[s] romantic love from her life . . . concentrate[s] almost entirely on her children and on her small ambitions'.[52] Meanwhile Julian Carlisle, ever in attendance, helps her raise her children and serves as a platonic companion during her needy years. She reasons that love is 'a competitive business, demanding dedication, self-denial, discipline, continuous practice, cunning manoeuvres, guerilla tactics: the same, she suppose[s], as in any other profession'.[53]

In Belize, Pavana's children are kidnapped by Alex's half brother, Stoner, in an effort to force Alex to resign his position and speak out against the heads of agreement. Pavana approaches Alex for help in locating their children. Pavana is, at this point, near the breaking point. Yet Alex views her vulnerability merely as an opportunity. After he unbraids Pavana's hair in a moment which for him signals the chance for conquest, he explains, '"It [her free flowing hair] reminds me of you when you were you"'.[54] The 'you' that Alex chooses to remember is that of Pavana, the needy ingenue in London. He defines and shapes and hence controls Pavana during their student years abroad. Because Helga died two years before, he is free, and offers Pavana a proposal of marriage. She rejects both his advances and the proposal. In so doing, she rejects victimization explaining that '"People's needs change"'.[55] She has recently discovered that she does indeed love Julian, a person with whom she can achieve equanimity.

Alex symbolizes the new Caribbean in that he is deficient and disappointing. Though educated and a skilful orator, he remains a case study in domination. A politician who still regards women as traditional objects to serve his needs and aspirations, he has 'a cold and arrogant side' to his personality that debilitates Pavana. For all his good intentions about the development of Belize, he never considers the question of women. Alex victimizes his wife Helga and Pavana as well as his sister for personal gain. His sister Moria, a constant companion in London and Belize, is also his lover. He brags after Pavana's rejection of him that he has '"achieved the ultimate in machismo! No door is closed to me, no bedroom door for sure, not even that of my [sister]"'.[56] Pavana examines, during the course of the novel, those attributes that stifle her well-being. When she decides to leave Julian and the United World Agency, she confesses to Julian,

'[A] lot of people, myself included, find development attractive but disturbing at the same time. . . . At home I'll try to discover what those values, attitudes, traditions and so on are that keep us 'developing' but never 'developed.'[57]

Development, the novel suggests, is an internal enterprise. In sum, it implies that the key to the dilemma rests with the condition of the women in the country. Indeed, Alex inspires her to the understanding of the importance of her work with the Women's Unit, 'not only on behalf of women but on behalf of men'.[58]

Moreover, women had long been regarded by male politicians as 'traditional territory, to serve their needs and aspirations'.[59] Hence, the entire notion of women and development is antithetical to the present government. As one of the few ministers who actually supports Pavana's appointment explains,

'Women's liberation. We don't need that here. Our women are free to rise as high as they please, if they wish to do so, which I don't believe they do, at least I haven't met many.'[60]

Traditional ideas about Belizean women abound in the novel. These notions are themselves aided and abetted by male-identified women who unwittingly contribute to their own oppression.

The condition of women, treated tangentially in *Beka Lamb* is fully explored in this novel. Where Toycie breaks down, Pavana expresses the possibilities of existing as mother and professional.

Motherhood seems to fuel Pavana throughout the novel. It is the source from which Pavana draws her strength, motivation, and conviction. Pavana is a mix of the 'terrible Caribbean mother' featured in Sybil Seaforth's *Growing Up with Miss Milly* and Jamaica Kincaid's *Annie John*. Given the socio-political realities, if not economic realities, of the Caribbean, motherhood is uneasily informed by tough love and possession/companionship. Yet Pavana is also the mother of independence, who refuses to be victimized by man or government – a government which still believes in the notion of rights over women.

While the new may be spurned by the people of Belize, Pavana grows into the knowledge that victims are victims so long as they permit themselves to be. Pavana accepts the position as Director of the Women's Unit in the Ministry of Community Development in 1981 against the backdrop of political and social upheaval. Still a colony of England, the inhabitants of Belize 'called a temporary halt to most overt hostilities' as they are faced with the immediate threat of Guatemalan expansion. Protest against the government's policy of 'victimization' follows. Similarly, an uneasy truce exists between Pavana and Alex as the threat to their children magnifies.

The story was inspired by an actual event, 'two brothers actually killed each other over this. They were on opposing sides'.[61] In the end, as calm is restored to the country, Pavana laments the death of Alex as the death of an era in which educated idealists returned to Belize to effect real social and political change in the country. Pavana reflects:

> These sounds, signalling the resumption of life's routine, seemed out of place, ordinary, belonging to another period of time, one which had ended. Shouldn't there be mourning in the streets, the blowing of trumpets, the beating of drums, some signal that another less innocent era had begun? What happened in a country when one or more of its heroes died?[62]

Sacrifice (Alex's sacrificing his life for Stoner and Pavana's sacrifice to the cause of development for women), it would appear, is the key to the development of a person and country. She ultimately understands that 'sometimes in the heart of defeat is hidden eternal victory'.[63] The end, then, signals the move to yet another stage of life.

Working on two levels, *Beka Lamb* is the story of a young girl's foray into adulthood and the story of a developing nation's foray into sovereignty. *In Times Like These* is the story of a young woman's exploration of self, of choices and ways of being in the world, as well as the choice of leadership for a nation. Edgell's latest novel was published in 1997. Told from the perspective of a Mestizo woman, *The Festival of San Joaquin* is based on a real incident, the arrest of a woman for the murder of her common-law husband. Edgell's commitment to Belize, women, and pluralism continues.

Notes

1. B. Ergood, 'Belize: An Introduction', *Latin American Research Review*, 26:3 (Summer 1991) p. 258.
2. Ibid.
3. I. McClaurin, 'A Writer's Life: a Country's Transition', *Americas*, 46:4 (July–Aug. 1994–5) p. 38.
4. G. Wilentz, '"One Life is not Enough": An Interview with Zee Edgell', *Obsidian II*, 9:2 (Fall/Winter 1994) p. 31.
5. C. Hunter, 'LITERATURE: Belize's First Novel, *Beka Lamb*', *Belizean Studies*, 10:6 (December 1982) p. 14.
6. Ibid., p. 17 and p. 19.
7. R.H. Shea, 'The Person She Wants to Be', *Belle Lettres*, 8:1 (Fall 1992) p. 38.
8. R. Bromley, 'Reaching a Clearing: Gender and Politics in *Beka Lamb*', *Wasafiri*, 2 (1985) p. 10.
9. Ibid.
10. P. Grimshaw, A Review of Trinh T. Minh-ha's *Woman, Native, Other* in *Explorations in Sights and Sounds*, II (Summer 1991) p. 41.
11. T.T. Minh-ha, *Woman, Native, Other* (Bloomington: Indiana University Press, 1989) p. 120.
12. C. Hunter, 'LITERATURE: Belize's First Novel, *Beka Lamb*', *Belizean Studies*, 10:6 (December 1982) p. 15.
13. Z. Edgell, *Beka Lamb* (Oxford: Heinemann, 1982) p. 12.
14. I. McClaurin, 'A Writer's Life: a Country's Transition', *Americas*, p. 41.
15. It won the 1982 Fawcett Society Book Prize, and was included in the CXE (Caribbean Examination Council) syllabus.
16. C. Hunter, 'LITERATURE: Belize's First Novel, *Beka Lamb*', *Belizean Studies*, 10:6 (December 1982) p. 17.
17. Z. Edgell, *Beka Lamb*, p. 1.
18. Cited in Ergood p. 263.
19. Z. Edgell's, *Beka Lamb*, p. 2.

20. L. Down, 'Singing Her Own Song: Women and Selfhood in Zee Edgell's *Beka Lamb*', *Ariel*, 18:4 (1987) p. 45.
21. Z. Edgell, *Beka Lamb*, p. 17.
22. Ibid., pp. 6–7.
23. Ibid., p. 44.
24. Ibid., p. 66.
25. G. Wilentz, '"One Life is not Enough"', *Obsidian II*, 9:2 (Fall/Winter 1994) p. 32.
26. L. Down, 'Singing Her Own Song: Women and Selfhood in Zee Edgell's *Beka Lamb*', *Ariel*, 18:4 (1987) p. 39.
27. Z. Edgell, *Beka Lamb*, p. 59.
28. Ibid., p. 9.
29. Ibid., p. 10.
30. Ibid., p. 2.
31. Ibid., p. 41.
32. Ibid., pp. 41–2.
33. Ibid., p. 62.
34. Ibid., p. 34.
35. Ibid., p. 47.
36. Ibid., p. 24.
37. Ibid., p. 47.
38. Ibid., p. 71.
39. Ibid., p. 167.
40. G. Wilentz, '"One Life is not Enough": An Interview with Zee Edgell', *Obsidian II*, 9:2 (Fall/Winter 1994) p. 35.
41. Z. Edgell, *In Times Like These* (Oxford: Heinemann, 1991) p. 16.
42. Z. Edgell, *Beka Lamb*, p. 20.
43. Z. Edgell, *In Times Like These*, p. 18.
44. Ibid., p. 46.
45. R.H. Shea, 'The Person She Wants to Be', *Belle Lettres*, 8:1 (Fall 1992) p. 38.
46. Z. Edgell, *In Times Like These*, p. 126.
47. Ibid., p. 163.
48. Ibid., p. 209.
49. Ibid., p. 65.
50. Ibid., p. 291.
51. Ibid., p. 35.
52. Ibid., p. 125.
53. Ibid.
54. Ibid., p. 279.
55. Ibid., p. 284.
56. Ibid., p. 280.
57. Ibid., p. 23.
58. Ibid., p. 283.
59. Ibid., p. 195.
60. Ibid., p. 133.
61. G. Wilentz, '"One Life is Not Enough": An Interview with Zee Edgell', *Obsidian II*, 9:2 (Fall/Winter 1994) p. 42.
62. Z. Edgell, *In Times Like These*, p. 306.
63. Ibid., p. 307.

Bibliography

Angelou, M. *I Know Why the Caged Bird Sings.* New York: Bantam Books, 1970.

Blain, V., P. Clements and I. Grundy. 'Zee Edgell' in *The Feminist Companion to Literature in English.* New Haven: Yale University Press, 1990.

Bromley, R. 'Reaching a Clearing: Gender and Politics in *Beka Lamb'*, *Wasafiri*, 2 (1985) pp. 10–14.

Down, L. 'Singing Her Own Song: Women and Selfhood in Zee Edgell's *Beka Lamb'*, *Ariel*, 18:4 (1987) pp. 39–50.

Ergood, B. 'Belize: An Introduction', *Latin American Research Review*, 26:3 (Summer 1991) pp. 257–65.

Grimshaw, P. A review of Trinh T. Minh-ha's *Woman, Native, Other* in *Explorations in Sights and Sounds*, 11 (Summer 1991) pp. 40–1.

Hodge, M. *Crick Crack, Monkey.* London: Heinemann, 1970.

Hunter, C. 'LITERATURE: Belize's First Novel, *Beka Lamb'*, *Belizean Studies*, 10:6 (December 1982) pp. 14–21.

McClaurin, I. 'A Writer's Life: a Country's Transition', *Americas*, 46:4 (July–Aug 1994) pp. 38–43.

Minh-ha, T.T. *Woman, Native, Other.* Bloomington: Indiana University Press, 1989.

Morrison, T. *The Bluest Eye.* New York: Washington Square Press, 1970.

Newson, A.S. A review of *In Times Like These* in *Shooting Star Review*, 7:1 pp. 44–5.

Shea, R.H. 'The Person She Wants to Be', *Belle Lettres*, 8:1 (Fall 1992) p. 38.

Wilentz, G. '"One Life is not Enough": An Interview with Zee Edgell', *Obsidian II*, 9:2 (Fall/Winter 1994) pp. 27–45.

12

Dionne Brand:
Writing the Margins

Charlotte Sturgess

'There is always something that must be remembered, some-thing that cannot be forgotten, something that must be weighed.'[1]

In Dionne Brand's writing the effort of the 'not forgetting', the necessity of a confrontation between past and present, demands to be examined in the light of her particular experience. As Francesco Loriggio has said of Brand's writing, 'It designates sub-types, the degree of distance towards the cultural past and the cultural present, of insidership or of outsidership one can or one does assume'.[2] As a Trinidadian Canadian black lesbian feminist, Dionne Brand folds her particular ethnic experience into a political consciousness. Writing itself determines the agenda of her commitment, marks out the possibilities of revision, does the 'unforgetting'. Both her poetry and her prose actively seek to problematize those perceptions of race, gender and sexuality which continually reject the Other to the margins in order to reproduce a white, heterosexual, phallic 'centre'. The ways in which her writing investigates such cultural spaces will be the object of this essay. For if writing for Brand is centred on the release from oppres-sion, structuring, as Carol Morrell states, a 'subject-position as a tool for political intervention',[3] the two-way pull of where one is (on the margins) and the signifying, recuperatory potential of that space, produces complex relations to language. Strong referentiality focuses Brand's political ethos in the redefinition, repositioning and dismantling of hierarchies. As Claire Harris, another Trinidadian Canadian black writer, says of her own political commitment:

> I write to displace the notion that the South and its people are not integral to modern Western civilization. . . . The reaction

of Europe, both in the Americas and at home, was to set its heart/its body/its head to scramble at the margins of backyard sinks, while its mind entertained in the drawing room.[4]

The importance of this statement would seem to lie in its gesturing to the multiple Othering that is the heritage and the medium of Caribbean writings; to the system of affiliations, desires and resistances which translate textually as borders, ruptures and erasures, and which inserts such writing within a historical context of collective violence and suffering. Colonial imaginary space is inherently split, the language of the experience of oppression at a symbolic distance from its origins in those European drawing-rooms of which Harris speaks. Contemporary racism and sexism, whether the backdrop to or the explicit themes of Brand's work, effect the erasure of the individual in the present, even as they retrace the erasure of origins in a colonial past. Presence itself has then to be constantly mediated through discontinuity, and the strategies, diversions and subversions which attest to its complicated allegiances in post-colonial time and space render the securing of the subject in language both crucial and highly problematical.

As Mireille Rosella states, the Caribbean exile has suffered a double displacement through the 'Middle Passage' and diasporic scattering.[5] If therefore there is a necessary dispersal at the heart of reflection on Caribbean literature, a multiplication of overlapping codes and images, this distance from a unified linear history creates in Brand's work a fundamental migrancy: a shifting of subject positions and of voice, and a crumpling of texture as narrative deals with erasure. Resistance takes the form of revision, particularly in poetry which re-enacts the symbolic dismemberment of the African body, its enforced migrancy and loss.

As in her poetry, the displaced individual, cultural silencing, absence and exile are the themes treated in Brand's collection of stories *Sans Souci*,[6] and as in her poetry, Brand's prose is interstitial, shifting on borders of meaning and concerned with the problem of finding voice as a racially and sexually inscribed Other. The story 'No rinsed blue sky, no red flower fences' announces the presence of absence in the title. It is written in an economy of the 'in between', conditioned by an arrival which incessantly rewrites departure and where living 'here' (in this case Toronto), means inscription on the margins of a 'there' where solitude reigns and personal history falls away.

This narrative of semantic fluctuations, seepages, and conden-
sations is structured by an anonymous Black woman's combat
with estrangement in a concrete cityscape. Her rented apartment
constitutes a trope of fixity in the story, establishing a chain of
meaning as questions of ontological boundaries and continuity
provide an interface with the development of her life in Toronto.
If plot development collapses, increasingly concerned with individual alienation in a city dotted with empty spaces – 'bachelor
apartments she could not afford' – it is a narrative in which
boundaries are both policed and disputed, in which the condition of presence itself is challenged. Ideological discourse at odds
with personal history causes the collision of codes in the story as
the concentration of values and power represented by high-rise
blocks and urban consumer life-styles establishes hierarchy, whilst
the irruption of images from 'elsewhere' establishes fluidity and
dispersal. The apartment, painted yellow, then white, which
'[w]hen she had money ... sounded homely' but where '...
When she was flat broke and depressed, the sound of footsteps
outside the door made her jumpy'[7] is emblematic of the simultaneous imprisonment in and exclusion from a middle-class system
of values. The other reality, accessible only in fantasies or dreams,
therefore not attaining referential status in the narrative, belongs
to the fluid register of the image: 'The feel of the salt, blue and
moving water, rushing past her ears and jostling her body, cleaning
it, coming up a different person each time as she dove through
a curling wave'.[8]

Both contexts remain indeterminate and narrative authority loses
itself in the gaps, troubling the source of voice itself. For if the
image of renewal and conversion is accomplished as the slide
from referential to fantasy projection, the following statements:
'Not knowing how it would turn out. A feeling of touching something quite big'[9] slip out of the narrator's control and beyond
the character's consciousness. The narrative registers the questioning presence of an uncanny 'elsewhere' lodged at the centre
of the metaphor, as though the plunge into the ocean is a symbolic
vector to an authorial desire, emerging in the interstices of
discursive play. The richness, sensuality and fluidity of this and
other images in the story coincides with Marlene Nourbese Philip's
comment on the importance of the image or 'i-mage' citing 'the
Rastafarian practice of privileging the "I" in many words',[10] and
thus founding the images in Caribbean writing in determined

inscriptions of the self. The gradual slippage of the woman's identity in the story is filtered through a process of negation – her lack of a legal status in Canada, a fatherless baby sent 'home' after a pregnancy and birthing which are subsequently effaced from memory: 'But no one was there, no one knew and the name she had used was not hers. Nor did the baby exist. No papers'.[11]

The gradual succumbing to gaps and blanks which signify the unstitching of causality is increasingly the condition for the retreat of the 'real', both thematically, as the woman falls back into silence, and discursively, as fantasy projections increasingly disrupt linear flow, causing the apartment itself to shift perspective: '. . . her imagination tightened the walls of the apartment giving them a cavernous, gloomy look. . . . The phone would ring and startle her. The sound would blast around in her chest and she would pray for it to stop, never thinking to answer it'.[12] The eternal 'detour' of Caribbean writing, mentioned earlier, leads back through a self which is in a state of permanent flux, for, as the narrator admits, a 'girl in a wet T-shirt, the sea in back, the sun on her body' does not represent her home. Instead '[i]ts glamour shielded her from the cold outside and the dry hills back home at the same time'.[13] Suspended on the border between worlds, where the 'real' is deferred and transit assured, the character's displacement would seem above all to translate the impossible terms of discourse in a narrative where reference cannot be secured, and which seems aptly encoded in the narrator's comment on the apartment: 'The apartment had two rooms. She needed a place with two rooms. Each so that she could leave the other'.[14]

Another story concerned with unstitching seams of continuity which ponder an 'elsewhere', 'Photograph' clearly problematizes the structuring of a transparent secure 'real'. The opening sentence of the story is predictive: 'My grandmother has left no trace, no sign of her self'.[15] If the grandmother is at the centre of the plot (which is little concerned with event or action for their own sake), she is equally the filter through which concepts of voice and identity are examined. As in much Black women's writing she represents continuity and origins, but the narrative process of return to the source in memory proves in fact a circular quest, for continuity itself is problematic and unity of voice not accomplished. Instead, beginnings are continuously reactivated as threads of narrative disperse with a narrative texture caught up in indeterminacy. Such indeterminacy reveals itself as much a

function of unstable meanings as the obvious thematic development around the search for identity and a coherent source of
voice. In this respect the narrative is littered with references which
entail a questioning of the premises of representation. Such is
the case in a passage which, whilst thematically inscribing a collective identity through a description of the grandmother's house
and effects, is a dialectic of the discursive conditions for such an
identity and the causal premises for continuity:

> We never knew how anything got into the drawer, because
> we never saw things enter the house. Everything in the drawer
> was pressed and ironed and smelled of starch and ironing and
> newness and oldness. My grandmother guarded them often
> more like burden than treasure. Their depletion would make
> her anxious; their addition would pose problems of space in
> our tiny house.[16]

Is the reader here confronted with a process of accumulation or
of loss? Where is resolution to be found if an 'outside' capable of
structuring the narrative-represented space is an 'outside' of knowledge itself, denoted by 'We never knew' and 'we never saw'?
The absence of a secure boundary tracing the limit of the narrator's field of knowledge and manoeuvre seems to destabilize the
premises of represented space itself, questioning the ontology of
an 'inside' which does not refer back to a governing discursive
responsibility. It is as if the 'burden' of the drawer's 'treasure'
and its unresolvability in the contradictory oldness-newness,
depletion-addition, is the saturation point heralding a crisis of
meaning itself.

Connections can be made with the critic Patricia Smart's definition of what is at stake in women's writing, that is: '[C]ette
lutte éminemment textuelle entre la texture et la Loi [qui] se
répercute en effet sur l'instance narrative et se traduit dans les
rapports entre les personnages masculins et féminins' (the textual
confrontation between texture and the Law which affects modes
of narration and is at work in the interaction between male and
female characters).[17] Those institutional, ideological and symbolic
(thus discursive) structures of history and continuity associated
with 'the Law', which in narrative are influential in establishing
boundaries and contours of representation, are singularly problematic in 'Photograph'. Apart from a singular appearance of the

grandfather, folded into one of the grandmother's rolling narratives, (thus gaining no referential status on the level of plot), male characters are conspicuous by their absence. This 'absent presence' of the masculine pole is registered in the way the narrative seems unable, through lack of defining codes, to organize and channel interconnecting networks of meaning. Instead, as the cited passage reveals, causality itself is halted on the border of the overtaxed and polarized maternal domain of the grandmother.

Another indication of the overdetermined maternal space, and the resulting slide into indeterminacy, is the concentration of objective reference itself at certain points, as though Otherness is registered through its concerted repression, thus undermining from within the terms of accumulation. This implies the gradual slippage from the specific to the general, the particular to the abstract, losing reference en route. For if the grandmother's possessions are a source of curiosity for the numerous children in her charge, their investigation provokes the type of tension which finds relief, not rift:

> ... we would try on her dresses or her hat, or open the bottom drawer of the wardrobe where she kept sheets, pillowcases and underwear ... pieces of cloth for headties and dresses and curtains, ... We would wrap ourselves in pieces of cloth, pretending we were African queens; ... we were always on the lookout for the next chance to interfere in my grand-mother's sacred things.[18]

The shifts from the mundane to registers of fantasy – 'pillowcases' to 'African queens' – from plural to the indeterminate 'pieces' sets up an internal dissonance just as it provokes a saturation of reference in the effort to secure a viable 'real'. In a similar way the children themselves fail to secure individual status, generating such appellations as 'We were an ever growing bunch of cousins, sisters and brothers',[19] falling prey to the narrative's difficulty in structuring difference. Such is surely the significance of their collapse into 'lawlessness' as soon as the grandmother's back is turned, and the impossibility of 'assigning blame' for, as the narrator says: 'We were all implicated and my grandmother always beat everyone, no matter who committed the crime'.[20]

If the conditions of agency and responsibility are constantly at risk, the grandmother patrols the borders of a space in which threads of story both circulate and tail off and the hierarchy of genealogy gives in to her authority. As the narrator states: 'We had always lived with my grandmother. None of us could recollect our mothers, except as letters from England or occasional visits from women who came on weekends'.[21] Time itself seems to be arrested in a continuum where 'always' reverberates through the erasure of memory of the mother. Just as an autonomous past and future is unimaginable because all roads cross and recross the grandmother's territory, so the anchoring of dynastic history falls short on the once more indeterminate description of 'women who came on weekends' which rejects them to the margins of representation. After working in England, the metropolitan, colonial 'elsewhere', the mother's return to the Caribbean signals her arrival as the 'strange and foreign' outsider. Instead of a nurturing presence and a central link in family continuity, she signals a crisis of authority which is resolved in her taking on the role of Other, thus focusing the propensity of the narrative to create internal crisis. Attempting to forge a niche in the hierarchy of the household, her authority is literally 'unimaginable' and she passes through a period of estranged recognition to that of alienation, eventually falling into silence. In much the same way that a troubled relation to masculine structures of 'the Law' affects the circulation of meaning in 'Photograph', so the colonial presence takes shape (if a shadowy, uncanny shape), through the inability to pin a defining contour of identity to the figure of the returning mother.

Both the focus of envy, where the narrator should 'go away and live well', or the place where Winter kills and 'white cannibals' devour Black children, or the 'Away-away' of drifting fantasy, 'England' is unable to be secured as a stable reference, but instead signifies as a disruptive presence through the mother who focuses such contradictory discourses. She is in fact 'Othered' to such an extent that the only material shape she could take in the narrator's imagination is the racial Other: 'To tell the truth, we were expecting a white woman to come through the door'.[22] Through her violent disruption of order, her place shifting between both worlds but accepted in neither, and mediating as she does in displaced fashion the legacy of colonization, the mother's unstable presence could equally be seen as the site where the dilemma of post-colonial language itself is invested. The strategies of silencing that relegate her to the status of the 'unnameable' are sufficiently insistent to make us ponder the ontological trace of the silence itself. The passage which establishes her presence in the household is entirely given up to the problem of how to address her and begins, 'We had debated what to call my mother over and over again and came to no conclusions' in order to end fourteen lines later with 'Finally, we never called my mother'.[23] Resistance, denial and final repression are also accomplished within the flow of stories which characterize the grandmother's signifying mode, protecting the 'inside' of privileged discourse from a disruptive presence by the violence of arrested communication: 'In the end, we closed our scenes ostentatiously in her presence'.[24]

This ambivalence towards the maternal heritage, which reveals identification to be fraught with conflict, can also be linked to the fundamental ambivalences of female-centred plots in relation to writing and history. As Marianne Hirsch comments, speaking of black women's writing and maternal discourse:

> . . . if the fantasy is a shared and loving connection rather than separation, the realities of the texts themselves reveal the fantasy to be mixed with ambivalence, fear, and anger. Between these mothers and daughters, whose lives remain intertwined with each other in plots that never lead to separation, much remains unspeakable and indeed unspoken.[25]

'Home' territory is very much the nurturing body of the grandmother, whose voice is a 'tongue lapping over a new story', but it is also the site where the narrator loses her own voice, signalling her incapacity to fill the gaps or bridge the absence which threatens continuity. Feminine homogeneity is such that not only are male characters absent from the plot, but the masculine pole of sexual difference caves in when menstruation, that female rite of passage, becomes a source of potential indeterminacy:

> . . . a rumour blazed its way through all the children just let out from school that there was a male sanitary napkin at the side of the road. . . . all the girls whipped their fingers at the boys on the street singing, "Boys have periods TOOOOOO!"[26]

If alterity and fragmentation thus threaten narrative on the level of symbolic displacement and referential instability (the problem of voice), this narrating self is steadily subjected to a splitting and dividing, and the unity of speech posited by the reiterated 'I', 'our', 'we', is at risk of dispersal. One of the signs of this disputed control of voice can perhaps be identified as the constant effort by the narrator to appropriate a 'settled' speech through the continual return to these pronouns as a reaffirmation of the experience or speaking self, as though narrative could not weave its way into plot but that instead a constant 'policing' of self-presence were the only way to maintain and stabilize operations. Likewise, the reiterated use of 'My grandmother' throughout the narrative indicates the failure to construct her discursively. As her place in the referential 'real' is not assured, discourse returns repeatedly to the point of departure. We could take this further by examining those points of breakage and restitching which characterize the narrator's speech, in order to discover what ideological premises underlie such breakage.

One function of the narrating voice is to establish the premises of loss and absence which, from the beginning, situate the act of telling as the site of negative affirmation. The 'no trace' of the first sentence studied previously sets up a discursive mode through which negation becomes the activating force which triggers memory. This is followed by '[w]e never knew', 'we never saw', '[n]one of us could recollect', '[n]obody knows', to cite only some examples. But since the epistemological absence structuring investigation implicates the narrator's own access to knowledge, the source and authority of such telling is challenged. Linked to the constant securing of the self, and the simultaneous displacement of responsibility for logic and coherence, is the constant filtering of information through the grandmother, who is, if not the source of speech, the source of authority and family history in the story. It is as if a circular movement of deferred meaning were at work in the narrative, the narrator saying what she cannot know, since the grandmother mediates the system of authoritative versions, which themselves are subject to hearsay (for the grandmother herself does not pronounce them). Subjective presence is thus divorced from grounds of knowledge and family history, and engaged in stapling tentative identities to the surface of the narration, over the gap where history should reside. This fragile relation of presence to origins within the narrating function cannot but refer us back to the narrative's skewed relation to 'authority' itself in the sense of structuring codes, and the way discourse is permeated by 'official versions' of order and constraint. Such is the case when encoding the 'elsewhere' of the colonial metropolis:

> The clothes smelled of a good life in a country where white people lived and where bad-behaved children like us would not be tolerated. All this my grandmother said. There, children had manners and didn't play in mud and didn't dirty everything . . . and did not run through the house like warrahoons and did not act like little old niggers.[27]

If the 'doxa' takes root within a discourse riven to the 'unsayable' of family history, this complex of voice can be linked to the workings of ideology in narrative. Nancy Glazener, linking women's texts to Bhaktinian dialogics, comments interestingly on the relation between textual repression and ideology:

> Like the carnivalesque understanding of negation, ideology is not simply the abstract opposite of what is said but is rather the obverse, the implicated Other, of what is said. Experienced individually as an unconscious . . . it becomes socially intelligible according to what is unspeakable and thereby unthinkable: the unspeakable challenges to the *status quo* or the unspeakable assumptions that make the *status quo* possible.[28]

That the narrator's access to language and to presence is mediated, that her desire is thus also mediated, is obvious, for she states: 'All of the words which we knew belonged to my grandmother. All of them, a voluptuous body of endearment . . .',[29] referring us to the failure of the 'self-management' of desire which, as Glazener continues, is the prerequisite of the liberal bourgeois individual. If desire is displaced, the site where it finds expression (the grandmother's nurturing body), is itself a contested zone, 'mediated by the discourse of the *propre*: the relationship between property and propriety'[30] which are the foundations of social/institutional desire-management. The grandmother's edicts pertaining to this institutional *propre* are at odds with her status as source of nourishing 'lapping words', her fund of mythological narrative' . . . whose thickness we felt, rolling in and out of the veranda',[31] in which desire swamps narrative itself and is thus incompatible with the encoded reality of the household. The narrative attempts to harmonize not only two divergent forms of discourse, but two disparate systems of meaning emanating from divergent world views – the 'word' of the 'body' of Africa which expresses itself in myth and folklore versus the 'word' of the individualistic ethos of twentieth-century capitalism.

The episode of the mangoes in the story is an example of this concentration on discourses of the *propre* in the story and is emblematic of the confrontation between individual and community which finds no resolution. The tree in question spreads its bounty from a neighbour's garden into the grandmother's. Officially the property of the rich neighbours, the mangoes which fall on the grandmother's side are the object of debate as to which right should prevail, that of property or that of need. In the end the grandmother opts for self-deprivation, not because she respects the laws of property, but according to the logic already investigated, which is that of accumulation versus loss. Indeed the interest of the scene lies in the system of weights and balances which recalls the dilemma of the grandmother's possessions. As the narrator says, the tree itself, symbol of fertility and organic sensuality, 'was so huge, it spread half its body over their fence into our yard'. Figure of excess, object of desire, the tree conditions the exacerbated scripting of borders: 'their fence', 'our yard', 'mangoes . . . on our side . . . belonged to us . . . belonged to them'.[32] Borders of appropriation are also moral and philosophical: the grandmother supports the claims of the tree's owners, 'not because she thought that they were right, but she thought that if they were such greedy people, they should have the mangoes. Let them kill themselves on it, she said'.[33]

In this overdetermined, hybrid space, (for the tree envelops all just as it conditions breaches and transgressions from one side to another), the factor determining the system of appropriation, disappropriation and reappropriation is the static balance between accumulation on one side of the fence counterbalanced by loss on the other, but which significantly causes violence to erupt within the grandmother's domain: 'Let them kill themselves on it'.[34] Unable to establish coherence between 'having' and 'being', finally the only way out of the dilemma is subterfuge, as the booty is secreted away: 'From time to time, we . . . hid them in a stash under the house or deep in the back yard under leaves'.[35]

The chaotic potential of poverty and family disorder, the impingement of the 'doxa' (thus the collapse of structure), the need to repress and transform – 'she said that changing furni-

ture around was a sign to people that we didn't have any money'
– and its threat to linearity in the flow of casual links, continually posits an 'outside' of the text itself where the fissures and
disruptions signal the radical inscription of a symbolic mobility
and cultural silencing.

Discussion of the trope of the photograph has been left until
last, in spite of its obvious significance in the story, because the
governing concepts of identity debated in the story can be
harnessed to the propositions of representation and correspon-
dence it vehicles. The title itself is a clue: lacking an article, it
becomes an abstraction, thus posing a challenge to the referential status of the object it designates. But photographs themselves
are a recurring trace, and the beginning of the story announces
their importance in the establishing of the grandmother's identity card. Likewise the children's mothers' presence is caught in
photographs sent from indeterminate places abroad. What is more,
the narrator herself, along with some of the children, has a
photograph taken to send to England. Destined to accrue representation and to stabilize reality, these proofs of identity only serve
to highlight the distance between an ever elusive reference and
its 'framed' existence. For as we have seen, the grandmother herself
gains no true referential status in the narrative. Seemingly without boundaries, everywhere and therefore nowhere in particular,
she is the ontological zone where codes of language cross and
divide, and where words in fact fail, for symbolic structures of
the 'outside' collapse into indeterminacy. The narrator herself is
also an absence of representation in the photograph intended to
fix her presence, for as she says: 'Nobody knows that it's me in the
photograph, but my sisters and Genevieve look like themselves'.[36]

Curiously unrecognized, then, the narrator is a stranger to her
own image, the Other of the referential real. Thus the multiple
attempts to secure the real only attest to its displacement. Likewise the birth certificates (which attest not only to identity but
to appropriation, for the narrator designates them as the 'proof
that my grandmother own[s] us'[37]) slide on to a sensual register
with 'their musty smell and yellowing water-marked coarse
paper',[38] thus once more injecting the real with alterity. One could
say, then, that the taking and sending of photographs serves to
designate the characters' ultimately shifting identities and perhaps,
further, to signal the narrative's inability to adequately master,
control, and channel meaning itself.

In this way, the multiple displacement in the narrative, the conflict of discursive modes, the 'tunnelling' voice which is a function of a subject of speech spoken through by symbolic dispersal, can but invite on to the stage of the representation an authorial presence of multiple transgressions – Dionne Brand, the lesbian feminist black Trinidadian Canadian. Her own shifting identity which mediates exile and displacement, just as it signifies rootedness in a Black consciousness, renders crucial the responsibility of authorship as an identifiable trait of the textual 'real'. As Francesco Loriggio comments:

> At the heart of literary ethnicity are, then, two processes, which may interlock but do not have to. In one respect, ethnicity is a perspective: it occurs when ethnics assume voice, speak about themselves, when there is a vision from within, writing with inside knowledge. In a second manner, ethnicity presupposes an indirect act of reference, one that does not willy-nilly link the text to the world or the "reality" it is presumed to hark back to, but relies on the figure of the author, and, more specifically his or her social identity, for mediation. . . . ethnic authorship is authoritativeness.[39]

In Brand's fiction 'authorship' conflated with 'authority' is marked textually by characters whose inscription in the linear teleologic 'real' is precarious, where fissures and gaps speak to 'texture' as poetic signifying strata rather than to narrative closure. It is writing in and of the post-colonial experience, which can also be linked to writing in a specifically Canadian context, where ' . . . alienation in that space will enter and undercut writing, making it recoil upon itself, become a problem to itself'.[40] Speaking against a white, middle-class 'centre' and to a constantly deferred Caribbean origin, Brand both claims ethnic authorship and is 'authored' herself within the terms of a realism submitting to the discontinuities of a fractured, post-colonial imaginary.

Notes

1. D. Brand, 'Bread Out Of Stone' in C. Morrell (ed.), *Grammar and Dissent: Poetry and Prose by Claire Harris, M. Nourbese Philip, Dionne Brand* (Fredericton, New Brunswick: Goose Lane Editions, 1994) p. 180.

2. F. Loriggio, 'The Question of the Corpus: Ethnicity and Canadian Literature' in John Moss (ed.), *Future Indicative: Literary Theory and Canadian Literature* (Ottawa: University of Ottawa Press, 1987) p. 57.
3. C. Morrell (ed.), *Grammar and Dissent: Poetry and Prose by Claire Harris, M. Nourbese Philip, Dionne Brand* (Fredericton, New Brunswick: Goose Lane Editions, 1994) p. 13.
4. C. Harris, 'Why Do I Write?' in C. Morrell (ed.), *Grammar and Dissent: Poetry and Prose by Claire Harris, M. Nourbese Philip, Dionne Brand* (Fredericton, New Brunswick: Goose Lane Editions, 1994) p. 30.
5. For discussion on Exile and the Caribbean writer see Chapter 4 of M. Rosello's *Littérature et identité creole aux Antilles* (Paris: Editions Karthala, 1992) pp. 91–112.
6. D. Brand, *Sans Souci and other Stories* (Stratford, Ontario: Williams-Wallace, 1988).
7. Ibid., p. 86.
8. Ibid., p. 87.
9. Ibid.
10. M. Nourbese Philip, 'The Absence of Writing or How I Almost Became A Spy' in C. Morrell (ed.), *Grammar and Dissent: poetry and prose by Claire Harris, M. Nourbese Philip, Dionne Brand* (Fredericton, New Brunswick: Goose Lane Editions, 1994) p. 101.
11. D. Brand, *Sans Souci*, p. 89.
12. Ibid., p. 88.
13. Ibid., p. 89.
14. Ibid., p. 88.
15. Ibid., p. 53.
16. Ibid., p. 55.
17. P. Smart, *Ecrire dans la maison du père* (Montréal: Québec/Amérique, 1988) p. 27. (Translation mine).
18. D. Brand, *Sans Souci*, p. 54.
19. Ibid.
20. Ibid., p. 56.
21. Ibid., p. 57.
22. Ibid., p. 69.
23. Ibid., p. 74.
24. Ibid., p. 71.
25. M. Hirsch, *The Mother/Daughter Plot: Narrative, Psychoanalysis, Feminism* (Bloomington and Indianapolis: Indiana University Press, 1989) p. 178.
26. D. Brand, *Sans Souci*, p. 68.
27. Ibid., pp. 57–8.
28. N. Glazener, 'Dialogic Subversion: Bakhtin, the novel and Gertrude Stein' in Ken Hirschkop and David Shepherd (eds), *Bakhtin and cultural theory* (Manchester/New York: Manchester University Press, 1989) pp. 124–5.
29. D. Brand, *Sans Souci*, p. 74.
30. N. Glazener, 'Dialogic Subversion: Bakhtin, the novel and Gertrude Stein' in Ken Hirschkop and David Shepherd (eds), *Bakhtin and cultural theory* (Manchester/New York: Manchester University Press, 1989) p. 123.

31. D. Brand, *Sans Souci*, p. 72.
32. Ibid., p. 65.
33. Ibid., pp. 65–6.
34. Ibid., p. 66.
35. Ibid.
36. Ibid., p. 59.
37. Ibid., p. 56.
38. Ibid.
39. Francesco Loriggio, 'The Question of the Corpus: Ethnicity and Canadian Literature' in John Moss (ed.), *Future Indicative: Literary Theory and Canadian Literature* (Ottawa: University of Ottawa Press, 1987) p. 55.
40. D. Lee, 'Cadence, Country, Silence: Writing in a Colonial Space', *Boundary*, 23 1 (1974) p. 36.

Bibliography

Brand, D. *Sans Souci and other Stories*. Stratford, Ontario: Williams-Wallace, 1988.
Glazener, N. 'Dialogic Subversion: Bakhtin, the Novel and Gertrude Stein' in Ken Hirschkop and David Shepherd (eds). *Bakhtin and Cultural Theory*. Manchester/New York: Manchester University Press, 1989.
Hirsch, M. *The Mother/Daughter Plot: Narrative, Psychoanalysis, Feminism*. Bloomington and Indianapolis: Indiana University Press, 1989.
Lee, D. 'Cadence, Country, Silence: Writing in a Colonial Space', *Boundary*, 23 1 (1974).
Loriggio, F. 'The Question of the Corpus: Ethnicity and Canadian Literature' in John Moss (ed.). *Future Indicative: Literary Theory and Canadian Literature*. Ottawa: University of Ottawa Press, 1987.
Morrell, C. (ed.). *Grammar and Dissent: Poetry and Prose by Claire Harris, M. Nourbese Philip, Dionne Brand*. Fredericton, New Brunswick: Goose Lane Editions, 1994.
Rosello, M. *Littérature et identité creole aux Antilles*. Paris: Editions Karthala, 1992 pp. 91–112.
Smart, P. *Ecrire dans la maison du père*. Montréal: Québec/Amérique, 1988.

Part III
A Guide to Fiction by Caribbean Women Writers

A to Z of Authors and Works by Country of Origin

Antigua
Jamaica Kincaid
Annie John (1983)
At the Bottom of the River (stories) (1983)
A Small Place (essay) (1988)
Lucy (1990)
The Autobiography of My Mother (1996)

Barbados
June Henfrey
Coming home and other stories (1994)
Paule Marshall
Brown Girl, Brownstones (1959)
The Chosen Place, The Timeless People (1968)
Merle: a novella and other stories (1983)
Praisesong for the Widow (1983)
Daughters (1991)
Hazelle Palmer
Tales from the Gardens and Beyond (1995)

Belize
Zee Edgell
Beka Lamb (1982)
In Times Like These (1991)
The Festival of San Joaquin (1997)

Carriacou
Audre Lorde
Zami: A New Spelling of My Name (1982)

Cuba
Cristina Garcia
Dreaming in Cuban (1992)

Dominica
Phyllis Shand Allfrey
The Orchid House (1953)

Jean Rhys
The Left Bank and Other Stories (1927)
Quartet (1928) (first published as *Postures*)
After Leaving Mr Mackenzie (1930)
Voyage in the Dark (1934)
Good Morning, Midnight (1939)
Wide Sargasso Sea (1966)
Tigers Are Better-Looking (1968)
Sleep It Off Lady (1976)
Tales of the Wide Caribbean: a New Collection of Short Stories (1985)

Grenada
Jean Buffong
Under the Silk Cotton Tree (1992)
Snowflakes in the Sun (1996)
Merle Collins
Angel (1987)
Rain Darling (stories) (1990)
The Colour of Forgetting (1995)
Nellie Payne and Jean Buffong
Jump-Up-and-Kiss-Me: Two stories from Grenada (1990)

Guyana
Joan Cambridge
Clarise Cumberbatch Want to Go Home (1987)
Norma De Haarte
Guyana Betrayal (1991)
Beryl Gilroy
Black Teacher (autobiography) (1976)
Frangipani House (1986)
Boy-Sandwich (1989)
Stedman and Joanna – A Love in Bondage (1991)
Sunlight on Sweet Water (autobiography) (1994)
Gather the Faces (1996)
In Praise of Love and Children (1996)
Inkle and Yarico (1996)
Denise Harris
Web of Secrets (1996)
Meiling Jin
Song of the Boatwoman (1996)
Pauline Melville
Shape-shifter (1990)
The Ventriloquist's Tale (1997)
The Migration of Ghosts (stories) (1998)
Grace Nichols
Whole of a Morning Sky (1986)
Narmala Shewcharan
Tomorrow Is Another Day (1994)

Jan Shinebourne
Timepiece (1986)
The Last English Plantation (1988)

Haiti
Edwidge Danticat
Breath, Eyes, Memory (1994)
Krik? Krak! (stories) (1996)

Jamaica
Opal Palmer Adisa
Bake-Face and Other Guava Stories (1986)
It Begins With Tears (1997)
Erna Brodber
Jane and Louisa Will Soon Come Home (1980)
Myal (1988)
Louisiana (1994)
Hazel D. Campbell
The Rag Doll, and other stories (1978)
Woman's Tongue: stories (1985)
Singerman (stories) (1992)
Michelle Cliff
Abeng (1984)
No Telephone to Heaven (1987)
Bodies of Water (stories) (1990)
Free Enterprise (1993)
Judith Woolcock Colombo
The Fablesinger (1989)
Christine Craig
Mint Tea and other stories (1993)
Vernella Fuller
Going Back Home (1992)
Unlike Normal Women (1995)
Lorna Goodison
Baby Mother and the King of Swords (stories) (1990)
Jean Goulbourne
Excavation (1997)
Andrea Levy
Every Light in the House Burnin' (1994)
Never Far from Nowhere (1996)
Alecia McKenzie
Satellite City and other stories (1992)
Dianne Maguire
Dry Land Tourist and other stories (1991)
Velma Pollard
Considering Women (stories) (1989)
Homestretch (1994)
Karl and other stories (1994)

Patricia Powell
  Me Dying Trial (1993)
  A Small Gathering of Bones (1994)
Joan Riley
  The Unbelonging (1985)
  Waiting in the Twilight (1987)
  Romance (1988)
  A Kindness to the Children (1992)
Sybil Seaforth
  Growing Up with Miss Milly (1988)
Olive Senior
  Summer Lightning and other stories (1986)
  Arrival of the Snake-Woman and other stories (1989)
  Discerner of Hearts and other stories (1995)
Makeda Silvera
  Remembering G and other stories (1991)
  Her Head A Village (stories) (1994)
Vanessa Spence
  The Roads Are Down (1993)
Elean Thomas
  The Last Room (1991)
Jeanne Wilson
  Model for Murder (1993)

Puerto Rico
Esmeralda Santiago
  América's Dream (1996)

Tobago
Marlene Nourbese Philip
  Harriet's Daughter (1988)

Trinidad
Valerie Belgrave
  Ti Marie (1988)
Dionne Brand
  Sans Souci and other stories (1988)
  In Another Place, Not Here (1996)
Brenda Flanagan
  You Alone Are Dancing (1990)
Rosa Guy
  A Measure of Time (1983)
Claire Harris
  Drawing Down a Daughter (1992)
Merle Hodge
  Crick Crack, Monkey (1970)
  For the Life of Laetitia (1993)

Amryl Johnson
  Sequins for a Ragged Hem (travel book) (1988)
Marina Ama Omowale Maxwell
  Chopstix in Mauby: A Novel of Magical Realism (1996)
Elizabeth Nunez
  When Rocks Dance (1986)
  Bruised Hibiscus (1994)
Lakshmi Persaud
  Butterfly in the Wind (1990)
  Sastra (1993)

Further Reading

Anim-Addo, J. (ed.). *Framing the Word: Gender and Genre in Caribbean Women's Writing*. London: Whiting and Birch, 1996.

Ashcroft, B., G. Griffiths and H. Tiffin. *The Empire Writes Back: Theory and Practice in Post-colonial Literatures*. London: Routledge, 1989.

———. *The Post-Colonial Studies Reader*. London: Routledge, 1995.

Bardolph, J. (ed.). *Short Fiction in the New Literatures in English: Proceedings of the Nice Conference of the European Association for Commonwealth Literature and Language Studies*. Nice: Faculté des Lettres et Sciences Humaines de Nice, 1988.

Barfoot, C.C. and Theo D'haen (eds). *Shades of Empire in Colonial and Post-Colonial Literatures*. Amsterdam: Rodopi, 1993.

Birbalsingh, F. (ed.). *Frontiers of Caribbean Literature in English*. London and Basingstoke: Macmillan Educational, 1996.

Boehmer, E. *Colonial and Postcolonial Literature: Migrant Metaphors*. Oxford: Oxford University Press, 1995.

Boucher, P.P. *Cannibal Encounters: Europeans and Island Caribs, 1492–1763*. Baltimore: Johns Hopkins University Press, 1992.

Broe, M.L. and A. Ingram (eds). *Women's Writing in Exile*. Chapel Hill and London: University of North Carolina Press, 1989.

Brown, S. (ed.). *Caribbean New Wave: Contemporary Short Stories*. Oxford: Heinemann, 1990.

Busby, M. (ed.). *Daughters of Africa: an International Anthology of Words and Writings by Women of African Descent from the Ancient Egyptian to the Present*. London: Jonathan Cape, 1992.

Butcher, M. *Tibisiri: Caribbean Writers and Critics*. Sydney: Dangaroo Press, 1989.

Carter, E., J. Donald and J. Squires (eds) *Space and Place: Theories of Identity and Location*. London: Lawrence and Wishart, 1993.

Chamberlain, M. (ed.). *Writing Lives: Conversations Between Women Writers*. London: Virago, 1988.

Chew, S. and A. Rutherford. *Unbecoming Daughters of the Empire*. Sydney: Dangaroo Press, 1993.

Christian, B. *Black Feminist Criticism: Perspectives on Black Women Writers*. New York: Pergamon Press, 1985.

Clarke, E. *My Mother Who Fathered Me: a Study of the Family in Three Selected Communities in Jamaica*. London: Allen and Unwin, 1957.

Cobham, R. and M. Collins (eds). *Watchers and Seekers: Creative Writing by Black Women in Britain*. London: Women's Press, 1987.

Collier, G. (ed.). *Us/Them: Translation, Transcription and Identity in Post-Colonial Literary Cultures*. Amsterdam: Rodopi, 1992.

Cooper, C. *Noises in the Blood: Orality, Gender and the 'Vulgar' Body of Jamaican Popular Culture*. London and Basingstoke: Macmillan Education, 1993.

Coser, S. *Bridging the Americas: The Literature of Toni Morrison, Paule Marshall, and Gayl Jones.* Philadelphia: Temple University Press, 1995.

Cudjoe, S. (ed.). *Caribbean Women Writers.* Wellesley: Calaloux, 1990.

Dabydeen, D. (ed.). *India in the Caribbean.* London: Hansib, 1987.

Dabydeen, D. and N. Wilson-Tagoe. *A Reader's Guide to West Indian and Black British Literature.* London: Hansib, 1988.

Dance, D.C. *New World Adams: Conversations with Contemporary West Indian Writers.* Leeds: Peepal Tree Press, 1992.

Davies, C.B. and E. Fido (eds). *Out of the Kumbla: Caribbean Women and Literature.* Trenton, New Jersey: Africa World Press, 1990.

Davies, C.B. *Black Women, Writing and Identity: Migrations of the subject.* London and New York: Routledge, 1994.

——. *Moving Beyond Boundaries* (2 vols.) London: Pluto Press, 1995.

Davis, A. *Women, Race and Class.* New York: Random House, 1981.

Davis, G. (ed.). *Crisis and Creativity in the New Literatures in English: Canada.* Amsterdam: Rodopi, 1990.

Donnell, A. and S. Lawson Welsh (eds). *The Routledge Reader in Caribbean Literature.* London: Routledge, 1996.

Duncker, P. *Sisters and Strangers: An Introduction to Contemporary Feminist Fiction.* Oxford: Blackwell, 1992.

Ferguson, M. *Jamaica Kincaid: Where the Land Meets the Body.* Charlottesville: University of Virginia Press, 1994.

Gates jnr., H.L. (ed.). *Black Literature and Literary Theory.* New York and London: Methuen, 1984.

——. *'Race', Writing, and Difference.* Chicago: University of Chicago Press, 1986.

George, R.M. *The Politics of Home: Postcolonial Relocations and Twentieth-century Fiction.* Cambridge: Cambridge University Press, 1996.

Gikandi, S. *Writing in Limbo: Modernism and Caribbean Literature.* Ithaca, New York: Cornell University Press, 1992.

Goulbourne, H. *Black Politics in Britain.* Aldershot: Avebury, 1990.

Guptara, P. *Black British Literature: an Annotated Bibliography.* Mundelstrup, Dangaroo Press, 1986.

Gurr, A. *Writers in Exile: The Identity of Home in Modern Literature.* Brighton: Harvester Press, 1981.

Hull, G.T., P.B. Scott and B. Smith (eds) *All the Women are White, All the Blacks are Men, But Some of Us are Brave: Black Women's Studies.* Old Westbury, New York: The Feminist Press, 1982.

Hulme, P. *Colonial Encounters: Europe and the Native Caribbean, 1492–1797.* London: Routledge, 1986.

Jonas, J. *Anancy in the Great House: Ways of Reading West Indian Fiction.* New York, Westport, Connecticut and London: Greenwood Press, 1990.

Juneja, R. *Caribbean Transactions: West Indian Culture in Literature.* London: Macmillan, 1996.

Keating, A. *Women Reading Women Writing: Self-Invention in Paula Gunn Allen, Gloria Anzaldúa and Audre Lorde.* Philadelphia: Temple University Press, 1996.

Kenyon, O. *Writing Women: Contemporary Women Novelists.* London: Pluto Press, 1991.

King, B. (ed.). *The Commonwealth Novel Since 1960.* London: Macmillan, 1991.

——. *West Indian Literature.* (2nd edn) London and Basingstoke: Macmillan Educational, 1995.

King, R. J. Connell and P. White (eds). *Writing Across Worlds: Literature and Migrations.* London and New York: Routledge, 1995.

Lalla, B. *Defining Jamaican Fiction: Marronage and the Discourse of Survival.* Tuscaloosa and London: University of Alabama Press, 1996.

Lashgari, D. (ed.). *Violence, Silence, and Anger: Women's Writing as Transgression.* Charlottesville: University Press of Virginia, 1995.

Lee, A.R. (ed.). *Other Britain, Other British: Contemporary Multicultural Fiction.* London: Pluto Press, 1995.

Lowenthal, D. *West Indian Societies.* New York, London and Toronto: Oxford University Press, 1972.

Mariani, P. (ed.). *Critical Fictions: The Politics of Imaginative Writing.* Seattle: Bay Press, 1991.

Minh-ha, T.T. *Woman, Native, Other,: Writing Postcoloniality and Feminism.* Bloomington and Indianapolis: Indiana University Press, 1989.

Mohanram, R. and G. Rajan (eds). *English Postcoloniality: Literatures from Around the World.* New York, Westport, Connecticut and London: Greenwood Press, 1996.

Mohanty, C.T., A. Russo and L. Torres (eds). *Third World Women and the Politics of Feminism.* Bloomington: Indiana University Press, 1991.

Moon, M. and C.N. Davidson (eds). *Subjects and Citizens: Nation, Race, and Gender from 'Oroonoko' to Anita Hill.* Durham: Duke University Press, 1995.

Mordecai, P. and B. Wilson (eds). *Her True-True Name: an Anthology of Women's Writing from the Caribbean.* London: Heinemann, 1989.

Morrell, C. (ed.). *Grammar of Dissent: Poetry and Prose by Claire Harris, M. Nourbese Philip, Dionne Brand.* Fredericton, New Brunswick: Goose Lane, 1994.

Morris, M. (ed.). *Faber Book of Contemporary Caribbean Short Stories.* London: Faber, 1990.

Morris, P. *Literature and Feminism: an Introduction.* Oxford: Blackwell, 1993.

Nasta, S. (ed.). *Motherlands: Black Women's Writing from Africa, the Caribbean and South Asia.* London: Women's Press, 1991.

Newman, J. *The Ballistic Bard.* London: Arnold, 1995.

Newton, J. and D. Rosenfelt (eds). *Feminist Criticism and Social Change: Sex, Class and Race in Literature and Culture.* New York and London: Methuen, 1985.

Ngcobo, L. (ed.). *Let It Be Told: Black Women Writers in Britain.* London: Virago, 1987.

O'Callaghan, E. *Woman Version: Theoretical Approaches to West Indian Fiction by Women.* London: Macmillan, 1993.

Pagden, A. *The Fall of Natural Man: the American Indian and the Origins of Comparative Ethnology.* Cambridge: Cambridge University Press, 1982.

Pettis, J. *Toward Wholeness in Paule Marshall's Fiction.* Charlottesville: University Press of Virginia, 1995.

Philip, M.N. *She Tries Her Tongue, Her Silence Softly Breaks*. London: Women's Press, 1989.

——. *Frontiers: Selected Essays and Writings on Racism and Culture, 1984–1992*. Stratford, Ontario: Mercury Press, 1992.

Ramchand, K. *The West Indian Novel and its Background*. (2nd edn) London: Faber, 1983.

Riley, J. and B. Wood (eds). *Leave To Stay: Stories of Exile and Belonging*. London: Virago, 1996.

Saakana, A.S. *The Colonial Legacy in Caribbean Literature*. Vol. I, London: Karnak House, 1987.

Scheier, L., S. Sheard and E. Wachtel (eds). *Language in Her Eye: Views on Writing and Gender by Canadian Women Writing in English*. Toronto: Coach House Press, 1990.

Senior, O. *Working miracles: Women's Lives in the English-speaking Caribbean*. London: James Currey and Bloomington: Indiana University Press, 1991.

Silvera, M. *Silenced: Talks with Working Class Caribbean Women about Their Lives and Struggles as Domestic Workers in Canada*. Toronto: Sister Vision, 1983.

Simmons, D. *Jamaica Kincaid*. New York: Twayne, 1994.

Sistren with H.F. Smith. *Lionheart Gal: Life Stories of Jamaican Women*. London: Women's Press, 1986.

Slemon, S. and H. Tiffin (eds). *After Europe: Critical Theory and Post-colonial Writing*. Coventry: Dangaroo Press, 1989.

Springfield, C.L. (ed.). *Daughters of Caliban: Caribbean Women in the Twentieth Century*. Indiana: Indiana University Press, 1997.

Thiongo, N.W. *Homecoming: Essays on African and Caribbean Literature, Culture and Politics*. London, Ibadan and Nairobi: Heinemann, 1972.

Wall, C.A. (ed.). *Changing Our Own Words: Essays on Criticism, Theory, and Writing by Black Women*. Rutgers, New Jersey: Rutgers University Press, 1989.

Walmsley, A. *The Caribbean Artists Movement 1966–1972: a Literary and Cultural History*. London: New Beacon Books, 1992.

Ware, V. *Beyond the Pale: White Women, Racism and History*. London and New York: Verso, 1992.

Williamson, J. (ed.). *Sounding Differences: Conversations with Seventeen Canadian Women Writers*. Toronto, Buffalo and London: University of Toronto Press, 1993.

Wisker, G. (ed.). *Black Women's Writing*. Basingstoke: Macmillan, 1993.

Index

Wasafiri, 43
Washington, Booker T., 13
Welsh, Sarah Lawson, 5
West-Indies/West-Indian, 15, 33, 45, 78, 86, 104, 111–12, 137, 146, 151, 167 n.24, 194
West Indies Federation, 1
Wilentz, Gay, 185
Williams, Aubrey, 162

Williams, Sherley Anne, 3
Dessa Rose, 3
Willis, Susan, 78, 86
Wilson, Betty, 173
Wiser, William, 48

Zola, Emile, 53
Nana, 53–4
zombification, 107–8, 110